Events as a Strategic Marketing Tool

2nd Edition

Events as a Strategic Marketing Tool

2nd Edition

Dorothé Gerritsen
Ronald van Olderen

With the cooperation of:

Jacco van Mierlo
Margo Rooijackers
Thomas van Velthoven

CABI

CABI is a trading name of CAB International

CABI
Nosworthy Way
Wallingford
Oxfordshire OX10 8DE
UK

Tel: +44 (0)1491 832111
Fax: +44 (0)1491 833508
E-mail: info@cabi.org
Website: www.cabi.org

CABI
WeWork, One Lincoln St
24th Floor
Boston, MA 02111
USA

Tel: +1 (617)682-9015
E-mail: cabi-nao@cabi.org

Originally published in Dutch under the title *Het event als strategisch marketing instrument* by Dorothé Gerritsen and Ronald van Olderen. © Uitgeverij Coutinho b.v. 2011/2017

© Dorothé Gerritsen and Ronald van Olderen 2020. All rights reserved. No part of this publication may be reproduced in any form or by any means, electronically, mechanically, by photocopying, recording or otherwise, without the prior permission of the copyright owners.

A catalogue record for this book is available from the British Library, London, UK.

Library of Congress Cataloging-in-Publication Data

Names: Gerritsen, Dorothé, author. | Olderen, Ronald van, author. | Mierlo, Jacco van, author. | Rooijackers, Margo, author. | Velthoven, Thomas van, author. | Eerdmans, Eef, translator. | Leijten-Kupers, Esther, translator.
Title: Events as a strategic marketing tool / Dorothé Gerritsen, Ronald van Olderen, with the cooperation of Jacco van Mierlo, Margo Rooijackers, Thomas van Velthoven ; translators, Eef Eerdmans and Esther Kupers.
Other titles: Event als strategisch marketinginstrument. English
Description: 2nd edition. | Wallingford, Oxfordshire, UK ; Boston, MA, USA : CAB International, [2020] | "Originally published in Dutch under the title Het event als strategisch marketing instrument by Dorothé Gerritsen and Ronald van Olderen"--Title page verso | Includes bibliographical references and index. | Summary: "An update to the popular first edition, providing an engaging resource for both students and professionals interested in Leisure, tourism and events. Including a wealth of internationally relevant examples, it gives a thorough insight into the way events can help reach strategic marketing goals"-- Provided by publisher.
Identifiers: LCCN 2019056043 (print) | LCCN 2019056044 (ebook) | ISBN 9781789242300 (paperback) | ISBN 9781789242928 (ebook) | ISBN 9781789242935 (epub)
Subjects: LCSH: Strategic planning. | Marketing. | Special events--Management.
Classification: LCC HD30.28 .G46813 2020 (print) | LCC HD30.28 (ebook) | DDC 658.8--dc23
LC record available at https://lccn.loc.gov/2019056043
LC ebook record available at https://lccn.loc.gov/2019056044

ISBN-13: 978 1 78924 230 0 (paperback)
       978 1 78924 292 8 (ePDF)
       978 1 78924 293 5 (ePub)

Commissioning Editor: Claire Parfitt
Editorial Assistant: Emma McCann
Production Editor: Tim Kapp
Translation: Esther Kupers

Typeset by SPi, Pondicherry, India
Printed and bound in the UK by Bell and Bain Ltd, Glasgow

Contents

About the Authors	vii
Preface	ix
PART I: PLAN	**1**
1 Introduction: Using Events as a Strategic Marketing Tool	3
2 Trends and Developments: Consumers' Pursuit of Happiness	16
3 Event Marketing	30
4 Events and Customer Relationship Marketing	50
5 Events and Marketing Communication	67
6 Events and Branding	88
7 Events and City Marketing: The Role of Events in Cities	116
PART II: DO	**139**
8 The Translation of Strategy into Concept	141
9 Touchpoints	164
Appendices to Chapter 9: Touchpoint Models for Trade Fairs and Corporate Events	183
Appendix 1 Touchpoint Model for Trade Fairs	184
Appendix 2 Touchpoint Model for Corporate Events	188
PART III: CHECK	**193**
10 Effect Measurement and Evaluation	195
Appendices to Chapter 10: Effect Measurement and Evaluation	215
Appendix 1 The ROI Model of Jack Phillips	216
Appendix 2 Economic Impact Study of the World Cyclo-Cross Championships 2014, Hoogerheide, the Netherlands	223
Illustrations	227
Bibliography	229
Professional Journals	233
Websites	235
Index	239

About the Authors

About the Lead Authors

Dorothé Gerritsen has been a Lecturer in Event Management, at the Academy for Leisure of Breda University of Applied Sciences, the Netherlands, since 1995. She studied communication science in Nijmegen. In one of the specialist areas open to students, event management, she initiates and supervises, together with Ronald van Olderen, research projects in the field of event marketing. In the past, she has also been a member of the Education Committee of the Centre for Live Communication, CLC-VECTA. The start of the research programme into event marketing inspired the creation of the book that you have before you now; a book that Dorothé lead-authored together with Ronald van Olderen.

Ronald van Olderen is a Lecturer in Event Management and the coordinator in the specialist area of event management at the Academy for Leisure of Breda University of Applied Sciences. He has been involved in the development of content for the specialist area of event management since 2001, focusing on corporate events in particular. Since 2004, he has been involved in initiating and supervising research in the field of event marketing, together with Dorothé Gerritsen. In this process, Ronald works closely with the Independent Dutch Event Association (IDEA) and the Dutch Association of Event Managers. In the past, he has held positions such as Marketing Manager at Sportief Holland Evenementen BV, and from 2005 to 2009 he was a member of the jury of the Gouden Giraffe Award, the award show for the business event industry in the Netherlands. In 2016 he worked for a major fundraising event called 'het Glazen Huis' within the project group of 3FM Serious Request Breda.

About the Co-authors

Jacco van Mierlo is a Lecturer in Event Management at the Academy for Leisure of Breda University of Applied Sciences. After earning his degree from the Dutch Academy of Physical Education, he studied leisure science at Tilburg University. Since 1994, he has worked at NHTV, as a coordinator in the specialist area of event management and as project leader of the Experience Centre Events Management (ECEM). Jacco's specific area of expertise is public events. In the past, he has been a board member of the International Festivals and Events Association Europe (IFEA), a member of the jury of the Dutch National Events Awards and he was on the advisory board of *Festivak* magazine.

Margo Rooijackers studied cultural psychology at Radboud University Nijmegen. Since 1993, Margo has worked as a Lecturer at the Academy for Leisure of Breda University of Applied Sciences. Her areas of expertise are consumer behaviour, imagineering and research. Moreover, she works as a student coach at the Imagineering Academy. She is also Coordinator of the Leisure, Health and Well-Being Project for the Academy for Leisure. Since 2012, she has been working with Rotterdam Festivals on a joint design research project aimed at monitoring, evaluating and improving visitor experiences during events. Margo has published numerous popular academic articles and is a member of the editorial committee of the *Trendrapport toerisme, recreatie en vrije tijd* van NRIT Media.

After his studies in development geography and social sciences at the new secondary school Teacher Training Institute in Tilburg, **Thomas van Velthoven** developed several public campaigns for Africa and he was one of the founders of the brand-building process for Novib. He positioned Memisa as the leading provider of structural support to health care organizations around the globe. Thomas reorganized marketing and communication practices for Red Cross Nederland and set up several innovative fund-raising initiatives in Europe for the International Federation of the Red Cross in Geneva. He switched from managing marketing departments within the charity market to consultancy work in the area of brand positioning for the commercial sector, for clients like Philips, Rabobank, Ben mobile telephony and BP. Since 2004, he has been working at the Academy for Leisure of Breda University of Applied Sciences. In addition, he is still undertaking consultancy work.

About the Photographer

Robert Aarts has been a professional photographer since 1995, specializing in event photography. After his studies at the St. Joost art academy in Breda, he started combining his passion for live music with photography. He joined the Dutch professional organization for professional photographers and started working for clients such as Arjan van Dijk Groep, Rotterdam Ahoy and Efteling, who all contributed greatly to the development of his craftsmanship. The convincing recording of live event messages and experiences became his trademark.

Preface

The Olympic Games are a classic example of a major international event that is strategically utilized by several parties. Typical characteristics of the event include: grand scale, live, global, having a massive economic impact and having consequences for the local infrastructure, the image of a country, sports development and for the people who live there, also called the host community. By way of illustration, we will present some statistical details on the last Olympic Games. In Beijing for example, three new subway lines were constructed – extending the city's total length of track from 42 km to 200 km, a new high-speed rail link from the airport to the city was launched and 31 new sports venues were built, including the National Aquatic Center, more commonly known as the 'Water Cube'. After the Olympic Games, the Water Cube attracted millions of visitors. A total of 4.7 billion people watched the Games on television, and the opening ceremony was an ambitious and spectacular show, watched by 2 billion people. A new image of China was born. A similar situation happened in Rio de Janeiro: 40,000 police officers were trained, 170 km of roads were constructed, US$200 million was invested in the heavily neglected dockland area and 7000 hotel rooms were built. Just the scale of it was huge. Dazzling numbers at the greatest event on earth.

The Games also fuel public debate, because the whole world is watching and so many interests are involved. Just think of discussions about the violation of human rights in China and the harsh measures in the slums of Rio de Janeiro and other cities in Brazil to create a 'safe' environment for the Olympic Games.

Events have impact; they are important and are ever more often utilized strategically, because they are perfectly suited to impressing people. Live meetings during an event are an effective way of engaging people on an emotional level; for instance, by means of a brand or a city. This book is primarily about the way in which organizations utilize events as a marketing tool to reach out to and connect with their visitors. It provides an insight into the strategic use of events, by means of marketing theories, interlaced with practical examples. Most other books focus on the practical management perspective of events. The idea for this book was conceived because of the increasing interest in event marketing among marketers. As it turned out, there was a need to study events as a means to achieving strategic marketing objectives. Over the years, the authors have gathered a wealth of material on this subject. Their knowledge has been brought together and organized in this book.

Many colleagues helped us during the writing of this book. We owe special thanks to those colleagues who wrote a chapter at our request because of their specific expertise: Margo Rooijackers (Chapter 2), Thomas van Velthoven (Chapter 6) and Jacco van Mierlo (Chapter 7).

Chapter 8 is based on a 2006 publication, *Imagine Your Event*, by our colleagues, Moniek Hover and Jacco van Mierlo. This chapter has been thoroughly edited and revised to conform with the rest of the book. We would like to thank them for making this possible.

Much of the knowledge and expertise presented in this book was gathered through students from Breda University of Applied Science. We would like to thank them for their efforts and hard work. Furthermore, our own industry contacts have provided us with many practice-based examples. Their input has made the book more engaging and was indispensable in presenting a clear and realistic picture of the industry.

For this second revised edition, the entire book has been updated; examples have been replaced or added and all texts have been critically examined. The structure, one of the strong points of this book, has been retained: the EVENTS model with the pre-, direct- and post-exposure phase forms a supporting guideline. Various universities of applied sciences in the

Netherlands and universities abroad have now been working with this book for a number of years. When you open this book, you will notice straight away that it is a full-colour edition. For a fascinating marketing instrument such as events, this is not only a very attractive but also a very important addition to the book's content. The material on the website has also been supplemented and updated.

Dorothé Gerritsen and Ronald van Olderen
Breda, spring 2020

Part I

Plan

Part I

Part I is about the planning phase of the strategic use of events, which involves the left side of the EVENTS model (see Fig. 1.3).

After two introductory chapters, we will deal first with the subject of event marketing as a tool. After that, we will present four forms of marketing in which this tool is used.

1. Introduction: Using Events as a Strategic Marketing Tool
2. Trends and Developments: Consumers' Pursuit of Happiness
3. Event Marketing
4. Events and Customer Relationship Marketing
5. Events and Marketing Communication
6. Events and Branding
7. Events and City Marketing: The Role of Events in Cities

1 Introduction: Using Events as a Strategic Marketing Tool

In this chapter we will explain what events are and how organizations can use them strategically. Moreover, we will discuss several types of events and introduce the EVENTS model. Finally, the structure of this book is described, with a preview of Chapters 2 through 10.

Learning Targets

After studying this chapter, you will have learnt:
- how events can be used strategically;
- what a strategically used event is;
- which types of events there are;
- what the main differences between the various types of events are; and
- how the EVENTS model works.

The Strategic Use of Events

This book is about the strategic use of events; about the ways in which organizations use events like air races to achieve underlying objectives. This is referred to as a strategic use of events because the event is part of a strategy – a carefully thought-out plan to achieve a certain goal. The event is the carrier of the message: in other words, it is a communication tool. Marketers and other communication professionals use events to get their message across to a specific target group or to increase customer loyalty. Messages range from 'Buy this product' to 'Nothing beats Groningen'.

The Emergence of Events as a Strategic Marketing Tool

Marketers and communication professionals use events as a strategic marketing tool more and more often. According to MOSAIC (www.eventmarketer.com), the corporate community is currently spending about 25% of its marketing budget on organizing events.

Where does this increasing popularity come from? We believe there are three explanations:

1. Target groups are becoming increasingly intangible to marketers. Many traditional marketing communication tools have lost much of their ability to capture the target group's attention. Newspaper subscriptions have been declining for many years, for instance. This means that marketers today reach fewer people through newspaper advertising. The same holds true for radio and television: due to the steady growth in radio and television channels, viewer and listener attention becomes fragmented. All this has forced marketers to look for alternative means of communication. Strategic events are one of these alternative means.

2. Events are effective tools to ingrain your message in the audience's mind. They are perfectly suitable for adding a layer of emotional value to a product or service. Visitors to an event undergo the event and experience it, and the event gives them lasting memories to cherish. As a result, the message of the event will stick – provided that it is communicated in the right way, of course. In a time when products and services, and cities too, become more and more alike, this is a good way to distinguish yourself.

3. Events are excellent tools to contribute to the quality of life in a company or, for instance, in a city or part of a city. Events foster social cohesion, thanks to their interactive character.

Introduction: Using Events as a Strategic Marketing Tool

The sound of a roaring engine: a small plane skims past a gigantic, cone-shaped pylon, turning in the direction of a slender white bridge. When the pilot manoeuvres his plane under the bridge, the crowd holds its breath: will the daredevil survive this stunt?

Red Bull has created an international series of air races (see also Chapter 6) in which competitors have to navigate a challenging obstacle course. Pilots fly individually against the clock and have to complete tight turns through a slalom course consisting of pylons and bridges. Admission to the event is free, and it draws huge crowds. Red Bull manufactures the popular energy drink of the same name, and finds itself in the same league as Vrumona, Spa and Heineken. Its core business is producing, bottling and distributing energy drinks. Why would this company engage in organizing air races?

Red Bull has created the air race series for marketing purposes. The air races are part of a sophisticated strategy. The company organizes the races to give the Red Bull brand a sporty and adventurous image. This image is supposed to help Red Bull distinguish itself from its competitors, who sell more or less similar energy drinks. The adventurous image is supposed to tempt customers to single out Red Bull rather than, for instance, a can of Slammers.

To Red Bull, the air race is therefore not an end but a means: the drinks manufacturer organizes the races for strategic reasons – for brand strategy reasons, to be precise. The event is a tool to achieve the underlying objective of creating an adventurous and sporty image. This does not mean, however, that the specific nature of the event is irrelevant. Red Bull deliberately opted for air races and not poetry reading sessions.

Event Marketing

The discipline that involves using events as a live means of communication is referred to as event marketing. Event marketing is marketing practices based on the use of events. In event marketing, events are part of, for instance, a communication campaign or a branding strategy. Sometimes the events are organized once (on a one-off basis), sometimes several times (on a regular basis). Chapter 3 addresses the subject of event marketing more extensively.

Event marketing is applied primarily in four types of marketing:

1. *Customer relationship marketing*: building, maintaining and intensifying relations with various parties (see Chapter 4).
2. *Marketing communication*: marketing products and services by influencing the visitor's knowledge, attitude and behaviour (see Chapter 5).
3. *Branding*: influencing, creating or changing valuable associations that a visitor has with a brand (external branding) and/or influencing, creating or changing valuable associations that an employee has in order to increase employee engagement and optimize the customer experience (internal branding) (see Chapter 6).
4. *City marketing*: 'selling' a municipality or region to current and potential residents, visitors/tourists and businesses or organizations (see Chapter 7).

These four types of marketing will be covered in Part I of this book.

Using Events as a Strategic Marketing Tool

Using events as a strategic marketing tool: now what does this mean precisely? In this book, we use the following definition:

> Using an event as a strategic marketing tool involves planning a unique event or series of events for one or more target groups where people come together, either physically or virtually, at the invitation and initiation of a company/business, government body or non-profit organization. The client wishes to achieve an emotional added value by means of an experience, to support a predefined objective (communicative or otherwise) that has to be achieved among one or more of the target groups identified.

This type of event has a number of characteristics. The event:

- is a planned, unique, physical or virtual event or series of events for one or more target groups;
- is held at the invitation of an organizing party; this invitation may also be public, so for everyone;
- is aimed at achieving an emotional added value to support the communicative objective of the organizing party;
- creates an emotional added value by means of an experience.

Several of these elements are reflected in our Red Bull example. After all, it involves:

- a planned event: the race and its spectators;
- a target group: consumers who are interested in spectacular adventurous sports;
- an invitation: Red Bull announces to the general public when and where the races will take place;
- an emotional added value: the aim of the race is to create a distinct image for the brand;
- an experience: spectators experience the excitement and sensation of the race.

Experiences

The definition in the section above shows that experiences are an important factor in the strategic use of events. But how does this work? Why does Red Bull expect that the spectators at the air race will associate the brand with sports and adventure afterwards? In a nutshell, it works as follows – before, during and after the event. Visitors to an event are exposed continuously to sensory impressions. They see, hear and undergo all sorts of things. These impressions lead to an emotion; for instance, enthusiasm or aversion. As a result, the visitor experiences the event as either pleasant or terrible. After the event, the visitor takes stock (unconsciously). The event as a whole has then become an experience. It is precisely because events are sensory experiences that the visitor is especially open to any messages communicated during the event. The visitor to the race organized by Red Bull is part of the spectacle. He feels the excitement, is engaged emotionally and feels a connection with the values of Red Bull. From now on, spectators will associate Red Bull with adventure and spectacle, either consciously or unconsciously.

The explanation we have given here is a strong simplification and certainly not based on any academic sources. The psychological processes that are involved in acquiring experiences and associations are complex. There are numerous factors that play a part in the visitor's experience of an event: the visitor's mood, interests, previously acquired experiences, social environment and background. The better an event aligns with these personal factors, the more meaningful the event will be to the visitor concerned. Chapters 8 and 9 of this book will consider this in more detail.

Touchpoints

The way in which an event is experienced is determined to a high degree by the visitor's experience of what are referred to as *touchpoints*. Touchpoints are interaction points between the organizer of the event and the visitors to the event; in other words, all communication and contacts between visitors and representatives of the organization. Sometimes, these points of contact are orchestrated carefully and deliberately by the organizer, and sometimes they occur accidentally. Touchpoints occur not only during the event but also before and afterwards. Take, for example, the Red Bull air races. In the pre-event phase, the organization announces the event to the target group, the general public. During the event itself, the energy drinks manufacturer is also unmistakably present, with its logos scattered around the site and its many representatives. And afterwards, the company posts photographs of the event on a freely accessible website, so as to allow visitors to enjoy the memory of the event.

When creating an emotional added value for a product or service, it is important for the organizer to pinpoint those points of contact that are crucial to the visitor. After all, bad experiences with the organization in any one of the three phases may have a negative impact on the experience as a whole. Fortunately, the opposite is equally true. The helpfulness of an organizer in rebooking a reservation or accommodating any special diet needs will give the visitor a positive first impression.

Corporate and Public Events

We can make a rough distinction between two types of events: corporate events and public events. Both types can be used in a strategic manner.

The points of departure in corporate events are the objective and the target group. The client or financier organizes corporate events to achieve something with a certain target audience (an exclusive event); for example, personnel events, company anniversaries, events for customers or the launch of a new car model.

Corporate events usually involve three categories of events, which we will explain briefly below.
- *Business-to-business events*: visitors are invited for business motives, and visitors go to the event for business reasons too. This does not mean that all leisure purposes are excluded. Examples are: trade shows, events for customers, anniversaries, conferences, or special events for customers as a part of major public sports events.

- *Business-to-consumer events*: visitors are invited for business reasons, but they visit the event for leisure motives. Examples are brand events, such as Lego Kids Fest in various cities in the USA (Detroit, Richmond, Denver and Cincinnati); the Red Bull Air Race in Rotterdam, the Netherlands; public trade events like the national boat show in the Coca-Cola Dome in Johannesburg, South Africa; and the Volvo Ocean Race.
- *Business-to-employee events*: the target group is the employees of a company. The aim may be to create a sense of solidarity (through team-building) or to reward and thank employees for their efforts. Examples of this are the staff party of Unilever or Shell; the team-building days of ICT company EDS; a special event on the occasion of a merger for members of staff from both companies involved; or a staff outing to a major sports event.

Types of corporate events
Business events (business-to-business)
Events based on business interests and organized for corporate contacts:

- product presentations;
- opening ceremonies;
- dealer conventions;
- kick-off meetings;
- press presentations;
- shareholders' meetings;
- sports events;
- small-scale business receptions;
- large-scale business receptions;
- national trade shows; and
- national conferences or symposiums.

Personnel events (business-to-employee)
Events organized by a company or organization for the employees of that company or organization:

- product presentations;
- opening ceremonies;
- company anniversaries;
- kick-off meetings;
- sports events;
- open days;
- incentives;
- staff parties;
- events for retired employees;
- seasonal events; and
- corporate retreats, big meetings.

(Source: Verhaar, 2014; NIDAP, 2016.)

The point of departure in public events often centres around the contents. They are organized, for instance, for idealistic reasons, to entertain or elevate visitors or to satisfy a certain public need. Public events are public, organized for the sake of their contents and intended for consumers; for example, pop festivals, music festivals and cultural festivals, but also dance events, charity events and sports events.

According to Kuiper and Kamp (2015), public events have four main objectives.

- *Aesthetic objective*: the organizer wants to show the public how attractive his product or type of product is; for instance, arts or cultural events.
- *Idealistic objective (educational/social)*: an event can be organized for political, religious or social purposes – a demonstration, for example.
- *Entertainment objective*: the event is centred around entertainment. These kinds of events are usually organized for commercial reasons; they are low-threshold and attract large crowds. Examples are funfairs and dance events.
- *Commercial objective*: events can also be organized for pure economic considerations and without any specific entertainment objective, such as annual fairs or trade shows.

Public events often have several overlapping objectives. The main objectives described above are therefore not mutually exclusive. Many events with an aesthetic objective, for instance, also contain elements of entertainment. Entertainment is used increasingly to encourage people to buy something (commercial value) or to believe something (idealistic, persuasive value). And, as already mentioned, public events are used by the business-to-business branch as a platform for inviting business contacts.

Types of public events
Festivals
- music festivals (e.g. dance, jazz and multicultural festivals);
- film festivals (national and international festivals);
- theatre festivals (e.g. street theatre and theatre on location); and
- arts festivals (a mix of theatre, dance, music, visual arts, film and new media).

Exhibitions/trade shows
Concerts/musical performances

Rallies

Sports events

Attractions, including funfairs

Markets
- tourist markets;
- arts markets;
- pasar malam (Indonesian word for evening market);
- folkloristic annual markets, cheese and flea markets; and
- village fairs.

Commemorations and ceremonies
- centennial events;
- public holidays and other commemorations of historical significance, such as liberation parties and official holidays related to the royal family;
- silent marches;
- speeches;
- unregulated street markets;
- concerts (including benefit concerts);
- weddings;
- funerals and births/baptisms (members of the royal family or other celebrities); and
- day of the Queen's/King's speech.

Parades
- carnival parades and lantern parades;
- demonstrations;
- flower parades; and
- dance parade, love parade and gay parade.

Culinary events

(Source: Verhaar, 2014.)

Fading Boundaries Between Corporate and Public Events

From the perspective of the strategic objective, the boundaries between corporate and public events are fading. The objectives of public events are moving increasingly in the direction of those of corporate events.

On the one hand, public events are used to an increasing extent by organizations to arrange business-to-business events in which the public event constitutes the central platform. An example of these kinds of events is the 'trade day' (day for professionals only) of the ITB (holiday trade show). One day of the ITB for consumers is reserved for industry professionals. Tourism professionals meet each other on that day at several symposiums, workshops and networking sessions. This 'trade day' can be regarded as a business-to-business event in which a public event (the ITB) is the main event, the central platform. Other examples are: VIP lounges, networking sessions during the Olympic Games, World Football Championships, the Australian Open in Melbourne and the ABN AMRO World Tennis Tournament in Rotterdam. A recent phenomenon is the development of concepts such as 'congrestivals', corporate festivals and business festivals.

Introduction: Using Events as a Strategic Marketing Tool

Here, the objectives of a business event or conference are playfully combined with the festive and relaxed festival atmosphere. It is this different mindset that makes it easier for the objectives regarding the business target group to be achieved – whether it concerns employees, customers or other business contacts.

On the other hand, public events seem to be taking on corporate characteristics to an increasing extent. Commercial interests are getting bigger and bigger. Organizers of public events often have no alternative but to seek sponsor funds, because government subsidies are diminishing. This brings with it its share of obligations towards the sponsors concerned, such as setting up a special (separate) space for sponsors during the event. Public events with commercial interests can shift even further towards the corporate end of the spectrum, thus becoming a platform for the initiation of countless commercial activities. A good example in this respect is the Tour de France. Originally a cycling contest, the event has become a commercial public event with major sponsorship interests. Organizations use this platform to initiate their own events. For instance, local bank branches invited their own customers to a client event on the first day of the Tour de France.

Business-to-consumer events in particular, such as the ITB Berlin (the world's leading travel trade show) or the International Motor Show in Geneva, Switzerland, occur at the interface between corporate and public events. They have a business and/or commercial goal, but are open to everyone who is interested.

The fading boundaries between corporate and public events have been visualized in Fig. 1.1, which will be explained further below. The figure is about events that have overlapping objectives. What is important in this respect is the perspective of the target group, as well as that of the commissioner of the event.

Corporate events

1. Business-to-business events (BtoB):
   1a The trade show 'Event' or a dealers meeting.
   1b Events for clients during Roland Garros in Paris.
2. Business-to-employee events (BtoE):
   2a Shell or Unilever staff party or staff team-building day.
   2b Staff outing to a major sports event.
3. Business-to-consumer events (BtoC): Red Bull Air Race, World Championship in several cities like New York (USA, the Hudson River), Lisbon (Portugal, Tagus River), Abu Dhabi or ITB Berlin, or the introduction of a new car model to the public.

Public events

4. Public events:
   4a Opening ceremony of the Nike Brand Store in Basel, Switzerland, or the arts festival 'The Fringe' in Edinburgh, Scotland.
   4b Castlebar International Four Days' Walks in Ireland, with sponsorship programme.
   4c Start of the Tour de France, with numerous side events organized by sponsors.

Fig. 1.1. Examples of overlapping between corporate and public events.

The Importance of Managing Events

Management is an important aspect in the strategic use of events. After all, the organizing party invests a great deal of money and effort in the event and consequently wants something in return. That is why the organizer will monitor the effects of the event (both during and afterwards) on visitors and, if necessary, make alterations to the project or parts of the project.

The management process consists of four steps:

- *Plan*: the organization decides to use an event to achieve one or more objectives within a certain period of time.
- *Do*: the actual organization of the event. In this process, it is very important for the event to be aligned with the objectives formulated previously, both in terms of category and set-up.
- *Check*: the assessment of objective attainment during and after the event. The organizer checks whether the objectives determined in the plan phase have been achieved. This phase involves effect measurement and evaluation.
- *Act*: the integration of the effect measurement results into the strategy. Depending on the outcome of the effect measurement, the organizer makes alterations to the strategy. Upon a successful outcome, for instance, it may be decided to organize the event again in the future (because it was successful) or, conversely, not to organize the event again in the future (because the goal was achieved).

And thus the circle is complete. The four steps together constitute what is referred to as the *Plan–Do–Check–Act* cycle (see Fig. 1.2).

In everyday practice, however, the cycle is not entirely completed. Effect measurement and evaluation are often overlooked, because some goals are difficult to measure or because all energy and attention is directed towards organizing the event. As a result, the party who commissioned the event will not have any information as to whether or not the efforts were actually productive and worthwhile.

The EVENTS Model

This book has been written by means of what is referred to as the EVENTS model. The model was developed at the Breda University of Applied Sciences as a tool to study systematically the strategic use of events (see also Box 1.1). 'EVENTS' is an acronym of 'Environment', 'Value', 'Effect', 'New', 'Touchpoint' and 'Strategy'. Events are strongly connected with their **E**nvironment and with the core **V**alues and the **S**trategy of the organizing party. The **N**ew concept and design for the event must be in alignment with these values and with the strategy. The visitor experience of the event starts as early as when the event is announced or invitations are sent out. During and after the event, visitors also come into contact (**T**ouchpoint) with the event. Finally, it is important to measure the **E**ffect of the event in order to be able to ascertain just how much it contributed towards achieving the strategic objectives formulated in advance.

Fig. 1.2. The PDCA cycle or Deming cycle. (Source: Truscott, 2003.)

Fig. 1.3. The EVENTS model.

> **Box 1.1.**
> Figure 1.3 illustrates the EVENTS model. It consists of a core and a layer around it. The layer represents the broader context in which event marketing is performed. The outer layer of the model symbolizes the macro- and mesoenvironments that affect event marketing strategies. These environments exert influence on the organization. In these environments, there are quite a few parties that exert influence – either directly or indirectly – on the organization that seeks to engage in event marketing. The behaviour of competitors or target groups may also necessitate organizations to change their practices. Economic trends and developments also affect the marketing strategies of organizations.
>
> The core represents the entire PDCA cycle. To the left of the model, we see an axis with four vanes. As already mentioned, this part of the figure represents the 'plan' phase. The axis represents event marketing. Each of the four vanes represents a marketing sub-area in which event marketing is used as a tool. As already mentioned, these sub-areas are customer relationship marketing, marketing communication, branding and city marketing. The arrow exiting from the axis illustrates the translation of the general strategy to the concept and design of a specific event. To the right of the vanes, we see an oval on its side, which represents the 'do' phase. It displays the three stages of an event: pre-exposure, direct exposure and post-exposure. These are the stages before, during and after an event, which we discussed in the section on touchpoints. The touchpoints themselves are depicted by the dots in the oval.
>
> Finally, to the right of the model, we have the 'check' phase. The large arrow to the right represents the phase of effect measurement. The fact that effect measurements are not only carried out afterwards but also during the event is shown by the small arrows in the oval.
>
> The arrow at the bottom of the figure symbolizes the feedback of the effect measurements results. If necessary, alterations will be made to the strategy, which brings us back to the 'plan' phase.

The EVENTS model is an elaboration of the PDCA cycle. Just like this cycle, the model has four steps: plan, do, check, act. The model shows how these four steps are taken in the strategic use of events.

The Structure of This Book

Chapters 2–10 inclusive, following this introductory chapter, are divided into three parts. The first part concerns the plan phase from the EVENTS model, the second part covers the do phase and the third part relates to the check phase.

In Part I, which is about the plan phase, we will deal first with a number of economic theories in which experiences and events play an important part. In this process, we will explain – basically by means of the experience and happiness economy – why events have become such a popular tool over the past decade (Chapter 2). We will also show why the contents and form of events are going to change over the years to come. Other themes dealt with in Part I are event marketing (Chapter 3) and the marketing sub-areas in which event marketing is applied. Customer relationship marketing, marketing communication, branding and city marketing will be dealt with successively (Chapters 4–7 inclusive).

Part II revolves around the do phase. We will describe how strategic objectives are translated to event concepts and designs. Chapter 8 presents answers to questions such as 'What is a good concept?' and 'What is the difference between an experience and perception?'. Moreover, we will go into detail about the methods to optimize the visitor experience (Chapter 9).

The final part of the book is about the check phase. In Chapter 10, we will explain how event organizers can measure the effects of their events and evaluate the research results. We will conclude the book with an overview of models for effect measurement and a practical example of effect measurement.

Event management, the elaboration of the concept and the organization of events in actual practice are themes that are not covered in this book.

Online Study Material

At https://www.cabi.org/openresources/42300 you will find the online study material for this book. This material consists of:

- open questions;
- a practice test including answers; and
- useful appendices to Chapters 9 and 10.

Answers to the open questions, multiple-choice questions with answers and PowerPoint presentations are available for lecturers.

2 Trends and Developments: Consumers' Pursuit of Happiness

Margo Rooijackers

In this chapter, we will focus on a number of economic and sociocultural developments that play a direct or indirect role in the strategic use of events. We will discuss what is termed the experience economy and the future happiness economy. In conclusion, we will explain how these developments present opportunities in terms of the strategic use of events.

Learning Targets

After studying this chapter, you will have learnt:

- which macro-level influences there are on events;
- what the consequences are (or have been) of the experience economy for the event sector;
- how trends affect events;
- what developments are taking place that will happen after the experience economy;
- when events can be meaningful to people; and
- why insights into trends and developments are important to professionals in the events sector.

The Experience Economy

If there were one economic development that accounts for the popularity of events, it would be the emergence of the experience economy. The experience economy is centred around the creation of experiences. In other words, this economy is not about products or services but about authentic experiences.

The term 'experience economy' was introduced by the economists Pine and Gilmore (1999, 2000). At the end of the previous century, they identified five stages of economic development that are characterized by a specific way of value creation and a distinct 'consumer orientation', the criterion that determines whether or not the consumer makes a purchase (see also Table 2.1):

- *Agrarian economy*: in this economy, emphasis is placed on extracting commodities from the natural world. At this stage, consumer sensitivity is connected with the availability of these commodities. Once they are available, a mutual exchange can take place.
- *Industrial economy*: in this stage, the manufacturer concentrates on the production of goods. The focus shifts towards the cost factor. Price is a critical factor in the consumer's decision-making process.
- *Service economy*: in the service economy, there is a shift from offering products to delivering services. Rather than price, quality is now the decisive purchase criterion for the consumer.
- *Experience economy*: in this stage, the consumer wants to be engaged on an emotional level, and consumer sensitivity shifts from service quality to experience authenticity.
- *Transformation economy:* in this stage, companies will take on the challenge of trying to achieve transformations or permanent changes in the lives of consumers. The decisive factor for the consumer's purchasing decisions is not specified by Pine and Gilmore in this phase.

Table 2.1. The progression of economic value in combination with the consumer's purchase criterion. (Source: Pine and Gilmore, 2000.)

Economic stage	Supplier's focus	Consumer's focus
Agrarian economy	Extracting commodities	Availability
Industrial economy	Manufacturing products	Price
Service economy	Delivering services	Quality
Experience economy	Staging experiences	Authenticity
Transformation economy (happiness economy)		

Pine and Gilmore concluded that, at that time, the economy had reached the fourth stage, which they referred to as the *experience economy* (Pine and Gilmore, 2000), and they argued that the transformation economy would gain more and more ground in the future. We will come back to this matter later in this chapter. But first, we will take a closer look at the experience economy.

The aggregate experience

Traditionally, the event manager operates in the area of real-life experiences. Organizers make sizeable investments in the 'aggregate experience' and pull out all the stops to stimulate visitors' senses. It is not an exaggeration to say that the era of the experience economy has reached maturity. Suppliers are aware as never before of the fact that the product focus no longer suffices and that the consumer wants to be engaged on an emotional level. They try everything to turn their products or services into unique and distinctive experiences. They do so by means of sensory awareness, distinctive themes or developing compelling *storylines*, but preferably by blending every conceivable experience tool – in combination with each other – into their offerings (see Chapter 8 for an explanation of experience tools). For instance, angling is not particularly known as an exciting pastime. Still, every year in Ahoy (a venue in Rotterdam), a public angling exhibition is organized where every effort is made to create an optimal visitor experience (Box 2.1).

More than just live meetings

The explosive growth of events-related online communities demonstrates that the sector is no longer just about live meetings alone. As for the future of the event sector, an intensified crossover between real-life and virtual experiences is to be expected. Technological innovations will contribute to this development even further. In conjunction with developments such as globalization and the emergence of a hyper-connected world, technological innovations will amplify this situation.

In 2007 DNB Media already proved that the event sector was going to venture beyond mere live meetings. This media company organized a virtual concert of the Dutch band, Di-rect, which was simultaneously held in the TMF studios and Second Life: a pioneering initiative for that time.

Another illustration of the fading boundaries between the real and the artificial world is the remarkable alliance between the theatre and cinema branch. For a couple of years now, the Metropolitan Opera in New York has been featuring operas that are recorded live and shown simultaneously in a number of Pathé cinemas across Europe. For opera fans from Amsterdam, this means that they can enjoy Richard Wagner's *Das Rheingold* at the same time as their Swedish

> **Box 2.1. Visma**
>
> Visma is Europe's biggest fishing show, which is held at the Ahoy venue in Rotterdam. This trade show is characterized by a wide range of exhibitors in four segments – wholesale, retail, fish tourism and boats – which makes the show interesting to all anglers, from carp anglers to predator anglers and from sea fishermen to whitefish anglers. Visma is positioned as the place where anglers come to meet other angling enthusiasts, to buy fishing equipment and to gather information. In the Discovery Theatre, top anglers share their knowledge with visitors; there are casting courses where fly fishing demonstrations take place; and casting competitions and belly boat presentations are held in a large water basin. Elsewhere, visitors can enjoy freshly smoked fish or learn how to fillet fish properly. The 'Stekkie Kidsroute', designed especially for children, serves the young anglers among the audience. And to stay up to speed all year round, visitors may subscribe to Visma's YouTube channel or follow the trade show on Facebook and/or Twitter. (Source: www.visma.nl)

'colleagues' in Lund, put on stage by the Metropolitan in New York before a *live audience*. An interesting question here would be whether the different audiences have comparable opera experiences, or whether the experience of the cinema visitors in the European cities is of a different calibre from the live theatre experiences of the audience in New York. An initial exploration of visitor experiences produced reasons to believe the latter. Additional research will be required to confirm this finding. The outcomes of studies of this sort may serve as a basis in examining how artificial experiences in the future can gain in authenticity and visitor impact, and how live and non-live meetings can reinforce each other.

Sharing economy and co-creation

Another relevant trend is the emergence of the sharing economy (or *peer-to-peer economy*). This can be regarded as the return of the traditional barter system, in a revamped form, enabled by technological innovations such as the development of the Internet. Well-known pioneers in the sharing economy are Airbnb, the online home rental platform, and alternative taxi service Uber – both of which have meanwhile been elevated to such high levels of professionalism that one may wonder what is left of the 'sharing' principle. Another example is BlaBlaCar, an online carpooling platform that connects drivers and passengers travelling to the same destination with each other. This service is popular with, for instance, young festival visitors.

The emerging sharing economy is based on the phenomenon of co-creation. This trend refers to the changing relationship between supply and demand. As a result of technological advancements and the advent of new media, it has become easier for consumers and producers to enter into dialogue with each other. Consumers are becoming 'prosumers' (producer and consumer in one) who work together with suppliers. According to Boswijk *et al.* (2008), it is no longer just the service provider who creates experiences — the customer can also take the initiative and have more control over the production process. In this respect, it is the service provider's task to build a bond of trust with the customer. In their book, *The Experience Economy: A New Perspective*, the authors present the following definition:

> Dialogue or interaction between organizations and consumers constitutes the basis for the co-creation of personalized value and/or experiences.

Jensen (2005, presentation, not published) predicted that the relationship between suppliers and customers will become so diffuse that consumers will know better where to find each other and will become a serious threat – as 'ama-profs' (a combination of amateur and professional) – to the continued existence of commercial event agencies. Just think of Stukafest, a student room festival that was started on a small scale by a handful of students in a small number of student rooms. Now, the festival features more than 250 artists and performers at numerous locations throughout the Netherlands (www.stukafest.nl). In line with this development, it is not difficult to imagine that, in the long run, the professional sector will turn its focus primarily towards the business market and the market of large-scale public events, and that professional amateurs will seek involvement in the niche markets of intimate and small-scale events for like-minded people drawn together for a common purpose. Commercial event providers would do well to monitor innovations in other sectors and consider the implications of this for their own sector.

Worth mentioning in this respect are 'secret events'. This concerns events which are accessible only to a select target group of fans, connoisseurs or close friends, who notify each other at the last minute via social media channels about the location and time of their event: a forbidden car race at a deserted industrial site, a dance party at a secret location or an illegal dog fight. Due to the secret and more or less closed character of this type of event, visitors tend to experience them as especially thrilling, and it also gives them the positive feeling of belonging to a select group of chosen ones.

The same human need is the driving force behind the emergence of what are called 'speak-easy bars' all over the world. Difficult to find for ordinary visitors, these are establishments that are often only accessible by invitation or via a password. An example of this is the second edition of Popmonument, a music festival in Bergen op Zoom featuring pop acts in special heritage locations, where a speak-easy bar was set up in the basement of the old city hall. Festival visitors who were able to find the location were welcomed with a cocktail and treated like VIPs. It is important for professionals in the events sector to examine how they can add similar elements of excitement and exclusiveness to their range of products and services. The future will certainly see a growth of secret events and VIP treatments, in all shapes and sizes.

Devaluation of the experience concept

The above-mentioned trends and developments all hint at the fact that the concept of 'experiences' has become an inextricable part of the event sector. The other side of the success coin is that the experience concept is exploited excessively. When every local annual fair featuring traditional craft demonstrations is announced as an event that you must not miss, the credulous visitors of these events will stroll around hopefully, looking for something that, unfortunately, they are not going to find. The devaluation of the experience concept has been set in motion and the process is irreversible, meaning that inevitably the concept will become eroded and unusable at some point. At the same time, today's globally oriented communication society has resulted in consumers who are much better informed, as well as more articulate and demanding. A decrease in available leisure time is accompanied by an increase in disposable income and an increased propensity to consume. Today's event visitors want more in a smaller amount of time, and for this they are willing to open up their wallets. Add to the equation the strong growth in supply and it will be clear that an important challenge is awaiting the event manager of the future. After all, what will come after the 'Live Life to the Max' principle of modern consumers with the attendant adage of 'Seen it, done it, got the T-shirt'?

The Advance of Happiness: The Happiness Economy

At the same time as the first cracks in the experience concept appear, the alternative is making a cautious advance. By now, countless names for this economic stage have popped up all around the world. In this chapter, we have already introduced the term 'transformation economy' (Pine and Gilmore, 2000, 2011). Alternatives are 'economy of meaning' (Kuiper and Smit, 2011), 'happiness economy' (Layard, 2011) and 'purpose economy' (Hurst, 2014). Characteristic of this new economic stage is that suppliers are taking on the challenge of bringing about permanent changes in the consumer and to help him give his life meaning (or more meaning). The key purchase criterion in this stage can be designated as 'happiness' (Rooijackers, 2007). Event suppliers would do well to take a closer look at the happiness concept and make it their business (Table 2.2).

Happiness is the ultimate goal that every individual pursues in his life. However, scientists, politicians or managers prefer not to burn their fingers on this subject. Why is it that scepticism sets in whenever the topic of the manipulability of happiness is raised?

Happiness cannot be programmed or organized, according to philosopher René ten Bos (presentation, July 2016). It is a subjective concept that is part of the realm of coincidence, selectivity and uncontrollability. According to many authors, happiness is self-transcending and presupposes receptivity. The ability to control one's own individual psychological condition is supposedly limited. If you try too hard to become happy, you will overreach yourself, the hedonist paradox says. As Immanuel Kant put it, 'the essence cannot be found in how we may make ourselves happy, but in how we make ourselves worthy of happiness' (Dijkhuis, 1999).

Enabling happiness

In contemporary psychology, an opposing view is expressed as far as the manipulability of happiness is concerned. Traditionally, behavioural scientists concentrate on divergent behaviour or behaviour that can be classified as unhealthy, such as depression, anorexia and stress. According

Table 2.2. Happiness economy as an economic stage.

Economic stage	Supplier's focus	Consumer's focus
Happiness economy	Facilitating permanent changes	Happiness

to the International Positive Psychology Association (IPPA) (www.ippanetwork.org), positive psychology is concerned with 'the scientific study of what enables individuals and communities to thrive'. What makes individuals feel happy, experience their existence as positive and useful, and believe that they matter? In positive psychology, the happiness concept is an explicit object of study. The focus is shifting to terms like quality of life, subjective well-being, optimism, positive emotions and flow. One of the representatives of positive psychology is Martin Seligman, known for his book, *Authentic Happiness*. He distinguishes three components of happiness:

- positive emotions (such as fun, surprise, gratitude);
- commitment (family, work, free time); and
- meaning and purpose (knowing and using your own talents for the purpose of something that is bigger than you).

As it turns out, the two latter dimensions appear to be the most important to fulfilment in life. Other researchers have come up with similar findings. According to Diener and Biswas-Diener (2008), family and friends, sense of direction, and meaning and purpose in life are critical to quality of life. Veenhoven, a Dutch sociologist, asserts that what people think makes them happy will not necessarily be what actually makes them happy (see https://worlddatabaseofhappiness.eur.nl/). His studies have shown that happiness bears a strong correlation to having a good marriage, participating in clubs and associations, and having a job but, remarkably enough, not to having children. Veenhoven also believes that a person's context is important. According to him, fulfilment in life depends on the fit between the liveability of the external environment on the one hand (e.g. level of prosperity, legal system, freedom) and the life skills of the individual on the other hand (e.g. the ability to take action, independence, forgiveness). As it happens, objective societal characteristics account for about three-quarters of the differences in happiness across nations.

Orchestrated happiness

How are people's life skills improved, how is social cohesion in communities strengthened and how can a well-oiled society be accomplished? The application of positive psychology is a key concern of the Centre for Applied Positive Psychology (CAPP). Attention is directed towards talent development in schools; coaching; leadership development; and community development. The guiding principle is that every individual has (latent) authentic talents that give him energy and allow him to function optimally, if he is able to put them to use. The trick is to make these talents flourish, not only in the interest of the individual himself, but also in the interest of the community in which he resides.

The management and organization sector has also become aware of the happiness concept. The renowned firm of Schouten & Nelissen promoted the concept by means of the 'Geluk in uitvoering' ('Happiness in progress') conference in 2006. The central question was 'Could you enable happiness?' and, if so, 'How can professional organizations stimulate happiness in the workplace?'. Leading national and international scholars answer this crucial question with a wholehearted 'yes'. The happiness factor is a relevant dimension in achieving rational organizational goals in terms of efficiency and profit maximization. Hutten, a company specializing in culinary and hospitality catering, fully endorses this perspective: 'Hutten is a company that has the vision of being the best, the funniest and the happiest. Happiness, including happiness at work, is of paramount importance to us. Only then will you, as a company, be able to guarantee continuity, quality and "always more attention"' (www.hutten.eu). Within the company, employees are invariably referred to as cooperators, who are given every opportunity to develop their talents.

The notion of the enabling of happiness should be an eye-opener for leisure managers. If it is worthwhile for organizations to make serious business of managing happiness in the workplace, there must certainly be opportunities in the leisure sphere. After all, the leisure context comes second to none where it concerns individuals making their own choices. In sectors like labour and health care, the perception of free choice is considerably lower, because of current concepts like performance, obligations and responsibility. Events in particular would be useful in 'happiness management', since it concerns staging live encounters between people, with the intention of giving these encounters a positive emotional dimension. The challenge for the future is for events to be not only memorable but also transformational. In other words, the visitor is changed in a positive sense because of the event. Moreover, this change should be permanent rather than temporary. For instance, the visitor may learn or experience something at the event that causes him to take a different perspective on a certain issue; for example, the Festival Mundial, a large-scale world music event in Tilburg (the Netherlands) with the aim of fostering an open and tolerant attitude towards other cultures. Another example is ZigZagCity, an architecture festival in Rotterdam, each edition zooming in on a specific part of the city. Regular visitors to this event are enthusiastic as it allows them to keep discovering (or rediscovering) different parts of Rotterdam, which strengthens their bond with the city.

But it may also be about boosting ties with friends with whom one attends a music event or about discovering one's own passion or talent while participating in a sporting event.

If the feeling of happiness can be influenced, the leisure or event managers of the future should not be experience stagers but happiness managers, with expertise in the area of '*quality of life*'. They should have knowledge of factors that promote the consumer's individual well-being and be able to put this knowledge to use in the context of events. In this way, event management creates the enabling conditions within which the consumer can express his personal identity and within which he can strengthen and expand his relationships with others. Moreover, the ultimate event allows its visitors to add meaning to their lives and encourages altruistic behaviour. And this is only a small selection from the range of determinants that are related to the concept of 'quality of life'.

Helping people to help themselves

There is, however, a certain ethical risk to happiness management. The all-important point of departure is that the individual's autonomy must not be compromised by patronizing or manipulating his emotions. In this respect, a parallel can be drawn with the entertainment concept from the literature on recreation. The aim of entertainment is not so much to help people, but to help people help themselves. Give children on the beach toy buckets and shovels and they will entertain themselves and each other; all day long. This is also what facilitating happiness is all about. It is crucial to create possibilities to allow individuals to follow their own dreams.

The successful event manager of the future will enable visitors to discover their hidden passions and develop their latent talents. Ideally, he will succeed in challenging visitors to make a difference by means of a meaningful contribution to a greater whole. Attention for meaning and purpose in the design and programming of events will inspire a permanent change in the visitor that increases the quality of his life, as opposed to a temporary climax.

Meaningful leisure products

With its 'Open Happiness' marketing campaign, the Coca-Cola Company was one of the first organizations operating worldwide in 2009 that aimed to create an association of happiness with its product. In the same period we saw Center Parcs, operating in the accommodation and recreation sector, rolling out a promotional campaign themed 'a state of happiness'.

And what about the 'holiday package with added value' as offered by Club Med in cooperation with DUOjob. This holiday programme, especially designed for stress-sensitive managers, comprises a series of workshops to learn to restore the work–life balance. These examples illustrate an attention shift from experiences to meaning. The focus of products and services has shifted from the temporary flow experience towards the lasting optimization of the leisure user's contentment with life. Beneficial effects, supposed to last until long after the holiday itself, are pursued. The growth of convent tourism can also be explained by people's growing need for spiritual healing and purpose in life. This development can even be seen in the fitness and beauty sector, which traditionally focused on the exterior (the body) only. Health and wellness centres have blended their traditional physical exercise and dietetic offerings with mental coaching and spiritual workshops. All this takes place, preferably, in a setting in which mutual interaction between like-minded people is stimulated and the sense of community is promoted.

Events with added value

The event sector has been directing its attention towards the concept of meaning and purpose for quite some time now. Everyone is well aware of national and international charity campaigns. The most famous charity event ever organized was undoubtedly Live Aid in 1985. With this benefit concert, organizers Bob Geldof and Midge Ure wanted to raise funds for relief in the ongoing Ethiopian famine. The concert lasted 16 hours and featured simultaneous performances by famous musicians in several places across the world, and it was broadcast live across many countries.

Events of a somewhat smaller scale, but also clearly focusing on meaning, are the events of the SoccorsoClowns in Italy: the music show, *SoccorsoClowns in Concert*, and the *SoccorsoClowns Theatre Tour*. Both events take place at different times and different locations in Italy and they have been designed especially for children with an illness or disability, the idea being that by going to one of these shows, they can be children again, if only for a little while (www.cliniclowns.nl).

Comparable initiatives are seen in the sports sector. The Johan Cruyff Foundation, for example, is committed to getting young people moving. The foundation does so by means of events such as the Johan Cruyff Games. A similar initiative is the charity, the Rafael Nadal Foundation.

This foundation offers educational programmes using sport as a tool for personal and social integration, passing on values such as effort, self-improvement and respect in order to encourage self-esteem and confidence (www.cruyff-foundation.org and www.tennisdailynews.net).

Corporate social responsibility

There are plenty of examples of companies that have made social responsibility part of their corporate philosophy. The starting principle in a strategy of this kind is to take the balance between *people, planet* and *profit* into consideration in all business decisions. Corporate and other events can be used as a tool in putting the corporate social responsibility principle into action. This too is a development that is part of the happiness economy.

An example in this respect is HEMA's annual 'Helping Hands' programme. HEMA is a famous Dutch department store, with shops in the Netherlands, Belgium and France. During this 2-day corporate event, employees of HEMA headquarters do volunteer work for a good cause: hosting a high tea in a nursing home in Amsterdam, Brussels and Paris, or fixing up a children's farm in a residential community.

Siemens has taken action on its social responsibility by means of the Siemens Caring Hands. Employees can nominate an event for a donation from Siemens. This donation involves a financial contribution or help in the form of Siemens volunteers.

Many event organizers have already made the importance of investing in corporate social responsibility part of their business strategy. For example, employees of Artishock, an events and marketing agency in 's-Hertogenbosch, are allowed to spend 10% of their billable hours on social projects in their home city (www.artishockevents.nl).

A range of appealing initiatives has already been accomplished. Nevertheless, the reality is probably a little more unmanageable. Too often, well-intended strategic organizational objectives get bogged down in the reality of every day, and factual activities cannot seem to escape the appearance of 'window dressing'.

Still, the examples mentioned in this section clearly illustrate that the attention to meaning and purpose is not a new phenomenon in the event sector. Strangely enough, commercial event businesses have hardly made use of this angle up to now. It is clear that this is where their challenge for the future lies.

Innovation Opportunities

The progression from the experience economy to the happiness economy is characterized by a shift of focus from experiences to happiness and quality of life. The changing economic context creates opportunities for innovation. The time has come for stakeholders in the event sector to reflect on the question of how to define their core business: creating experiences for consumers or generating meaning for people or society? What is typical of the happiness economy is the pursuit to increase the quality of life on an individual, social and societal level. Consequently, the event manager's focus area is shifting from staging optimal experiences to facilitating happiness. The ultimate goal on an individual level is to achieve an increased sense of happiness in the visitor. On a social level, it concerns optimizing the quality of life of society in general, and in particular to strengthen social cohesion within and between the various groups and subgroups that make up society. In this new economy, it is highly conceivable that the consumer will make a deliberate choice to visit events that contribute to his contentment with life and/or that have a positive influence on the quality of life in the social, political–economic and/or ecological context in which he finds himself.

The challenge for the event manager of the future is to create innovative event concepts – consistent with the happiness perspective – and develop an accompanying set of management tools or toolbox, in order to successfully shape these events, both offline and online.

Scenario Analysis

A scenario analysis is a method to analyse possible future events by considering alternative possible outcomes and it is used as a tool to formulate strategic management recommendations.

A scenario analysis consists of the following seven steps (Van Notten *et al.*, 2003):

Step 1. Formulating a project plan (objective, design and contents).
Step 2. Carrying out a general trend analysis.
Step 3. Reducing trends to a limited number of key trends.
Step 4. Describing key trends.
Step 5. Constructing alternative scenarios.
Step 6. Developing storyboards for each scenario.
Step 7. Formulating recommendations.

Step 1 is the step of formulating a project plan. In this stage, the objective of the analysis is formulated and choices are made with regard to the design and contents of the analysis.

During Step 2, a general trend analysis is carried out. This can be done by means of the DESTEP model, which addresses trends and developments in demographic, economic, socio-cultural, technological, ecological and political areas.

The next step, taking the client's problem as a point of departure, involves reducing the large number of trends to a limited number of key trends. The two selection criteria in determining these key trends are the degree of probability that the trend concerned will persist and the degree of impact that is attached to this trend. The result of Step 3 can be represented in what is called a probability impact diagram.

After determining the key trends, Step 4 focuses on an extensive description of each of these trends, in which a line is drawn from the past through the present to the future.

In Step 5, based on the information from this in-depth trend analysis, a number of possible future scenarios are drawn up. Usually, two to four scenarios are developed. Depending on the client's needs, this may result in a probable, possible and preferable alternative and/or a profit, non-profit or public sector scenario. A commonly used approach is to select and compare two main trends, creating a system of axes with four different scenarios. An example of this is shown in Fig. 2.1. Another option for developing scenarios is to take the various intervention alternatives available to the stakeholders involved as a starting point and to present the consequences of each intervention in a corresponding future scenario.

Fig. 2.1. Four scenarios for the future of 'Live Communication 3.0'. (From NHTV Minorgroep CLC-Vecta, 2015.)

CLC-VECTA

An example of an organization in the event industry that considers it absolutely crucial to closely follow trends and developments and anticipate the future, is CLC-VECTA Centrum voor Live Communication. CLC-VECTA is a sector association for organizations that are professionally involved in organizing, accommodating and facilitating trade shows, meetings and conferences, events, entertainment and incentives. It looks after the interests of its more than 200 members by informing, advising, supporting and inspiring them in various ways (www.clcvecta.nl).

In collaboration with Breda University of Applied Sciences and Stenden Hogeschool Leeuwarden, CLC-VECTA has launched a long-term research programme entitled 'Live Communication 3.0'. One of the sub-studies from this programme is a scenario study to answer the question of what challenges the near and distant future of live communication poses and what this means for the strategic policy of the CLC-VECTA members.

Steps 6 and 7, in conclusion, consist of designing storyboards for the various scenarios and formulating recommendations in the area of strategic management for the client.

As part of the CLC-VECTA scenario study, specific attention was paid in the trend analysis to technological trends and developments in live communication. In this process, the study zeroed in on trends like content amplification, Bluetooth low energy, micro locations, and iBeacons and wearables, but also on mobile devices and event apps, robotics, virtual reality and 3D printing, and holograms (Hasanoglu and Dopheide, 2016).

For the development of the future scenarios, two developments that are decisive to the future of the live communication sector were selected and compared with each other. The horizontal axis was labelled as crowd (physical, live encounters) versus cloud (digital encounters). The vertical axis involves the scope of the encounters, with large-scale, mass events versus small-scale, intimate encounters at the axis extremes. This approach results in four alternative scenarios.

What's typical of the scenarios on the left side of the diagram is a permanent emphasis on organizing live encounters between people. This is where the strength of trade shows and events can be found traditionally. What characterizes the scenarios on the right side of the diagram is that they reflect the importance of the increased digitization of life in general and the realization that digital encounters can be equally valuable to interpersonal relationships, and may sometimes even replace live encounters altogether. The scenarios at the top of the diagram are characterized by an emphasis on the organization of large-scale, mass events, whereas the underlying quadrants are all about encounters that focus on small scale and intimacy.

It may be useful, in line with the aforementioned perspective of happiness, to add a third axis to Fig. 2.1, with experience versus meaning as the axis extremes. This will give the diagram a three-dimensional character and also raises the question of whether the future will revolve around creating experiences or accomplishing meaningful transformations.

The future scenarios for live communication as set out above can be described as ideal-type scenarios that are unlikely to manifest themselves in their pure form. The relevance of the study lies in the fact that it is made clear, instantly, that the industry has to acknowledge that there is work to be done. Where in the past all that event organizers had to do was organize professional (large-scale) live encounters of a high quality (top-left quadrant), they will be faced in the future with the challenge of creating optimal offline and online combinations in new forms of 'live events' and with the question of how they are planning to orchestrate even more meaningful encounters. If the current members are not prepared to innovate and think about aspects such as cross-media distribution, building lasting and meaningful customer relationships, differentiating between main and side events, and so on, new providers will seize their opportunities (NHTV Minorgroep CLC-VECTA, 2015; CLC-VECTA, 2016).

The research presented offers a sector association such as CLC-VECTA clear tools and guidelines to promote and enhance the professionalism of its members. It clearly shows that, at the moment, the expertise of its members is not necessarily the expertise required in the future. This presents opportunities for developing and encouraging interventions to strengthen the members' innovative capacity in the desired direction. Just think of developing a range of training programmes in which members receive an answer to the question of how technological innovations can be optimally implemented in their own business operations. It may also involve facilitating interactive workshops in which members explore the possibilities of the happiness perspective for the future professional context in a process of collective creativity.

Summary

The experience economy no longer centres on products and services but on authentic emotions and experiences. Pine and Gilmore (2000, 2011) distinguish five economic stages, which are the agrarian economy, the industrial economy, the service economy, the experience economy and the transformation economy. Our current society is characterized by them as an experience economy. Events should have added emotional value to visitors and offer them an aggregate experience. The importance of developments like globalization, digitization, co-creation and sharing is expected to increase in the near future. If we look ahead a little further, the transformation or happiness economy may gain ground. The emphasis on experience will shift to a focus on meaning and instigating lasting changes in the visitor's life will become the ultimate goal.

The progression from experience economy to happiness economy presents opportunities for innovation. Events can be used, for instance, as a tool to promote social cohesion and personal well-being. How to give shape to this exactly is the challenge for the professionals of the future.

3 Event Marketing

Dorothé Gerritsen and Ronald van Olderen

We will start this chapter with an explanation of what event marketing means. Then, we will place this form of marketing in a broader context. After a description of the various types of event marketing, we will present its advantages and disadvantages. We will finish this chapter with a number of tips relating to the application of event management.

Learning Targets

After studying this chapter, you will have learnt:

- how event marketing emerged;
- which approaches there are within event marketing;
- what the strategic reasons may be for employing event marketing;
- what the position of event marketing is within the marketing mix;
- what types of event marketing we can distinguish;
- what the strength is of events and event marketing; and
- when event marketing can be employed.

Box 3.1. Smart

The introduction campaign of the new Smart car in Italy is a good example of a mediagenic event. To this end, Bureau Merlo Spa rolled out a series of events in Rome, Naples and Milan based on the concept of 'urban mobility' and through state-of-the-art technology and strong storytelling, obviously in line with the values of the brand and out-of-the-box communication campaigns. The creative idea consisted of an invasion of spherical UFOs cruising the streets of Rome, Milan and Naples as part of a teaser campaign that went viral. A countdown was organized in the weeks before 7 November, the date when the UFOs revealed their content: the new Smart. This led to more than 600,000 views via the viral campaign, 3,500,000 video impressions and more than 70,000 visits to the city-invasion.it website. Eight thousand people attended the opening of the UFOs in the three cities involved.

Source: beaworldfestival.com

Event Marketing

Event marketing is very much of current interest. Organizations are becoming increasingly alert to the strength of events as effective live means of communication. Events are used more and more often; for instance, by companies to bring their brands, products or services to the attention of current and potential customers, thus attempting to create a positive brand attitude. Since event marketing is only at the beginning of a glorious career, it is important at this point to define the concept.

The words 'event marketing' generate about 3 million hits on Google. All these websites exhibit a great diversity of definitions and descriptions: organizing events; creatively turning the message into a theme and a programme; the relationship of an event with other marketing and communication means; emotions and experiences; marketing of events; alignment of the event with the company's brand values, and so on. In the battle for the consumer's attention, brands, companies, countries, cities and even royal families are opting ever more often for non-traditional means of communication. Sponsoring, social media and event marketing are rapidly growing communication tools. The fact is that the event has secured an important position in the field of marketing.

The above example (Box 3.1) shows that Smart achieved maximum results with limited resources by organizing an event. Traditional marketing and communication means, such as advertisements and printed media, are very expensive. Smart realized that the essence was the live experience of the launch of a new car. This would probably enthuse the primary target group much more than, for instance, an advertisement, with greater follow-up and media coverage as a result. In this example, Smart deliberately incorporated the event into its marketing and communication strategy. Additionally, the event generated an excellent platform for the account managers to get in touch with the media, with local Smart dealers and with consumers. All in all, this example shows how an event can be used strategically as a means to achieve certain goals: event marketing.

A Definition

Event marketing involves marketing, events and communication. It is a concept that is attracting increasing attention from businesses, organizations and the media. By now, the term has become widely used, but it has not yet found a place in the *Oxford English Dictionary*. In the section on using events as a strategic marketing tool in Chapter 1, we have already presented a definition of the word 'event'. The word 'marketing' is a contraction of the words 'market' and 'getting'. Market getting became marketing.

> Marketing is the process of developing, pricing, promoting and distributing products, services or ideas that are tailored to the market; it includes all other activities that create value and systematically lead to increased sales or another desired response, establish a good reputation and ongoing relationships with customers, so that all stakeholders achieve their objectives. (Verhage, 2009)

Communication is an essential component in the definition of events as well as that of marketing. As far as events are concerned, the communication objective is all-important; and as far as marketing is concerned, promotion is one of the tools to achieve the marketing objective. In Chapter 5 of this book, we will explore the relationship between events and communication more extensively.

Marketing and the Emergence of Experiences

Over the past few decades, marketing has shifted its focus from an entirely product-oriented approach to a more communication-oriented approach. Several decades ago, companies that had a marketing plan had a definite lead on their competitors. Today, 90% of all companies in the industry apply the same marketing and research techniques, as well as means of communication.

In other words, it is becoming increasingly difficult for a company to 'stand out from the crowd'. Figure 3.1 presents the evolution of business practices.

Marketing originated from the economics discipline. Initially, businesses primarily had a product orientation: the product was the focus within 'marketing'. Product-oriented companies distinguished themselves by means of the quality of their products. In those early days, the quality of products was very high, which was all a business needed to set itself apart from its competitors. Starting from the 1920s, marketing was employed from a more sales-oriented perspective. The difference in quality between products was negligible at that time, and competition was based mainly on price differences. The era of Kotler, the marketing-oriented period, was characterized by an emphasis on distribution. 'How and where do I sell my products?' was a key question in this phase. The four Ps – product, price, place and promotion (communication) – were the ingredients for successful market operations. According to Rijkenberg (2005), this was logical, because as it turned out, there was a huge demand for all sorts of products that generally made life more comfortable.

As time went by, companies came to realize that there was only little scope left for product innovations, and what is more, they required substantial investments in promotion. Meanwhile, the consumer hardly cared about product innovations any more. The consumer was far more concerned with immaterial needs, intensification and experiences. Nowadays, businesses are acknowledging that – rather than the product – the crucial factor is customer retention, causing a shift to occur from transaction-oriented marketing to relationship marketing, the subject of Chapter 4. There is a need for 'added value' of the product, as a result of which society in the 21st century has developed a much more distinctive communication orientation. Brand values have become important in this phase. Consumers want to identify themselves by means of a brand.

Phase	Focus in marketing mix	Consumer needs (from physical to mental)
		Physical
Product orientation (traditional)	Product	Functional needs
Sales orientation (from 1920)	Price	Functional and convenience needs
Marketing orientation (from 1956: Kotler)	Place	Material needs, Status, Recognition
Communication orientation (from 2000)	Promotion	Immaterial needs, Intensification, Experiences, Self-development
		Mental

Fig. 3.1. The evolution of business practices. (Source: Rijkenberg, 2005.)

Experience Marketing

Subsequently, a shift occurred from traditional marketing practices to experience marketing. Experience marketing is an extra marketing tool and is, in fact, also a development in the field of marketing, which involves the creation of non-tangible and memorable experiences. It is about a subjective customer or consumer experience. Due to economic progress, products and services have become so easily available and mutually comparable that organizations are forced to look for new tools in order to protect their margins. According to Pine and Gilmore (2000, 2011), the solution can be found in adding theatricality and entertainment: buying and consuming must be turned into an experience. It is all about engaging the customer on an emotional level. Far from settling for the pure function of a product or service, consumers today want added value in the form of an experience. The experience is worth more to them than the mere fulfilment of a need. Furthermore, products and services in contemporary Western societies are only rarely designed to meet consumers' basic primary needs.

To be able to distinguish properly among products, services and experiences, the principle of value addition is crucial. In the case of an experience, the value addition can be found in the people themselves; the experience of the customer or visitor is the actual product. An experience is the result of the interaction between the event organized and the person concerned. A service, for instance, can become part of an experience when it is delivered in such a way that customers have an experience they will remember later, because it left an impression on them. The next example will show that the service of 'showing a film in a cinema' is turned into a unique experience through the application of event marketing. The cinema's marketing objective is to attract new crowds. This is done by offering event concepts with experiential elements to new target groups. More and more cinemas and cinema chains have discovered the power of these types of events and are organizing live events in their cinemas.

Developments in Marketing Communication

Over the years, marketing communication has seen its share of important changes as a consequence of changes in production methods and market circumstances. Important developments in this respect are:

- big advertising budgets (starting from 1960);
- greater availability of marketing communication budgets;
- one-to-one communication; and
- experience communication.

The most important development occurred around the 1960s, when consumer marketing made its entrance. Producers came to recognize the importance of products and services and directed their attention to mass communication. In the early 1980s, producers started engaging in advertising, promotion, sponsoring, direct marketing and public relations. Moreover, they acknowledged that there were two target groups to take into account: consumers and distributive trade.

From 2000 onwards, one-to-one communication has become increasingly important. Messages are geared as much as possible to the values, wishes and characteristics of the consumer. The enormous communication volume makes it harder to reach the target group, forcing brands and organizations to look for alternatives. One of these alternatives is experience communication, or, put differently, live communication (see Chapter 5).

The shift from traditional marketing to experience marketing has a clear link with event marketing. Within the field of communication, the emphasis has moved to the one-to-one relationship with the consumer. In this respect, events are a very appropriate medium: people can meet each other in person, all senses can be stimulated and an experience can be created. The event as a

> **Box 3.2. Sing-along cinema**
>
> The sing-along cinema is one of the concepts by means of which cinema chains try to attract new crowds. Their websites are swarming with 'events' and 'specials': Turkish films and Bollywood films in major cities, senior afternoons and ladies' nights ('Enjoy a glass of prosecco, as well as delicious canapés and finger foods!'). Live satellite broadcasts from the Metropolitan Opera in New York invariably lead to a sold-out Metropolis in Antwerp. And the latest invention by Pathé International: girls' afternoon. Normally, vampire films have to grow on the audience over time, but *Twilight* was sold out straight away. Youry Bredewold, from Pathé International, reported a theatre full of screaming teenage girls. Cinemas are going through changes. Nowadays, events account for some 3–5 % of Pathé International's turnover. They have capitalized on the wish of 'wanting to have an experience together with one's own kind of people'. The profit margin is attractive: a night out to the opera on the silver screen at Metropolis will set you back €32, a VIP ticket as much as €45. A bigger pond to fish from, that's the general idea. After all, cinemas are doing great. Most cinema visitors are aged between 16 and 31. It makes perfect sense to attract wealthy senior citizens to the cinema, too. And as it happens, events are an excellent way to do so.
>
> Source: Van Zwol, 2010, adapted by the authors.

communication platform offers excellent opportunities to forge closer ties between suppliers on the one hand – brands, cities, products, services or regions – and consumers on the other hand. The consumer is allowed to experience personally what the organization is all about and what it stands for.

Event Marketing: Two Perspectives

Event marketing has its origin in the fields of marketing as well as communication. Event marketing can be regarded from two perspectives:

1. Marketing for events.
2. Marketing through events.

Marketing for events

The point of departure in marketing for events is that the event is the product to be marketed: events such as IMEX (the international trade fair for event organizations), Salone Internazionale del Mobile in Milan (the famous design furniture fair), New Orleans Jazz and Heritage Festival, International Motor Show Geneva and Sensation White in various cities in the world like Sao Paulo (Brazil) and Bucharest (Romania) and in Taiwan. The event is the core business, and in most cases, a brand name, too. Everything that the organizer does is for the purpose of the event. In other words, the event is the starting point of all business operations and can be marketed by means of various strategic approaches: branding, relationship marketing, marketing and communication, and other disciplines. To put the product called 'event' on the market, a variety of resources and channels can be employed, such as the Internet, commercials, posters, social networks and advertisements. The ultimate goal is for the event:

- to be positioned effectively in relation to competing events;
- to contribute to the organization's strategic goals; and
- to contribute to the organization's continuity and profits.

Marketing through events

Events can be used as an important part of the marketing and communication policy of, for instance, brands, products and services. The organization uses the event for strategic and/or tactical considerations. The ultimate strategic goal is the organization's continuity.

This book focuses on the event as a means to achieve a certain goal, which falls into the category of marketing through events. Based on empirical research among professional event marketers, we will apply the following definition:

> Event marketing focuses on developing, intensifying and expanding a relationship (or brand relationship) with one or more target groups, in which the event or the series of events is used as a marketing and communication tool and in which emotion and experience are brought together. A clearly defined objective, message and target group, consistent with the organizer's policy, is a precondition in this respect.

So, an organization may choose to engage in event marketing because it wants to communicate a certain message. It is important for this message to be conveyed effectively. That is why clear and measurable objectives must be formulated in advance. Getting the right message across to the target group seems easier than it really is. There is no point in doggedly pursuing event marketing strategies, cost what it may. As it turns out, there are still a great many companies that use events in an ill-considered way.

Reasons to Opt for Event Marketing

The guiding principle of the various strategies dealt with in Chapters 4 through 7 is that the concept of event marketing is interpreted as broadly as possible. The goal of a strategy is to increase the sales of products or services and to ensure an organization's continuity or – for instance, in the case of a city – encourage economic activity.

There are various strategies based on which an event can be organized:

- *Relationship marketing strategy*: building, maintaining and intensifying relationships with various stakeholders.
- *Marketing communication strategy*: influencing the visitor's knowledge, attitude and behaviour.
- *External branding strategy*: influencing, creating or changing the visitor's valuable brand associations.
- *Internal branding strategy*: influencing, creating or changing the employee's valuable brand associations in order to increase employee involvement and optimize the customer experience.
- *City marketing strategy*: contributing to the objectives of a city.

We believe that achieving economic objectives by means of events is not the only concern. Events can also be used in the public sector (countries, regions or cities) to achieve strategic goals. In the end, these objectives will advance economic objectives. For instance, cities can use events to put their city on the map strategically. Winning the bid to host the start of the Tour de France may be interesting to the city of Utrecht for economic reasons, but it may also be an opportunity for the city to put itself on the map as the major cycling city of the Netherlands and/or generate more publicity with the aim of attracting more tourists (a promotional reason). Another reason – a social one – may be organizing various activities relating to the Tour de France for children from the city's urban regeneration districts. Of course, it usually involves a mix of all these motives.

That is why it is interesting, for economic reasons, for a city like Utrecht to win the bid to host the start of the Vuelta a España (a multi-day cycling race that is held every year in Spain), but what may also play a role is that the city of Utrecht wants to put itself on the map as one of the major sport cities of the Netherlands. Or the goal may be to generate more publicity, in order to attract more tourists (promotional motive). Another social reason may be to organize activities, relating to the Vuelta a España, for children from urban regeneration districts.

Below (Box 3.3), we give an example of a company that purposefully uses events to achieve strategic goals.

This example serves to show a number of things. Basically, Bogra wants to increase sales. The platforms to do so are a pre-trade show for top clients and a trade show for other client groups. At the international trade show, the company also concentrated on important potential clients. To Bogra, these platforms are excellent opportunities to have live contact with important clients. The events may not lead directly to increased sales, but indirectly they may strengthen the company's relationships with its clients or influence the mindset of current and potential clients with regard to the Bogra brand. So, it may be clear that the reasons for using the event (from a sales, customer relationship or branding perspective) should be formulated first of all.

Box 3.3. Bogra

Bogra is a producer and supplier of coffins, urns and other products that can be used before, during or after a funeral or cremation. Twenty per cent of its total production volume is exported to other countries, mostly to France and Belgium. Bogra delivers directly to customers (business-to-consumer) or via regional wholesalers, including funeral transport companies (business-to-business). A few years ago, Bogra was planning to introduce a new line of coffins to its main client group, the funeral companies, with the aim of increasing sales. To this end, Bogra called in the services of a specialized event agency, which developed a communication track themed 'Choose your coffin', focusing on the fact that choosing a coffin is often an emotional moment; after all, it involves a choice for the final goodbye. People on the street were asked what kind of coffin they would like to be buried in, by means of a catalogue describing the three categories (product lines):

1. Traditional/classic.
2. Modern/contemporary.
3. Deluxe/exclusive.

The results from this survey were then used during a pre-trade show, to which the main clients of Bogra were invited. The pre-trade show for important clients was held in the basement of a fortress. Emphasis was placed on interaction and product information by means of the three product lines. Subsequently, the concept was translated into a trade show stand concept (a life-sized white coffin), with visitors literally undergoing a 'coffin experience'.

Bogra presented itself at the international funeral trade show in Düsseldorf with the theme of 'I love Holland'. On their stand there were mainly ecological coffins in a décor of red tulips and little lambs in a field. Woollen coffins, a green alternative for burials, were also on display.

Source: Gouden Giraffe entry, 2005, unpublished; and www.bogra.nl, www.your-event.nl, adapted by the authors.

Event marketing can be undertaken as an integrated part of a communication campaign or on a periodical basis. It is also possible that it concerns an event or a series of events as a part of an overall campaign. With its 'Choose your coffin' theme, Bogra initiated a campaign to introduce new product lines. Within this campaign, a survey of the clients' needs was carried out, a pre-trade show was organized and the company arranged representation at an international trade show. Bogra intentionally opted for these means. The overall campaign was supported by diverse media and means of communication.

Events that are used from a branding perspective may involve either internal or external branding. Internal branding may comprise not only internal events (employee training programmes) but also team-building events and events to increase employee involvement. Personnel is a valuable asset to an organization, it is a precondition to achieve its objectives, which is the subject of Chapter 6.

The Bogra example is an example of external branding: getting the Bogra brand to stick in the customer's mind. If customers (including potential customers) attend the presentation of the product and experience the coffin for themselves, then this will have an impact on the customer's brand associations, and it may even change his attitude towards the product.

Events in the Marketing Mix

Even though there are many different interpretations and applications, the marketing mix still constitutes the basis of the marketing policy of many companies. The four Ps (product, price, place and promotion) make up the foundation of the marketing mix, but other components can be added to the traditional marketing mix. A fifth P was added to the marketing mix at a later stage, the P for personnel, based on the idea that personnel contribute to marketing. The inclusion of event marketing in the marketing mix has produced the discipline matrix (see Fig. 3.2). The discipline matrix is an expanded and updated version of the traditional marketing mix, with the addition of the fifth P for personnel. Furthermore, experience marketing and the attendant 'E' of emotion and experience are additional features.

Fig. 3.2. Discipline matrix. (Source: Michels, 2013, adapted by the authors.)

Experience marketing focuses on the subjective experiences and perceptions of consumers. The experience marketing parts are shown in shaded boxes, because they are tools that create live, three-dimensional and all-senses experiences of the brand, the product or the service. As we have shown, event marketing is an appropriate tool to evoke sensations and emotions in consumers.

The event is shown in the marketing mix as one of the communication tools, apart from sponsoring, marketing PR, advertising, the Internet, sales promotion and direct marketing (store communication and personal sales belong to the marketing communication mix). In event marketing, the event is the central point, which is supported by several means and channels of communication. The event can be regarded as a product. The purpose of the means and channels is to add strength to the event and also to extend the visitor experience. These means can be used in three phases:

- *The pre-exposure phase*: this is the phase that precedes the event, or series of events, in which visitors are encouraged to take part in or attend the event. The experience that is created during the event itself can also be spread out to the preliminary stage.
- *The direct exposure phase*: this phase involves the actual experience itself.
- *The post-exposure phase*: the phase after the event. What does the organization do to stay in touch with the visitor?

See Fig. 3.3 for a diagram of this.

Types of Event Marketing

We distinguish different types of event marketing. The supplier may:

1. Conceive and organize the event himself (e.g. brand events, relationship events or brand venues).
2. Team up with an existing event (e.g. sponsored events, side events and spectaculars).
3. Facilitate and/or finance the event: regional or national government bodies often host, facilitate and/or finance cultural or sporting events, by means of which they enter the arena of event marketing.

Conceiving and organizing an event of your own

Brand events

The 'Festival Anòlia Estrella Damm' (music festival from the beer brewery in Barcelona, Spain, in the old beer brewery) or the 'Audi Brand Event' are examples of brand events. At the Audi Brand Event, Audi organizes a dazzling show to launch its new A4 models, bringing to life the values of sportive, progressive and sophisticated. Due to the combination of audio-visual aspects, acts and entertainment, the overall concept exudes the core value of 'progression'. In this situation, Audi is the initiator, owner and main financier of the event.

So, brand events are events that revolve around a brand. Their organization may be in the hands of a professional event organizer. The sole purpose of the event is to create positive brand associations or reinforce existing brand associations. Through the event, closer ties must be forged with the target group, so that the brand becomes embedded even more strongly in their identity and lifestyle.

Brand events are organized to reach a specific target group, which is chosen on the basis of the brand values. The event provides for an experience in the target group, and its purpose is to increase brand familiarity and reinforce its image.

Brand venues

With its Holland Heineken House and the Heineken Experience, Dutch beer brewer, Heineken, has created two powerful brand venues in its multi-channel strategy, which is a strategy aimed at

Fig. 3.3. Pre-, direct and post-exposure.

communicating with the consumer through multiple channels. Heineken's objective is that the consumer comes into contact with the brand and experiences it. The associations that Heineken wishes to get across are conviviality and being together. A quick look at their website reveals that this involves, among other things, entertainment, music and sports.

Another interesting example is the Miele Inspirience Centres in Germany, MIC for short. As a manufacturer of high-end domestic appliances, Miele came to realize that customers were more inclined to purchase a product if they were given the opportunity of experiencing the product themselves. MIC is an inspiring showroom where cooking work shops and demonstrations are given and where conferences and seminars are organized on a regular basis.

In other words, brand venues are brand meeting places. They provide companies with the opportunity to establish a strong identity for their brand. Brand venues are also referred to with the term 'out-of-home marketing' and they fall within our definition of event marketing.

Relationship events

A good example of a relationship event which is centred around providing information to customers, as well as customer activation, is the Wella event for hair stylists, beauticians and trade press. The 'Wella family' continues to grow during this event (https://beaworldfestival.com/) by:

- Revealing the latest trends.
- Celebrating talent with the international TrendVisionAward.
- Showcasing innovations around Wella's brand portfolio. This generates new business and increases audience engagement outside this event through all the media attention. The concept of 'NewHorizons' was expressed in elements such as the location by the sea and aesthetic elements based on the horizon. During the event, participants had the opportunity to discover new horizons through presentations of trends, various hair shows and educational workshops.

Relationship events are an excellent opportunity for the various parties involved to meet each other in a different setting, not only for a company's top clients, but also for future clients or stakeholders.

Internal branding (internal brand events)

The Italian fashion brand, Diesel, has set up its own internal branding programme, titled 'Diesel Love Power Experience', targeted at employees who handle customer contacts. The Diesel Love Power Experience was, in fact, an employee motivation training programme highlighting the relationship between employees and retailers – a relationship that is supposed to balance between Love (long-lasting and personal relationships) and Power (commercial success and free enterprise). The programme comprised several elements: an introduction training session, a personnel party, a team-building event, a performance interview and a goodbye party. The outcome was impressive: better relationship of the employees with Diesel; motivation to boost sales; open feedback culture; willingness towards personal growth; departure of employees who did not fit in with the company profile; more attention in the Customer Service Department to the relationship with retailers; and a wish to improve internal cooperation in the Sales Department.

To sum up, branding events are events to connect employees better with the brand, in order to improve business results in the long term, based on the idea that personnel are a critical factor in sales success.

Teaming up with an existing event
Sponsored events

An example of a sponsored event is the ABN AMRO World Tennis Tournament, which has been in existence for almost 40 years. Sponsoring this event provides plenty of scope for the organization to foster relations with its target markets. ABN has developed special package deals to allow for live encounters with its target group. Other examples in this area include the Emirates Airline US Open Series (the famous tennis grand slam), Volvo Ocean Race and Red Bull Crashed Ice. What stands out is that these events are often sporting events; after all, sport is a pre-eminent platform for sharing and conveying emotions.

Sponsoring of events obviously presupposes interaction between the sponsor and the sponsored event. A sponsor provides money, goods, services and know-how. In exchange for this, the sponsored party commits itself to contributing to the achievement of the sponsor's communication objectives. Compared to other forms of marketing communication, this form has an indirect character. Sponsoring will only be effective if it is aligned properly with the other marketing communication tools of the organization. Events lend themselves well to sponsoring. Much the same as with brand events, a company can choose an event that evokes the right associations.

During events, a brand can also be present 'live', as a part of the main event. This can be done by using promotion teams. Chupa Chups promotion teams, for instance, hand out free lollipops at music events. Another example is the Glorix promotion team cleaning toilets – and making a grand display of it – at Mysteryland or other festivals.

Such a side event (Box 3.4) is a separate part of an existing bigger event. The supplier of the side event is not responsible for this bigger event, thus coasting along on the image that belongs to the main event, and the attendant target audience. Obviously, there has to be a clear link between the event visitor and the organization's target group.

Box 3.4. Side events

Olympic Experience The Hague

From 6–21 August 2016, the Olympic Experience event organized by TeamNL of NOC*NSF (Dutch Olympic Committee * Dutch Sports Federation) took place in The Hague. The sports beach of The Hague was transformed during the Games into an Olympic Rio where everyone could come and play, watch and experience sports. The Olympic Experience offered sports fans of all ages, families, sports clubs and the corporate community a chance to experience the Olympic Games and TeamNL's achievements to the fullest and offered space for 6000 visitors every day. During the day, people could practise all kinds of sports themselves under the guidance of 30 different sports associations. In the afternoons and evenings, visitors could watch the Olympic Games live and cheer on TeamNL via large television screens, including previews and reviews, entertainment and the presence of former top athletes and Olympians. What's more, there were live contacts with, among others, Holland Heineken House in Rio.

Source: www.teamnl.org

Campaigns

Campaigns cause commotion. The intention is to generate a one-off lasting memorable experience that generates a lot of free publicity. The campaign may either be pushing the edge of what is acceptable or be entirely legal.

Edge of Acceptability

Ambush marketing refers to the practice of appearing to align a brand with an event for which that brand has not paid for the right to be a sponsor. Events that are very suitable for this purpose, in terms of the media attention they attract and their image, are the Olympic Games or the European or World Football Championships. An example in this respect is Bavaria, which was planning to hand out special 'Leeuwenhoses' to the audience attending a match of the Dutch football team in the run-up to the World Championships in Germany. The Koninklijke Nederlandse Voetbalbond (KNVB), however, already had a sponsorship agreement with Heineken, so the special pairs of trousers did not make it past the stadium's entrance. Meanwhile, publicity for Bavaria was nevertheless created. Heineken had concocted a similar campaign 2 years earlier, during the European Football Championships in Portugal. Heineken horns were handed out to the audience, something that official sponsor Carlsberg was not particularly pleased with. At the World Championships in South Africa, Bavaria captured the media's attention with its Bavaria Babes. These ladies had entered the stadium as supporters of Denmark. In the second half, they caught everyone's attention, singing and dancing, after having changed to orange Bavaria dresses.

Legal

Finding ways to associate their brand with an event does not necessarily require businesses to be present at the event itself; they can also organize other events themselves, centred around the theme of the main event. For example, a supermarket chain had a campaign that allowed customers to save for tickets to a concert, and a newspaper gave away tickets to a concert by Adele at the Royal Albert Hall in London. The 'Beesies' (small teddy bears) of Albert Heijn (AH; Dutch supermarket chain) is another example. Although AH had nothing to do with the organization of the World Football Championships 2010, it managed to tie in with the 'football feeling' with its 'Beesies' campaign. Since 2016, Plus (another Dutch supermarket chain) has owned the premier league football rights. In this way, Plus is connecting its name with sports and health, as a result of which a link is established between the brand name and the emotions associated with football matches and football in general. The alliance also offers new possibilities for savings and loyalty campaigns for customers.

Relationship events

BNP Paribas offers its most important clients a Roland Garros Tennis Tournament VIP package. Being a sponsor of Roland Garros, BNP Paribas had an excellent opportunity to organize a range of hospitality events for its clients. A fun, sporty and pleasant day is the stage for expressing appreciation, a casual closer acquaintance with customers as well as a chance to exchange information. These relationship events all take place during the Roland Garros Tennis Tournament. In other words, Roland Garros is an existing event, which triggers all kinds of other smaller events.

Internal branding events

We have already discussed internal branding events earlier. Internal events can be part of an existing event. In the example of the Roland Garros Tennis Tournament, it is possible for BNP Paribas to develop a programme for its own staff members. Staff members may then visit tennis matches and listen to various lectures from the management of BNP Paribas. The aim of BNP Paribas in this example may be team-building or employee loyalty and/or commitment.

Hosting, facilitating or financing an event

National, regional and local government bodies may decide to host not only large-scale sporting events, such as Giro d'Italia, the Vuelta a España or the Tour de France, but also cultural events, dance events or international conferences such as the international 'Nuclear Security Summit' in The Hague. If these events are employed purposefully and strategically and supported by a government, then this falls into our definition of event marketing.

Event marketing has several forms of manifestation, with underlying objectives. The ultimate goal is to ensure business continuity and generate profits. Events are not always organized because of an economic objective; they can also create enabling conditions. The right goals have to be pursued in a well-considered manner, and it also has to be determined which goals can be achieved by means of which type of event. The classification we apply is obviously not the only classification possible. In practice, all kinds of combinations are possible.

The Advantages of Event Marketing

The use of events is gaining in popularity with many different variations, as has been seen above. But how can one explain the fact that companies or cities purposefully use events as a strategic choice? To be able to answer this question, we need to look at the power of events and their advantages and disadvantages. Experiences, emotions and values are becoming increasingly important in society today. The emergence of event marketing is a logical phenomenon within this development. The event is a means that can evoke sensations and emotions, thanks to:

- the direct contact;
- the possibility of interaction;
- the emotions and sensations and the impact;
- the possibility to increase customer loyalty and to engage in networking; and
- the possibility of conveying a message in a very targeted manner.

Due to the possibility of immediate interaction with the target group, the supplier of an event can also take immediate action when something is not in order – the music is too loud or the food is too cold.

The setting of an event takes people away from their everyday work environment. An informal get-together presents opportunities to get to know each other in a different way. This may lead to situations that would never occur in the everyday work environment.

Interaction is also connected with experiencing things. During the event, the customer takes part in communication, he participates in the event; this is referred to as experience communication. Thanks to the direct experience (sensation), the impact of communication will be greater. The visitors of an event participate and can learn from what they experience. Being in dialogue with other people is a part of interaction; the supplier, as a representative of the brand, and the customers (including potential customers) exchange opinions and ideas about the product. This is the biggest advantage of an event: direct, face-to-face communication. The participants have the opportunity for an encounter (due to efficient programming), they are interested in the programme of the event (or else they would not have come) and they are capable of understanding the message (which makes them easily influenced by the supplier).

Personalized approach

A company wants to get some kind of message across about its own brand. Communication of this message will have a positive influence on the knowledge, attitude and maybe even the behaviour of the target group. The event is a means to approach the consumer in a personal manner. The message can be communicated very clearly and the setting of an event allows for taking immediate action in the event of any obscurities. It is even possible to work on the relationship with the customer. Companies expect their events to leave a positive impression, as a result of which the relationship will improve (see Chapter 4).

Integrated communication

Events can be combined very adequately with other media and means of communication. Whereas in the past events used to focus on the 'fun' aspect, today much greater emphasis is placed on content, integrated communication (cross-media) and the application of new media. Furthermore, under the influence of new media, the importance of personal encounters – personal contacts with business partners, clients and prospects – is growing. Apart from the preliminary and subsequent stages, the event offers plenty of other communication opportunities.

Being different

With event marketing, through the choice of a certain type of event, a message can be conveyed to one or several target groups in a very targeted manner. The characteristics of the event can be fully aligned with the target group(s). So, the client determines who is invited to the event and which target group the event will focus on, to avoid unwanted guests showing up and to make sure that all money is directed towards useful marketing efforts. Business-to-consumer events are an exception in this respect. These events focus on a specific target group, although the organizers do not know in advance who will come to the event. Marketing campaigns concentrating on a specific target group will yield much greater returns than loose-cannon campaigns revolving around ill-defined target groups.

As opposed to printed media (such as advertisements or brochures), the event is a means to combine different target groups and different objectives.

Generating purposeful attention

If you want to get through to the consumer, regular means of communication hardly suffice any more. Too many messages are fired at consumers all the time, so they no longer take any notice. An attractive and original event can draw consumer attention. This is where event marketing is different from traditional, regular means of communication, which are often no longer fit for purpose. The event is a live and three-dimensional medium, with lots of possibilities for making a product or brand attractive. Senses play an important role in this respect. Scent machines, for instance, can be used to disperse the scent of grass, to evoke a spring feeling. The beat frequency in music can either create a thrill, a buzz or a quiet and harmonious ambiance. The event sector is also becoming increasingly aware of what coloured lights can do to create a certain mood.

Unleashing emotions
Interpersonal relations are based on emotions. During an event, emotions can be unleashed to make visitors more approachable. More often than not, there are 'unknown' aspects of a person's character to be discovered. It is also possible to evoke group effects deliberately for the purpose of intensifying the experience. The 'aaaaah' reaction from the crowd when the Red Bull stunt pilots flew right along the Statue of Liberty in New York is one example.

Building networking opportunities
The presence of other guests at an event may be reason enough for some people to come to the event, too. Despite the fact that people can get in touch at any time, seeing each other in person continues to be important. The informal aspect plays a role here, too. People who have good relations with a company may act as ambassadors in contexts of this sort.

Appealing to trade journalists
Events are perfectly suited to involving trade journals. An event that offers a product or brand experience will generate more press attention than, for instance, a new brochure or advertising of the product or brand. Moreover, it is possible to engage in two-way communication at events.

The Disadvantages of Event Marketing
One-offness
A major disadvantage of an event is that it usually involves just that one moment when everything that had been planned so carefully in advance comes together. The execution of the event is bound by a certain time limit. Will the concept be expressed well? Will guests experience the event as exuberantly as it was meant to be? Will the programme be effective? In other words, errors of judgement can be made at any point, which will have a huge impact on the message that was supposed to be communicated. In addition, influences from outside can interfere with the event. Consequently, there is a certain risk involved in the use of events. Experienced event organizers will try to eliminate risks as much as possible by means of their expertise, their ability to convert well-considered objectives into one all-embracing concept and a well-balanced programme. What is more, they will go about their projects in a systematic manner, making adjustments as and when necessary. Very accurate planning, especially in the case of an integrated approach, is an important prerequisite.

Costs
It is commonly known that the use of an event in the form of a project is a costly affair. Personnel have to be freed up in the preliminary stage, and as the event nears, the number of work-hours required increases dramatically. An event is a very labour-intensive matter and can have a great impact on an organization. Without a professional approach, the costs can get out of hand. Costs per contact are considerably higher compared to other means of communication, such as flyers, direct mailing, newsletters and banners on sites.

Complexity

Some events are not even possible without external expertise and support. Technological advancements have led to a higher degree of professionalism of events. Just a few years ago, using a website in the preliminary stage was not something that was normally done. Today, you are nobody if you do not have a website. This development has repercussions across a range of business sectors: security, communication, logistics, audio-visual aspects, and so on. It is almost impossible to be a specialist in all these areas. That is why events are increasingly contracted out to experienced professionals.

The Strategic Use of Events

Is it always possible to use events? When will event marketing actually help to achieve certain objectives? What are the dos and don'ts of event marketing? Theoretical and practical research has generated a number of key questions that need to be answered in advance.

1. What is the objective, originating from the organization's strategic policy?
2. What is the message that has to be conveyed?
3. Who is the target group?
4. Which tools, means and media are best suited to achieve the objective?

Objective

Formulating objectives is part of the process of developing a corporate strategic policy. The first question is, of course: what are these objectives? The objectives must be measurable. Objectives such as 'creating a memorable experience', 'customer retention', 'building and expanding relationships' or one of the goals mentioned in the earlier section on the reasons to opt for event marketing may lead to the decision to use events as a means.

Message

The second important question that an organization has to ask itself is: what is the message? The message has to be formulated very clearly, because it is the point of departure for many activities. The objective(s) and the message can be transformed into an event concept and design. In this process, the marketer has to be able to empathize with the visitor. Only then will it be possible to create meaningful experiences.

Target market

The next key question is: what is your target group? It is also important to analyse the interests, needs and values of your target market. What is important in the choice of an event is the specific target group that has to be reached. Is an event actually the best choice? To obtain an accurate insight into the choice of the target group(s), a customer pyramid is a useful tool (see Chapter 4). Successful event marketing involves a personal approach to the target market, interaction between the target market and the brand. The target group has to be able to relate to the values of the brand or the company.

Tools, means and media

If the use of an event turns out to be the best choice, then this involves a market-oriented approach. If the event is the means or one of the means from the marketing mix, then the organization will have to ask itself which marketing communication tools and means can be integrated in order to add strength to the message and the objective. In this case, event marketing is part of the marketing communication policy; the event can be integrated with, for instance, the

Internet, sponsoring or printed media. We have already written that events are also a good tool for free publicity. This will be explained in Chapter 5.

The choice for an event

The choice to use an event is dependent on several factors, some of which have already been dealt with:

- the objective;
- the target group;
- the event's expected contribution to the objective;
- the available alternatives in the area of marketing communication tools, means and media;
- the level of support within the organization;
- the level of feasibility within the organization (e.g. know-how and sufficient support);
- the risks involved in organizing an event;
- the time path; and
- the costs.

When every aspect has been considered, a budget allocation of the marketing means can be drawn up and an activation budget can be requested in time in the company.

Customization

An event must be custom-designed. If event marketing is used in the most optimal way, the objective and the message will be converted to an event concept and design in a creative and authentic manner. The event concept and design also comprise the organization's core values. They also ensure that as many senses as possible are appealed to, for the purpose of a multi-sensory experience. The event is easily accessible and either formal or informal, and apart from entertainment aspects, it offers depth and meaning. During the entire process, in the phases of pre-exposure, direct exposure and post-exposure, there must be a link with the values that have been elaborated to the smallest detail. The quality of the event and the integrated means mix (see Fig. 3.2) must be strictly monitored, and there must be regular feedback.

Follow-up

The effect of an event has to be measured in order to be able to determine its return on investment (ROI). Successful event management requires a long-term view, in addition to effective cooperation between client and contractor. This will allow for constant monitoring within a track in which all marketing communication tools have been integrated. The event will then be the biggest live marketing communication tool, creating a dynamic balance together with the other marketing communication tools. Effect measurement and event evaluation will be dealt with extensively in Chapter 10 and the Appendices.

Summary

Events are used more and more often as a live means of communication. Event marketing is the discipline where marketing, events and communication come together. In this respect, one can identify a development from product orientation towards communication orientation. Experience marketing provides for memorable experiences, an emotional added value which the customer is asking for. The event can be regarded as a communication platform within the developments in the area of marketing communication.

The event has a place of its own in the marketing mix as a communication tool, in addition to, for instance, sponsoring, the Internet and advertising. We distinguish three types of event marketing. An event can be an event in itself, it can be part of a bigger event, or it can be facilitated by regional or national governments.

There are many advantages to event marketing, including the personal approach, integrated communication and the opportunity to interest trade journalists. Disadvantages may be: the one-off nature, the costs involved and the complexity.

For a strategic use of events, it is obviously important to determine accurately the objective and the target group. An event must always involve customization.

4 Events and Customer Relationship Marketing

Dorothé Gerritsen and Ronald van Olderen

The central theme of this chapter is the role of events in relationship marketing. After a brief sketch of the history of this form of marketing, we will discuss the three Rs: reputation, relationships and reciprocity. Next, we will focus extensively on relationship events. We will finish the chapter with an analysis of the limits to customer relationship marketing.

Learning Targets

After studying this chapter, you will have learnt:

- how relationship marketing emerged;
- what relationship marketing is;
- in what way events are used in relationship marketing;
- why events are used for relationship marketing purposes; and
- what the limits are to using events in relationship marketing.

A quick browse of the Internet will tell you that social communities are gaining in popularity. Partly due to the developments in the field of social media, like-minded people can easily find each other. A Facebook event is easy to create and it allows companies quick access to a certain community. Examples of communities can be found in diverse areas: the Mazda MX-5 Club; sector organizations; football supporters; experts in the field of marketing, communication, events, and so on and so forth. The number of LinkedIn members – a professional networking site – is growing. People feel a need to connect with like-minded people and to share experiences with each other. Within these communities, events are often used for the purpose of virtual as well as live meetings. The Mazda MX-5 Club often organizes tours for its members. Sector organizations such as MPI (Meeting Planners International) or IFEA (International Festivals and Events Organization) meet their members at New Year receptions and conferences. In this way, networks are maintained, updated or built through various virtual and live channels. What is increasingly common, especially among the younger generation, is for an online meeting to take place before a live meeting is organized. Each social media platform has its own – often unwritten – rules to get and stay in touch with a certain community and developments in this area are progressing at lightning speed.

Organizations and companies too have become aware of the value of good customer relationships and of communities. More and more often, they incorporate systematic networking strategies into their policy frameworks, which is referred to as customer relationship management. Organizations have come to realize the necessity of regarding customers as partners, and thus of building new customer relationships as well as intensifying existing relationships. Existing customers require less attention and energy from an organization than customers yet to be acquired. Binding customers to your company, product or service plays a crucial role in this respect. Events may play an important role here. The fictitious example below shows how an event – by means of a game, app and social media – can be used to get in touch with an important partner group, the intermediaries, who are responsible for a crucial portion of the sales of Insurance Direct products and services.

The Emergence of Customer Relationship Marketing

Within marketing, there has been a shift from transaction-oriented thinking towards an approach that focuses on building and maintaining relationships. In Chapter 3, we said that, traditionally, marketing was about a transaction with an anonymous target group, without any preceding or following action, with the emphasis on attracting new customers. Price was always the most important component (price competition). A price that came about in a competitive market comprised all the essential information for both parties in order to accomplish the exchange. So, marketing activities were centred around an ad hoc transaction and the

> **Box 4.1. Relationship marketing at Insurance Direct**
>
> Insurance Direct is an innovative insurance company with around 1000 employees, offering a complete range of insurance products to both business and consumer markets. The company has an innovative view of insurance and operates exclusively through intermediaries.
>
> Insurance Direct's communication is handled through intermediaries, the company's primary distribution channel. A study carried out by Insurance Direct showed that the intermediaries were losing a portion of their distribution to direct writers (including Internet suppliers) and banks, due to shifting use of channels (via apps, social media, and so on) and changing consumer buying behaviour, especially among the younger generation. Furthermore, it turned out that the intermediaries were not entirely familiar with the support that Insurance Direct offered in terms of marketing and that they had a need for support (customization), especially in the area of know-how. In order to be able to position themselves as the 'partner in business' for marketing consultants, Insurance Direct organized a marketing event: an event game to increase the intermediaries' awareness of the changing environment and the opportunities that still existed in terms of the employment of social marketing tools. According to Insurance Direct, an event offers interactive possibilities for its participants to experience for themselves what these opportunities are. *Awareness* and *experience* are supposed to give the intermediary the feeling that REAAL is *the* partner in business.
>
> The intermediaries of Insurance Direct (top potentials, core and potentials) were invited by means of various channels: a personal e-mail, an app especially designed for the event and various posts on Instagram (in keeping with the marketing concepts of 'know your customer' and 'use several communication channels to reach your customer'). The company made sure that the event was imbued with its core values and the event fulfilled the objectives formulated in advance in various ways. The game that was developed as a part of the event was especially consistent with the image of Insurance Direct as a realistic insurer: Insurance Direct is alert because it keeps a close eye on market conditions, as well as trends and developments in society. At the event, a marketing film was played, showing consumers' capricious buying behaviour, the distribution channels that consumers use, their 'zapping' behaviour, and so on. A presentation was given to explain the importance of sound marketing. A marketing simulation game gave participants a live experience of which strategies might boost their contract portfolios. The execution of the event was consistent with Insurance Direct's image and national campaign. The company had deliberately opted for an out-of-the-ordinary setting: various event venues in De Spoorzone in Tilburg.
>
> The evaluation carried out afterwards revealed that the intermediaries appreciated the event and that they gained new ideas in the area of marketing and the effective use of social media – ideas that they said they were going to put into action. All in all, the event improved the capacity of Insurance Direct's staff members to get in touch with this particular client group.

ensuing exchange of a good or service against money. The customers were mostly anonymous. Marketing was, in other words, thinking up a good campaign for a target group. The four Ps – price, place, product and promotion – had a central place within transaction marketing. Nowadays, an extra P has been added to the marketing mix: personnel.

Transaction marketing is about earning money as quickly as possible, here and now. There is no long-term view. What is lacking in this approach is the potential for meaningful, lasting customer relationships.

Making profit from a transaction became increasingly difficult due to the increasing competition between suppliers, which at the same time made it more difficult to attract and retain customers. As a result, the nature of the relationship between suppliers and consumers changed: a shift occurred from the transaction focus – attracting customers and thinking in terms of market share – towards a focus on building and maintaining relationships, retaining customers and thinking in terms of customer share. When a company invests in customer loyalty, it will need fewer new customers. Whenever it has new products or services to offer, this company can focus on its existing customers. All in all, there have been a number of events and developments in both the internal and external environment that have led to a shift in focus from transactions towards relationships. What this also entails for companies is spending more time with their customers, and this is done largely through events. Sometimes, a company teams up with an existing event or sports event: the Sony Open in Hawaii or the Rolex 24 at Daytona (USA) are two examples. On the other hand, devising and developing events of your own, for customers and business partners, is also a possibility. CycloMedia for instance, a company that specializes in panoramic and aerial photography, had its own boat that was used for networking with clients. A day of sailing including high-end catering was an important event for this company in the context of relationship marketing.

Explanatory Developments

In this section, we will present an overview of the developments that account for the importance of relationship marketing and the role of events. Events are a magnificent tool for maintaining relationships. Meeting customers and communicating with them face-to-face in a leisure or business setting provides an organization with plenty of starting points for setting up an efficient relationship marketing policy.

Growing competition

Relationship marketing is growing in importance because markets have become a lot more transparent and because it has become easier for consumers to compare prices. The world in which we live is getting smaller and smaller, so to speak. A trip to America or Asia used to be a major and time-consuming undertaking, but today you just take the plane, which will bring you to your destination in less than no time. Thanks to new media and the Internet, relevant information is available to almost everyone. Companies have started looking for cheaper manufacturing operations and markets. The result is that the degree of competition is increasing.

Technological advancements

Freedom of choice has increased, due to technological advancements. It is becoming increasingly difficult for companies to set themselves and their products apart from the competition. Technology does not stand still and new technologies are easily available and transferable. That is why many products are very much alike and they are well matched in terms of quality. The necessity of the consumer remaining loyal to a particular company is becoming smaller as a result. Unparalleled freedom of choice and less distinction between products are the reasons why consumers have less pronounced preferences for a certain product variety and move between suppliers more easily.

The necessity to be loyal and/or stay with the same company, after all, is not that great, unless the supplier is capable of building direct and structural relationships with its customers.

Companies can do so, for instance, by means of event marketing, relationship marketing and a well-thought-out branding strategy (for branding, see Chapter 6). Due in part to the emergence of innovative companies such as Airbnb and Uber, but also payment processors and other innovative financial service providers, the established players will have no alternative but to invest in relationships and customer retention too.

Technological developments in the area of communication

Developments in the area of information technology offer marketers more and more scope for conveying their message to the individual consumer. Using traditional as well as new media, marketers can bring about a higher degree of interaction with consumers. Consumers are exposed to a lot of impressions and information. This information overkill has made consumers weary, to the extent that they are beginning to tune out information they do not want. They have become more critical in selecting information that is relevant to them.

Technological developments have also lowered communication costs with customers for businesses and organizations. Presently, it is possible to buy databases at a very low cost and fill them with accurate and up-to-date information. The decreasing costs have made it easier for companies to anticipate individual needs and desires.

Individualization

As a result of the individualization of society, marketers are struggling to find ways to approach individuals, who can no longer be regarded as members of a homogeneous group. We all have our own specific preferences and we want to be spoken to about matters that interest us. It is therefore getting harder to segregate the market on the basis of the traditional segregation criteria, which fail to accommodate individual needs, while consumers today are expecting to be approached and treated in a personalized manner. The purchase of a product or service continues to be important, but the process that follows the purchase is increasing in importance, too. To minimize dissatisfaction after the purchase, companies have to stay in touch with their customers. One might even say that the actual marketing process does not start until after the purchase process.

The necessity of direct communication

Owing to the developments outlined above, the emphasis is shifting towards customer retention. It is not the power of mass communication that is important here, but direct communication with the consumer. The focus of marketing is therefore shifting from the product to the organization itself. Short-term thinking has made way for a strategic view, in which the company is a decisive factor for customers. The new generation of marketers no longer thinks in terms of customers, but in terms of relationships. Where the four Ps were centred primarily on promotion (transaction thinking), in the future, relationships will become pivotal (see Fig. 4.1).

Transactions	➡	Relationships
Action	➡	Interaction
Static	➡	Dynamic
Decision oriented	➡	Implementation oriented
Short term	➡	Long term
Goods	➡	Services
Product focus	➡	Customer focus

Fig. 4.1. From transaction marketing to relationship marketing. (Source: Van Kempen, 2005.)

The ultimate goal will obviously still be the exchange or the transaction itself, but the exchange or transaction will be accomplished on the basis of good customer relationships.

From the Four Ps to the Three Rs

We have already shown that the four Ps are no longer adequate in terms of customer retention; they merely offer a tactical advantage. The three Rs stand for reputation, reciprocity and relationships. They constitute a strategic counterpart to facilitate real customer-centric operations. The three Rs are bound inextricably with each other and support each other.

The model displayed in this figure is based on the relationship between an organization and its customers, regardless of what type of organization. One example would be a company like AXA, a major global insurance company, which interacts with customers who have taken out an insurance policy with them, or a professional football organization like FC Barcelona, which maintains relations with sponsors.

Reputation

Reputation is based on the way people think and talk about the organization concerned, both inside and outside the organization. What do people say about the organization? The image of the organization in the eyes of others can be decisive to the organization's success. A good reputation will attract people, including potential customers. We will illustrate the importance of reputation by means of an example concerning a client and a contractor (an event agency).

> *Satis&Fy*, one of the leading full-service production companies in Europe, is selling a concept for an event to Levi Strauss. When the exchange has taken place or, in other words, when Levi's has instructed the agency to elaborate and execute the concept, Levi's may decide to assign the agency another event project. In this way, a relationship arises between the client and the contractor. In this respect, it is crucial that the client's expectations, in this case the expectations of Levi's, are exceeded every time. The relationship thus developed may confirm the event agency's reputation, which completes the circle.

A good relationship does not always need to begin with an organization's reputation, which is not what the model of the three Rs in Fig. 4.2 implies either. After all, it is also possible for a customer to have a positive experience with a supplier, giving his image of this supplier a positive influence, which may result in a lasting relationship.

Fig. 4.2. Reputation, reciprocity and relationships. (Source: Storm, 1992.)

Reputation does not come by accident. If an organization has opted for relationship marketing, this will require a certain line of approach: start thinking in terms of relationships instead of transactions. The people inside an organization must be fully aware of the fact that customer-centric operations are an absolute necessity and everyone must act accordingly. Computer systems are available for this purpose. A database, or customer relationship management system (CRM system) containing customer data, is a good place to start, but it is not the only possibility. It is the employees who will have to get things done, and to this end, their mode of action will have to change. An organization may have the most sophisticated computer systems in the world, containing every conceivable piece of information on its customers, but if it really wants to put this information to optimal use, its employees – especially those who have direct contact with customers – will have to act appropriately.

Customer relationships cannot be imposed; they have to be invited from inside the organization. One way of putting it is that the personnel of a company have to fit like a glove with the company's DNA. This is the key ingredient for a good reputation. Moreover, reputation is something that is determined by customers. This does not mean that once a good relationship has been built, it will continue for all eternity. Companies will have to prove themselves over and over again. The customer's expectations will have to be fulfilled – and even exceeded. With the advent of the three Rs, the four Ps have not become superfluous; they make up the foundations on which the three Rs model rests. If the visitors' needs are not satisfied, during or after an event, then the relationship will not be formed, let alone a good reputation. Reputations are, of course, also strongly influenced by what is said and written on platforms such as Twitter, Facebook and review sites.

Relationships

A customer is someone with whom an exchange is accomplished, based on a one-off activity. Diller's definition aptly describes the characteristics of a relationship:

> A relationship is an interactive process between a buyer and a seller, which involves the purchase and use of goods and/or services, which is driven by economic and non-economic goals, and which is direct, integrative and concerns more than one transaction.

(Schijns, 2000)

Apparently, a relationship implies a person with whom a connection is established through an interactive process, and this connection is of a higher order than the transaction itself. A relationship does not even have to be driven by economic goals. Relationships occur in a wide variety of forms: potential customers, customers, local residents, government bodies, suppliers, stakeholders, employees. The interactive process is decisive, since relationships have a behavioural as well as an experiential dimension. The effects of the interactive process depend on the factual contacts, and on the subjective assessment of those contacts. This is the reason why a company can lose a pitch – in which a spectacular concept for an event is presented – despite a long-existing relationship with a client. The pitch was good, but the click was just not there.

The why of relationships

Relationships are based on mutual benefits. A relationship must bring benefits to both the company and the customer. Organizations would do well to focus on specific customers:

- customers that strengthen the organization's reputation; and
- customers who are appropriate to the organization's knowledge and skills.

Entering into a relationship produces three advantages: interaction, understanding and stability.

First, interaction is important. A customer can give feedback on the company's performance via social media, in both a positive and a negative sense. It is not without reason that many companies have departments responsible for monitoring, responding to and communicating via the various social media channels. Negative feedback produces input to do better the next time; for instance, to fine-tune certain processes or to maximize contact intensity. Positive feedback can be important in establishing whether or not the company has listened well to the customer's needs and whether or not all of the customer's objectives have been achieved. The most important thing is that contacts between customer and company are maintained and that both parties keep talking to each other without reproaching each other. What is worse than a client who says that everything is all right but who thinks the opposite?

Second, sustained contacts between a potential customer and a supplier will give both parties a better insight into the business operations. What does the company stand for; what are its core values; what kind of people does the company employ? There are numerous questions that are not given any thought whenever a new exchange takes place. The company data are stored in the customer information systems and included in the customer processes as a matter of course. This will increase efficiency.

Third, and thanks to relationship marketing, customers will be less inclined to turn to competitors. Loyal customers are less sensitive to the advances of other parties or the possibility of a lower price.

Reciprocity

Reciprocity is what it is all about. The company's reputation and relationships may be excellent, but if there is no exchange, it will endanger its business continuity. The exchange not only must take place but also it must leave behind a positive feeling and confirm the company's reputation, especially so after the actual transaction. Just think of the evaluation of an event, after-sales care, effective complaints handling and quick and correct answering of questions.

Events and Customer Relationship Marketing

Through live encounters with, for instance, wonderful music, sensational theatre and strong catering concepts, it is possible to engage people emotionally. As a result, events are very suitable for use within a relationship marketing strategy.

Rather than making a profit on the transaction, relationship marketing is concerned primarily with making a profit on the relationship. This profit can be achieved only through exchanges with existing customers. In some cases, individual transactions will be loss making. But the aim of relationship marketing is building a profitable relationship. Relationship marketing involves satisfying and retaining customers in order to maximize the customer's lifelong value to the company in terms of profit.

We apply the following definition of relationship marketing.

> Relationship marketing is an integrated effort of the organization in order to identify, maintain and build a network with individual consumers, and continuously reinforce that network, to the advantage of both parties, by means of interactive, individualized and value-adding contacts that relate to several, successive transactions.
>
> (Schijns, 2000)

Customer satisfaction and long-term relationships are generated through the interactions among marketing, quality and the provision of service to customers. High-quality services are a condition for attracting and retaining customers.

As well as being the result of marketing, quality and service, relationship marketing is also a tool to build customer loyalty.

There are many relationship marketing tools, but it is always difficult to capture precisely why a customer turns to the competition. Research has shown that decisions regarding business transactions are often made on emotional grounds. This means that tools to influence the feelings, experiences and opinions of customers are becoming increasingly important.

The Target Group

Within a relationship marketing strategy, events are organized purposefully for a certain target group, which may be either an internal or an external target group. After all, organizations must not only develop relationships with existing and potential customers but also with suppliers, employees and influencers. If Levi Strauss, for instance, is planning to organize an event for its clients, then this not only involves its existing clients but also other interest groups on which Levi Strauss as a business depends. To offer added value to its customers, an organization also needs good relations with interest groups and external parties. Good relations with, for instance, a caterer may be decisive to the success of Levi Strauss's relationship event.

A concept will be more consistent if the organizations involved know each other and know how the other party operates. A shortage of drinks at a party, for example, can be solved by a telephone call to the company's own supplier, or another supplier with whom the company has good relations. It goes without saying that, as the relationship grows more intense, the parties involved will be willing to do more for each other. They may, for instance, waive the total cancellation costs as specified in the signed contract, charging 50% of the total amount instead. This is an example of the advantages that good relationship marketing can produce.

In relationship events, we distinguish the following target groups: prospects, customers, suppliers, competitors, influencers and employees. We will explain briefly each of these target groups in the following sections.

Prospects and customers

Establishing good relations with prospects and customers is priority number one. In the end, it is customers who make the company profitable. Furthermore, customers play a crucial role in spreading a business's reputation. When customers talk about your company in a positive way, they are an indirect source for potential new customers.

Suppliers

Organizations often work with subcontractors or suppliers. Good relations with one's suppliers often produce the greatest possible competitive advantages. Closer ties can be forged by, for instance, inviting these parties to the opening of a new office or a year-end closing party. Through events of this kind, the company shows its appreciation, which in turn may lead to greater synergy and closer collaboration.

Competitors

It is possible for competitors to work together. Take, for example, three companies pitching for an event. Rather than trying to edge each other out, they may choose to join forces based on each other's expertise, in order to design and organize the event together. It is not uncommon to invite competitors to informal gatherings.

Influencers

Government

Representatives of local or provincial government authorities are often invited to official functions, such as the opening of a new building or a first pile ceremony for a new construction project.

Financial institutions

It is very important to develop and maintain relations with financiers. The events to which financiers are invited will create a positive image for the company among the parties concerned. Members of financial interest groups, such as shareholders and members of the board, may also be invited to informal gatherings.

For instance, ING Bank regularly organizes ING Fundcoach evenings for its private investors. At these evenings, ING Bank tells participants about the latest developments in portfolio management, strategies to be pursued and 'treasures' in the market. The primary goal of ING Fundcoach evenings is to weave closer ties with private investors. The ultimate goal is for the parties involved to step up their investment activity (buying and selling investment products).

Press

The press plays an important role in terms of event reporting. The news value that is generated by an event may help to achieve the event's objectives. So, it is important for a company to build good relations with the press and invite journalists to its events. A journalist will focus primarily on what is considered news value to the target group of the medium for which he works (see Chapter 5).

Employees

Employees make up the foundation of every organization. Employees, and sometimes their partners and/or children, too, can be invited to the annual personnel party. In this way, a company can express its appreciation for the achievements of its employees over the past year.

An example of an event for employees is a gathering following a corporate takeover, an opportunity for employees of both sides to get to know each other and for synergy to be created.

Customer Segmentation

Acquiring knowledge of one's customers is essential in relationship marketing. An event can be organized more efficiently when more information is available on the target group concerned. Nearly all organizations that are interested in developing and maintaining direct relations with

> **Box 4.2. Samsung theme park**
>
> A good example of an event with huge spin-off benefits was Samsung's 'S7 Life Changer Park', a theme park by the Seine in Paris consisting of nine attractions – from ski jumps and surfing to a 'diving-with-dolphins' Zen Zone – combining reality and virtuality. The goal was to promote the latest Samsung Smartphone with a focus on virtual reality. The media mix consisted of an extensive campaign on social media such as Instagram and Facebook, but also a launch party, live broadcasts from the theme park, guerrilla marketing and press releases. In the end, this resulted in 42,000 visitors within 4 days, an enormous media reach and a positive image of virtual reality in general and Samsung in particular.
>
> Source: beaworldfestival.com

their customers and stakeholders engage in CRM. CRM is a corporate strategy that has taken a huge leap forward over the past few years. CRM involves gathering, storing and analysing – in a structural and continuous manner – information on individual customers in order to be able to develop and evaluate marketing activities specifically geared to these customers. IT applications and databases make up the basis for using this information. CRM processes affect the organization as a whole: marketing, IT, logistics, finances, production and development, human resources and management. That is why a CRM strategy must provide direction to every department or function within the company, taking the customer as a starting point.

These are the pillars of CRM:

1. Customer knowledge.
2. Customer relationship strategy.
3. Communication.
4. Individualized value proposition.

Customer knowledge

Knowledge of customers is indispensable in developing long-lasting relationships and delivering customized products and services. In this respect, it is important to record not only standard data but also emotional data on the customer: data on the values, attitudes, motives and social network of customers, and other matters that go beyond the mere individual characteristics. These kinds of data are essential in organizing relationship events. The customer's subjective assessment plays a decisive role. Did the event meet the customer's expectations? Did it respond to the customer's deeper motives and did it fit in with his or her perceptive framework? So, it is all about knowing what really touches someone on an emotional level. This will be explained in Chapter 8, in the section on 'The Psychosocial Framework'.

Customer databases are generally very big and diversified. Organizing databases of this kind requires proper registration and segmentation.

Registration of standard data

What most customer databases contain are standard details, such as *individual data* – name, address, place of residence, additional details on the factual customer, sales, frequencies and times of purchase – and *demographic data* – the data required to identify certain groups.

Emotional data

What is often missing in databases are *emotional data*: information on the values, attitudes, motives and social environments of customers, and other matters that go beyond individual characteristics. These types of data are essential in organizing a relationship event.

Behaviour and experience are crucial elements in relationships. The effect of a live encounter determines whether or not the visitor is satisfied with the event. The subjective assessment of the event obviously plays a decisive role. Did the event meet the client's expectations? Did it appeal to the deeper motives of the person in question? In other words, it is about knowing what really moves people.

> **DNA**
>
> Suppose you are invited to a birthday party. You are not sure yet what to bring as a present and you are considering the regular gift range: a book, a DVD voucher, a bunch of flowers, a bottle of wine, perfume or aftershave. These are presents you might give to anyone. What if the person inviting you asks for an experience? This would change your decision process. What you need to know now is what this person is interested in, what he likes to do; in short, you will have to get through to the person's 'DNA' in order to find a suitable gift or activity.

Groups of customers are often invited to attend appreciation events; for instance, a tennis tournament. The company assumes that everyone will enjoy this event, which – however – remains to be seen. This shows that having adequate emotional data in the customer database is conducive to a customer-centric approach.

Segmentation

Segmentation is indispensable to the registration of customer data. Jay Curry (1991) developed the customer pyramid to categorize customers, clarify customer behaviour and carry out analyses.

Fig. 4.3. Segmentation based on customer value. (Source: Curry, 1991; Hart, 1998; Kneepkens, 2005, adapted by the authors.)

Picture 1 displays the ladder of customer loyalty; picture 2, Curry's pyramid; and picture 3, Hart's (1998) marketing costs. The customer pyramid is a tool to gain an insight into the customer database; based on this information, analyses are carried out of the efforts that are made in order to attract more customers. The pyramid shows which customers are important to the business and what their needs are. By handling these needs appropriately (relationship marketing), the business tries to get its customers to rise on the customer loyalty ladder (picture 1) and, as such, make them more important customers. Satisfied customers will stay loyal to the organization for longer periods of time, will be more willing to take part in events and, in the end, will become the 'ambassadors' of the organization.

According to Curry (1991), many organizations are striving to generate business from non-customers. In his eyes, this is a waste of time. Companies had better concentrate on their existing customers. Curry (1991) advises them 'not to spend too much time on small customers; after all, it is the big customers that generate most of the business, and – in all probability – the most profit too'.

Segmentation is often made on the basis of profitability. The term 'customer value' indicates the individual customer's contribution to the company's profit. The majority of the customers fall into the segment of 'small customers', according to Curry (1991). Only 1% of the customers belong to the 'top' segment, 4% to the 'big' segment and 15% to the 'medium' segment. Small customers represent 80% of the customer base. Each of the top customers accounts for a substantial portion of the profit. And although medium and small customers are important to a company as a group, they are relatively insignificant on the level of the individual relationship. An event to which top clients are invited is the previously described example of Wella's NewHorizons event, see the section in Chapter 3 on 'Conceiving and Organizing an Event of Your Own'.

Inactive customers are those who have bought products or services in the past. This segment is one of the most important segments. After all, inactive customers are familiar with the company and can become active customers again relatively easily.

Prospects are persons who have not yet bought anything, but with whom a relationship has been built nevertheless. This relationship has been built through interest shown in the past. Prospects can become clients in a short space of time. Suspects, on the other hand, are persons with whom no relationship has yet been built, but to whom the company's products or services may be interesting. A suspect can become a prospect, and a prospect can become a customer.

The rest of the world has to be mapped out in order to identify which segments – persons or potential target groups – are not interesting to a company and which therefore do not require any marketing efforts.

It is possible, of course, to invite several customer groups to an event at the same time: potential customers, small customers or suspects. A precondition is that customers should have the potential to act as ambassadors and that small customers and suspects do not get lost in the crowd, because that is not what a relationship event is about.

Picture 3 in Fig. 4.3 shows that, in general, the marketing costs per customer at the top of the pyramid are the highest. The importance of customer retention grows as you move up the pyramid, and that is where a personal approach has more weight.

Customer relationship strategy

After gathering relevant customer knowledge comes developing a customer relationship strategy or loyalty strategy based on the corporate objectives. Depending on the nature of these objectives, a company can organize a relationship event, focusing on:

- achieving quick success; and
- building structural customer relationships.

With regard to relationship events focusing on structural customer relationships, we distinguish social strategies, psychological strategies and strategies of a temporal nature.

If the company is after quick success, the objective will be a tactical one and emphasis will be placed on the general or economic value. Price reductions or free services at events are examples of this. The company focuses on the value of the customer (in terms of money) in the short term. It goes without saying that this strategy may be detrimental to the company's profit margins.

If the company focuses on long-lasting, structural customer relationships, it has several strategies at its disposal: social, psychological or temporal strategies.

Social strategies may involve the role of the company's personnel during an event. How do the members of staff anticipate certain situations that will occur at the event? Empathic ability is crucial in this respect. When providing a service at an event, the personnel will have to judge each situation carefully and act accordingly. Creating a community around a brand or organization can also be a way to invest in a relationship. Social ties among the customers themselves are also likely to have an influence on customer loyalty towards the company. In conclusion, events can be an excellent tool for co-creation. Involving the customer in planning and designing the event is an example of this.

The strategies employed can also be of a psychological nature. After all, the purpose of events is to respond to the customer's needs, values and motives. With a comprehensive and accurate customer database, it is possible to employ a differentiated approach to reach customer segments. The customer's value to the company determines for whom the event is organized, how big it will be and in what form it will be offered (see also the customer pyramid). Another form of a customer relationship strategy concerns the creation of temporary values. Events can be used to generate process advantages to facilitate the availability of the product or service in order to save the consumer time. Companies give their customers certain privileges; for instance, by giving them the opportunity to check in earlier or order tickets earlier.

Evidently, the chosen strategy and approach, as well as the way in which the event is employed, are determined by the company's objectives. Recent studies have shown that the strategic embedment of events in customer relationship strategies is becoming increasingly common.

Communication
The best way to build dialogue with individual customers or customer segments has to be considered and determined on the basis of the company's objective and strategy. In other words: how can the objectives and strategy be transformed into communication? This involves the communication strategy, communication objectives, the message, the target groups, the media to be employed, the means of communication, and so on. A network of communication channels will have to be developed by means of which the company can engage in communication anytime, anyplace, anywhere. Numerous communication channels and means can be applied in a relationship event in order to ensure the event's success, such as digital projectors, flyers, programme booklets and face-to-face communication. The event experience, however, can be extended by carefully considering – in the pre-event and post-event phases – forms of communication that will involve customers in the event (see Chapter 3).

Individualized value proposition
The product, the service and the price need to be adapted to the individual customer's circumstances. Companies need to develop competencies to deliver customized services to their customers. As described previously, customization involves the right alignment between the target group or customer, the company itself (and its reputation) and the organization of the event.

Reasons to Use Events in Customer Relationship Marketing
Events are one of the tools or means that can be applied within the field of customer relationship marketing. The ultimate goal of relationship marketing is – either directly or indirectly – to retain profitable customers and increase spending per customer.

Reasons to use events as a relationship marketing tool include: showing the customer your appreciation, informing the customer, surprising the customer and motivating the customer.

Showing the customer your appreciation
Many events are meant to express appreciation for one's existing customers. Confirmation of the relationship plays an important role in this process. In principle, the company wants to thank its customers for their business in the past. Clients of AXA Insurance, for example, are offered opportunities to access various concerts, theatre shows and workshops. Customers and other key stakeholders are sent an invitation, and the setting is usually informal. It also happens that companies sponsor an event or a football club in exchange for free tickets or a VIP box. Subsequently, these sponsors invite their own customers. As a sponsor of the Roland Garros Tennis Tournament, BNP Paribas invites its own clients to this public event.

Informing the customer and confirming your reputation
Informing the customer is an objective that serves the fulfilment of the relationship (in which the relationship is connected with reputation). Events that are based on this objective are usually organized for customers and potential customers, and the programme generally has a more formal character. The event focuses on confirming the reputation that the company has built. The fictitious company Insurance Direct (see the beginning of this chapter) organized an event for all of Insurance Direct's insurance agents. At the event, the insurance agents were informed about the latest developments and changes with regard to several products of the company. There were several top speakers who talked about regulations and market developments. Information on other topics was presented by Insurance Direct itself. The presence of the top speakers contributed to the character of the event; a character that confirmed Insurance Direct's reputation and expertise.

Surprising the customer

Surprising customers is one of the ways for a company to show its appreciation, basically saying that the customer is very special to the company. The setting is usually informal and the strength lies in the spontaneous, unexpected effect. This does not always have to be a large-scale event. Sending a postcard, a bunch of flowers or a cake for someone's birthday can be something that surprises the customer and has a positive effect on him or her. On the other hand, larger-scale activities are possible, too; for instance, organizing a party for a person with whom the company has cooperated for 25 years. In situations like this, it is also possible to combine the surprise with an existing event. To give an example, individuals who have made a structural contribution to the event industry are put in the limelight they deserve during the award ceremony of IFEA World in the category of 'the Hall of Fame Award'.

Motivating the customer

Although generating sales is not the primary goal of a relationship event, it will often be the underlying thought. This also holds true for relationship events aiming to activate customers, in the process of which relationship fulfilment plays an important role. Customer activation events are usually organized for current and/or potential customers, and the formal programme also has an informal side to it. The event must obviously be geared to the company's reputation and to the target group. This dual challenge must be considered carefully all the time.

After all, it does happen quite a lot that an event does not address properly the target group's needs or is not organized on the basis of the company's core values.

The pre-trade show organized by Bogra, for instance, which we have already mentioned in Chapter 3, had a clear entertaining and informal character, apart from comprising elements of 'providing information' and 'motivating the customer'. There was a performance by a singer and there was time to talk with each other informally.

Obviously, the relationship experience (reciprocity connected with reputation) must be optimal in every relationship event. First of all, the event must be planned perfectly, it

Fig. 4.4. Relationship experience, relationship fulfilment and relationship confirmation. (Source: Storm, 1992.)

must be consistent with the target group's needs and aspirations, and it must reflect the company's DNA.

After an exchange transaction, the customer will assess whether or not the transaction satisfied his expectations, or perhaps even exceeded them. This, in turn, will have an effect on the relationship and reciprocity (see Fig. 4.4).

Limits to Customer Relationship Marketing

Are there any limits that should be taken into consideration in the use of events within the framework of relationship marketing? And what is perhaps even more important: who imposes these limits? In general, there are few to no limits imposed, except within the pharmaceutical industry (see the next section).

Companies can communicate with their clients directly and determine for themselves what the limits are. It goes without saying that, normally speaking, the event matches the company's standards and values, and stays within the budget available. This suggests some sort of limitation or restriction. Companies can also have a code of conduct, specifying guidelines for relationship events for personnel, for instance, and for giving away promotional gifts. Moreover, the budget for an event can be bound by fiscal constraints.

Summary

The increasing degree of competition and individualization, as well as technological developments, lead to a greater emphasis on relationships in the field of marketing. The three Rs – reputation, relationships, reciprocity – constitute the strategic counterpart to the four Ps.

The target group of events within relationship marketing can be either internal or external: clients, employees, suppliers, influencers (e.g. government bodies and the press). Customer knowledge is obviously very important in relationship marketing, including emotional data (which are often overlooked). Segmentation is essential to the registration of customer data.

Relationship marketing implies a relationship strategy, which may have a social, psychological and/or temporal character. A lasting relationship is the ultimate goal. Events are an effective means in relationship marketing, and they can be used for various reasons.

Apart from budget constraints, there are in principle no limits to relationship marketing other than the normal ethical standards that apply in society in general and in organizations in particular. An aspect that does need to be taken into account though, is the 'Werkkostenregeling' (Work-Related Expenses Scheme). An exception in this respect is the pharmaceutical industry.

5 Events and Marketing Communication

Dorothé Gerritsen and Ronald van Olderen

© Dorothé Gerritsen and Ronald van Olderen 2020. *Events as a Strategic Marketing Tool*, 2nd Edition (D. Gerritsen and R. van Olderen)

We will start this chapter with a definition of communication. Next, we will deal with the communication model and the position of events in this model. We will demonstrate that events have news value, while addressing the relationship between new media and events. We will conclude the chapter with a section on the practice of communication and events.

Learning Targets

After studying this chapter, you will have learnt:

- what is meant by communication;
- what the communication model is and what the position of events is in this model;
- what the function and effect of events is in marketing communication;
- the ways in which events affect knowledge, attitude and behaviour; and
- how communication messages can be transformed into events.

A Definition of Communication

Communication is a comprehensive term. It is used in various contexts and meanings: it may be about communication between two people, but also communication by way of a company's brochure. Events also fall into the category of communication.

The word 'communication' derives from the Latin word 'communio', which can be translated as 'community'. Consequently, communication can be taken to mean 'to make common', 'to share' or 'to understand each other'. The *Longman Dictionary of Contemporary English* describes communication as 'to exchange information', 'to tell people something' and 'to understand'.

Our definition of communication is as follows:

> Communication is the production and the exchange of information and meaning of verbal and/or non-verbal symbols which takes place between people, either wanted or unwanted. Information is conveyed, with a certain intention, after which this information is received and interpreted. (Michels, 2013)

The Communication Model

Communication is a process of interaction – either conscious or unconscious – between senders and recipients. Senders and recipients switch roles all the time. This process is often illustrated by means of a simple, elementary model, shown in Fig. 5.1, in which M stands for message.

Fig. 5.1. Simple communication model: S = senders; M = message; R = recipients. (Source: Michels, 2013.)

This model is far from complete; in this chapter we will be working towards a more complete model. Communication connects people. For example, direct or virtual communication (the Internet, the telephone), in which a message is transmitted immediately, but also communication in a more figurative sense: coming closer together, learning to understand each other by sharing thoughts, opinions, values and arguments. Apart from the message itself, the communication process also involves the channels or media through which the message is communicated.

An event can be considered as a communication tool in both these meanings; it is a platform where people can meet each other in person and where they can connect with each other as well, and it is the medium or the channel through which the message is conveyed. In order to elaborate the simple communication model further, we need to take a step back and first take a look at developments within the field of communication.

Live Communication and Events

Over the past few decades, the number of communication channels has increased, but the use of these channels has become less predictable. One-to-one communication has become important: messages are tailored as much as possible to the needs and characteristics of the individual consumer. As a result of the enormous volume of communication, it has become more difficult to reach the target group and increasingly companies are looking for alternatives. Events are one of these alternatives.

In this respect, communication professionals also speak of experience communication. The event is an experience that is orchestrated in such a way that the message is communicated to the target group. It involves an active dialogue between sender (organization/client) and recipient (visitor of the event), which is made possible by technological advancements. Consumers are turning into prosumers: they want to produce as well as consume. It is only logical that the sending is done from diverse groups and not just from one sender.

Communication professionals consider events as an effective tool and often describe them as the strongest form of communication; after all, it involves direct communication, something that cannot be ignored. As a consumer, one can experience a brand, try out a product or talk with like-minded individuals. This is a very direct form of communication.

Van der Zande (2007) has formulated the following definition for live communication:

> Live communication is an on-site sharing of information, in which sender and recipient communicate with each other in person and in a direct way. The message is supported by the sender's body language, emotions and charisma. In this process, the interaction possibility intensifies the recipient's involvement.

Live communication is a very effective form of communication for, among other things:

- creating experience moments;
- building outstanding PR;
- promoting a product or service in a unique way;
- generating attention for one's message; and
- establishing loyalty with the product, service or company.

The example of APM Terminals, a company that manages port and terminal facilities all over the world (see Box 5.1), shows how a communication issue can be transformed into the use of an event or live communication. As TV and radio are important media, which are primarily drawn by live events that are newsworthy, APM used an event to communicate its message live to various customer groups, followed by a huge spin-off to other media.

Box 5.1. APM Terminals MVII

The opening of the new APM Terminals MVII was celebrated by means of a concept created by Bureau Bind: a unique choreography of sea containers being moved within the terminals in the port of Rotterdam, accompanied by music composed just for this occasion. This choreography was supported by a visual show on 16 huge video screens. Guests could watch the show from a purpose-designed floating theatre complex in the port of Rotterdam, where they were transported to on a ship. The target group consisted of: customers and business relations of Maersk Line, international port authorities, suppliers and employees of the terminals, local, regional and national public sector employees, staff members of safety organizations and other public services that are important to the terminal's functioning, relevant newspapers and trade press, and residents of the Rotterdam region. The show was opened by the Dutch king.

The objective was to communicate that there were two actors involved: the terminal itself and the designers of the terminal, who created the most automated and environmentally friendly terminal in the world. The result was a spectacular event: the guests were overwhelmed and touched on an emotional level. A valuable side effect was the national and international coverage on television, online and in magazines (including professional magazines). And last but not least, the terminal employees were proud.

Source: Best of Events Awards 2015, beaworldfestival.com

Events in the Communication Model

In the APM Terminals example, the use of the medium of television alone did not suit the marketing communication objectives and the event turned out to be an adequate supplement: APM effectively conveyed its message through live communication with the target audience.

We can now add events to the simple communication model from Fig. 5.1 to create the model as depicted in Fig. 5.2.

The sender, in this case the organizer or client of the event, wants to get a message across to one or more target groups. In this process, he can choose a number of means, one of which is the

Fig. 5.2. Expanded communication model. (Source: Kneepkens, 2005; Michels, 2013, adapted by the authors.)

event. The advantage of using an event as a means is direct communication with the individual members of a target group, while at the same time stimulating their senses. Live communication is two-way communication. The recipient decodes the message and can provide feedback straight away. In other words, visitor reactions are out in the open, on the spot.

As a sender, you choose the words and/or images for your message with the intention of evoking a certain reaction in the recipient; it is all about encoding the message as effectively as possible. As a result, you stand a greater chance of the recipient interpreting the message as you intended it to be interpreted. The recipient will decode the message. What you want to make clear as a sender can be made clear in many ways. And remember that it is not just about the contents that you communicate. Form and content go hand in hand.

The example of the anniversary celebrations of Yacht (Box 5.2), a secondment firm for interim professionals, shows how the right mix of communication means is used for the purpose of the event in order to convey a message to the target group, in all stages (preliminary, main and subsequent).

The Four Aspects of a Message

There are four aspects to a message (Schulz von Thun, 1982):

1. The business aspect: it involves objective information like data, times, location.
2. The expressive aspect: when senders communicate, they always show something of themselves; in a conversation, this is expressed verbally as well as non-verbally.
3. The relational aspect: not only do senders show something of themselves, but by addressing the other party, they also show how they see the recipient.
4. The appealing aspect: the communication also has a clear goal. As a sender, one wants to get the recipients to do something.

We will explain these aspects using the example of the Wimbledon Tennis Tournament in London. Through various tennis clubs in the UK that are associated with the British LTA (Lawn Tennis Association), tennis enthusiasts are informed of and invited to order tickets

Box 5.2. Yacht 2402

A major 'anniversary party' titled 'Yacht 2402' at a secret location (Passenger Terminal, Amsterdam) for all employees (without partners) was the result of the board's briefing. On 16 December, Yacht marked its 2402-day anniversary (more than 6 years), and this was cause for a celebration. Yacht, part of the Randstad Groep Nederland, operates in the secondment of highly educated professionals in a large number of areas of expertise; professionals who are capable of achieving organizational goals together with clients. A sense of festivity and inspiration was what the event was supposed to convey to the 350 internal employees (Yacht office personnel), the 1950 interim professionals (personnel employed by Yacht) and 200 freelancers (who complete projects for Yacht with third parties). The idea that Yacht employees were a source of inspiration themselves was to be propagated by means of a stimulating, surprising message, imbued with the brand essence of Yacht: professional, result oriented, inspirational and with a distinct focus on value for money.

A brief summary of Yacht's objectives:
- increase the sense of solidarity among all target groups;
- improve customer loyalty, including interim professionals and freelancers; and
- foster a sense of pride.

The Yacht 2402 concept

In the realization of the concept, Yacht's brand essence constituted the point of departure. 'Being meaningful' is a key ingredient in this respect. Yacht's personnel can play a crucial role here, both internally and externally. This role was expressed in the composition and performance of the Yacht song '*van betekenis*' (including a rap version). 'Being meaningful' was also carried through in the invitation phase, during which all

Box 5.2. Continued.

Yacht employees were given the opportunity to contribute to the celebrations – and thus 'be meaningful' in an interactive way, via a website set up especially for the occasion. The four brand values were reflected in the styling and set-up of the party, by means of lounge areas scattered throughout the location; the colour setting in black and white (the Yacht colours); the dress code (black and white); HTML mailings in black and white; the website; the catering (finger foods); and the entertainers and artists programmed.

The preliminary stage

An extensive interactive communication track was developed for the event, with the aim of involving the Yacht employees (and a great number of external parties!) in the party, reinforcing the 'we' feeling and the 'by Yacht, for Yacht' feeling. Five months prior to the event, a 'mark the date' announcement was sent out by mail, accompanied by a fridge magnet with the date of Yacht 2402 on it. Two months later, the first HTML e-mail was sent out, containing a click option to a special event website. The website featured the first information on the event and a questionnaire about numerous aspects of the party for guests to decide on (smoking/non-smoking, type of music, type of snacks/finger foods, etc.), and a clock that counted down the minutes to the date of the party. During the preliminary stage, pieces of information were added regularly to the website. Everyone was kept updated on the latest developments via HTML e-mail. The event website constituted the central communication medium for sharing information: dress code tips from stylists, photos uploaded by employees, possibility to vote for one's favourite cocktail and for the Yacht 2402 music top ten, a registration and cancellation procedure, and information on logistics matters.

The board, comprising 13 directors, wanted to connect with the employees in a recognizable, non-traditional manner. The board's interactive contribution consisted of a live variant of the television programme *Job Swap*, a reality programme in which a team of specialists train people for another job in a short period of time. At the event, the board members exerted themselves as cook, oyster shucker, cocktail shaker, camera operator, switch technician, sushi chef and even DJ. Their learning process in the preliminary stage was recorded on video.

The event

Yacht employees were transported by bus from the regional offices to a secret location. On the bus, Yacht 2402 water bottles and snacks were handed out, and a video message from the director was played. On arrival, members of the board welcomed every guest personally with a glass of champagne, with lounge music playing in the background. At 19:00 h, an opera singer opened the event, after which a voice-over narrator welcomed the guests again and declared the buffets officially open, which was followed by an unplugged performance by a semi-acoustic band featuring various soloists. At 19:58 h sharp, a countdown clock was displayed on video screens. The climax was nearing. The Yacht employees yelled out the last 10 s of the 2402 days along with the clock. At 20:00 h, the opening film started, featuring quotes from the board, regional directors and 'ordinary' Yacht employees. The film also revisited briefly the not-so-wonderful moments of Yacht, including the recruitment freeze in the past. The film ended with an image of the Yacht logo consisting of the photos uploaded and posted by the employees present. After that, and amid great interest, the short job swap videos were played, with bloopers of the board's learning process. The activities of the members of the board were shown on

> **Box 5.2.** Continued.
>
> video screens live throughout the entire evening. The general director opened the dance floor, as a true DJ would, after which the party burst into full swing with a varied entertainment programme: a 'Yacht of the Proms' concert including a big live orchestra and soloists. A performance by Hans and Candy Dulfer, followed by a firework and confetti show, at 24:00 h sharp, concluded the evening. On their way out, the guests were given a Yacht bag with a Christmas present. Before getting on the bus, they had the opportunity to eat some chips at the Yacht snack van. On the bus, everyone was given fleece blankets, bottles of water and midnight snacks.
>
> **Subsequent stage**
>
> On the Monday following the event, the visitors were sent a text message to inform them of the fact that the website was updated with photos, the opening film and the job swap footage. Yacht employees could submit comments to appear in the guestbook, as well as upload photographs they took. A special art print displaying the Yacht logo was put up 2 days later in all Yacht offices.
>
> The board members of Yacht were so enthusiastic about the party that they ordered a special video report to be made of the evening, which was also placed on the website later.
>
> Source: Gouden Giraffe, www.gouden-giraffe.nl, adapted by the authors.

at a special group price. Information packs are sent to the management committees of the tennis clubs with a letter signed by the board of directors, presenting the dates of the matches, names of players who have committed to the event and the location. The information pack also contains a few posters of top-class tennis players, an answer form and a reference to the website.

Where do we find the four aspects in this message?

1. The business aspect. The dates of the matches and the location.
2. The expressive aspect. The expressive aspect can be found in the character of the information pack: professional set-up, posters that evoke a certain feeling.
3. The relational aspect. Wimbledon and the tournament managers demonstrate that they find the tennis clubs and their members important to the tournament's success. It is of major importance to have a sympathetic and enthusiastic audience.
4. The appealing aspect. The goal is for the managing committees of the tennis clubs to put up the posters in their canteens and encourage members to visit the tournament by filling in the answer form.

There are many different ways to get in touch with each other. You can communicate in writing, orally and digitally. Communication seems simple enough at first glance, but in reality, it is rather complex. How do you choose the right communication resources in a certain situation, how do you strike the right tone, how do you select the right visual material? Choosing the right combination will ensure that you achieve the intended effect. The multitude of possibilities makes communication a fascinating, but at the same time difficult, subject.

The Communication Modalities

The field of communication is rooted in a number of disciplines, such as psychology, sociology and economics. Events are used as a means to convey a message for information purposes, for

PR purposes and sometimes for advertising purposes. Although boundaries are fading due to technological advancements, it is useful to apply this distinction. It helps to formulate more targeted objectives. The boundaries between internal and external communication are fading too, especially because the Internet has made information accessible to everyone. Nevertheless, treating internal and external communication as distinctly separate processes will continue to be important in policy development. Events are very well suited to internal communication as well as external communication (see also the section on internal branding events in Chapter 6).

As an event organizer, you will be faced with the different modalities of communication, each with a different goal: the modality of information, education, PR, advertising and propaganda. Sometimes, you and your project team will be tackling the question of how and when the event had best be promoted among the target group. And sometimes you will be in a meeting to establish which information is crucial in which phase and at which point in time. If you look at the extent to which the recipient is influenced, you can determine which modality of communication is involved; for example, announcements or information about opening hours: the 'information' modality. It is purely about providing information, without any further intentions. On the other end of the spectrum, you will find an extreme form of influencing in the modality of 'propaganda'.

So, each of the modalities comes with a certain goal. Michels (2013) has given the following descriptions:

- *Information*: sharing knowledge with the recipient without any intention to influence.
- *Education*: transferring information to influence the recipient's knowledge, attitude and/or behaviour.
- *Public relations*: strengthening the sender's image and fostering mutual understanding between an organization and its target audiences.
- *Advertising*: influencing the target audience's knowledge, attitude and/or behaviour, and creating a distinct identity for a brand.
- *Propaganda*: communicating ideas with the aim of convincing others of an ideal (usually one-way communication).

Events as a Marketing Communication Tool

The choice for an event as a tool is a radical one: organizing an event costs a lot of time and energy, but this is counterbalanced by the enormous impact of the event. Once the choice has been made, all the stops must be pulled out to make the event a success. There are many parties involved in the organization of an event and the risks involved are relatively high. Apart from that, an event is usually a complex whole; it is a project within which and about which communication takes place. An event is an excellent opportunity to showcase your brand (or product, service, etc.) in the best possible light. That is why the management staff generally wants the organization of the event to be perfect. Nothing must go wrong – after all, the image is at stake. It is not for nothing that professional planners are often engaged in the organization of large-scale events. By now, there is a mature event management industry; there are event management study programmes, academic literature and sector organizations.

It may be clear that events are an important platform for marketing communication and contact with the various target groups. The event itself is a tool amid an enormous range of possible communication tools, from which a responsible choice has to be made. Each choice (tool) has its own particular advantages and disadvantages (see also the section on events in the marketing mix in Chapter 3).

Good communication is characterized by efficient coordination between:

- goal;
- message;
- means/tool;
- target group; and
- timing.

Despite the fact that countless physical and digital tools are available to us, there is no reason to doubt the event as one of the possible tools in which the marketing communication objective should obviously be directional. An important question in this respect is which role the event plays within the total field of marketing communication; it involves a strategic choice.

Events: Mass Communication or Interpersonal Communication?

The discipline of communication is commonly divided into two categories: mass communication and interpersonal communication. When an event is chosen as a means and when an event is communicated, the advantages and disadvantages of these two categories will have to be considered. Mass communication involves the sender communicating with a large group of people, whereas interpersonal communication is targeted at a limited number of persons, which allows for direct feedback. Thanks to modern technology, direct feedback has become easy in mass communication too. Snapchat, Twitter, Pinterest, Facebook (livestream functionality), and so on, allow people to share their feedback with the whole world at the touch of a button. Yet, of course, this medium is still reasonably anonymous.

Each category has its pluses and minuses, and the choice obviously depends on the company's objectives. Events can reach a wide range of substantial target audiences. Their advantage – compared to the medium of television, for instance – is that the effects can be seen immediately and that people can meet up in person. Michels (2013) compared mass communication and interpersonal communication with each other (see Table 5.1).

> **Box 5.3.** Veed.
>
> The Veed YouTube event in the Amsterdam Westergasfabriek is a wonderful example of the new way to get in touch with young target groups. YouTubers become known online and get many followers and subscribers if they are successful. The Veed event gives all of them an opportunity to meet up in person. Many marketing managers and brand storytellers regard this as an excellent inspirational opportunity to reach their target groups. Furthermore, the components of Veed Insight and Veed Awards are linked to the event, aimed at professionals in the field of marketing, storytelling and branding, who can learn here from YouTubers as influencers of today's younger generation.

Table 5.1. Mass communication and interpersonal communication. (Michels, 2013.)

Mass communication	Interpersonal communication
One-way communication	Two-way communication
Sender has little idea of the effect	Sender has a good impression of the effect
Difficult to customize to individual recipient	Easy to customize to individual recipient
Low cost per person reached	Reaches few people at the same time
Recipient can turn away easily	Recipient cannot turn away easily
It is more difficult to create behavioural change	It is easier to create behavioural change
Examples: radio, television, national papers	Examples: personal talk, telephone call, conference

Events and Communication Targets: Knowledge > Attitude > Behaviour (KAB)

Organizations have to think carefully about the levels at which they formulate their communication targets. It requires a vision and strategic thinking with regard to the use of communication (the message, the goal and the means). Traditionally, three levels are distinguished in this respect. In this section, we will explain how events may play a role on each of these three levels. Marketing communication specialists agree unanimously on the answer to the question of when communication can be typified as successful: this is the case if it meets the KAB principle (Michels, 2013). This is an abbreviation of the three main targets in the area of communication: aiming at changes in knowledge, attitude and behaviour (not necessarily in this order). The ultimate goal of event marketing is to effect change in knowledge, attitude and/or behaviour. It implies that people know what to do (knowledge) and understand the reasons (attitude) for what they have to do (behaviour).

Knowledge

The first level is knowledge. Many broadcast communication tools, such as television and radio commercials, but also newspaper advertisements and push messages, are aimed at publicizing a new product or campaign. If the tool is not used in a purposeful manner, the target group will not learn of its existence, which means that the product will not be sold. Determining the knowledge target is therefore crucial to the continuation of a business, and depending on the scope of the target group, certain channels will be opted for. A local shopkeeper will opt for his own show window for extra publicity; a multinational will decide on a prime-time television commercial. The strength of the tool depends on the question of whether the message reaches the target group in multiple places, at multiple moments and through multiple channels. As a result, people will talk about it with each other (through physical and virtual channels) and the objective of, for instance, 'publicizing a campaign' will be achieved. In other words, it is all about choosing the right channels, aimed at the right target group(s).

Attitude

The second level involves attitude. To ensure that the target group is not only aware of the existence of the organization or a new product but also forms a positive image and considers contacting the organization or buying the product, it is important to think about the contents of the message. What is it that you wish to communicate as an organization? What outcomes do you want to achieve in your target group? In most situations, you want the target group to think about the organization and the message, and to become enthusiastic. Tone and visualization are important in this process. When you do this right, as an organization, and when you manage to achieve the desired attitude change, you will have achieved the second-level communication target.

Behaviour

The final level is about behaviour. Communication is also a means to induce certain behaviour in people, such as deciding to buy a product. It is wonderful if the majority of the target group is familiar with the company, and what is more, has a positive image of the company, but if nobody buys or joins anything, or whatever it is that is being pursued, then you have not achieved much. It is all about making sure that people actually do something. Apart from the choice for the right distribution channels (which is, of course, crucial in this respect), you also want people to actually buy your product or service. This can be achieved by rewarding certain behaviour, for instance, by organizing a competition (in every conceivable form), repeating the message and initiating promotion campaigns and customer card schemes. Entrance tickets to leading public events are often used as rewards. But it can also be the other way around: a range of campaigns is initiated to 'sell' an event, which will trigger people to actually buy tickets to the event.

The role of events in influencing knowledge, attitude and behaviour

How do you increase people's knowledge? How do you change people's attitudes or influence their behaviour? By means of the following example, we will explain how the communication around an event – a musical – can be orchestrated to influence the knowledge, attitudes and behaviour of potential visitors. In this example, the event is a product that requires a marketing communication strategy and the right mix of instruments.

Box 5.4. Albert Heijn's musical

Albert Heijn, a Dutch supermarket chain, came up with a customer loyalty campaign under which customers could save for tickets to a musical. This campaign was communicated through commercials on national radio and television (the target group of Albert Heijn can be found across the Netherlands as a whole). Subsequently, customer savings cards were distributed door-to-door. The supermarkets were adorned with posters and information displays about the musical, and customers were asked at the checkout desk if they wanted stamps to save for tickets to the musical. All relevant information could be found on the website. At different points in time, in different places and in different ways, people were exposed to the campaign. The target group of Albert Heijn (supermarket customers) was informed extensively about the initiative. Just how successful the campaign was going to be depended on the target group's interest in musicals. Undoubtedly, a target group analysis had been carried out in advance, which revealed that customers of Albert Heijn are indeed regular musical visitors. Customers had a positive image of this campaign, as it appealed to certain values (beauty, art, family, see section on values in Chapter 8) and the preference for going to see musicals as a leisure pursuit.

Having customers save stamps and stick these on to savings cards is a way to get customers activated; their behaviour is influenced. The step from exchanging the savings cards for musical tickets is now only a very small one. Meanwhile, customers will have stopped by the supermarket several times, buying products they don't really need, and they will also have visited the website a couple of times. Impulse purchases (unplanned, spur-of-the-moment decisions to buy a product or service), which make up a substantial part of supermarket sales, are encouraged as a result. In addition, customers will feel positive about Albert Heijn and will talk about the promotion campaign with others. On the evening of the musical itself, people will no doubt talk about having acquired their tickets through Albert Heijn.

Events and the Multi-channel Strategy

A multi-channel strategy is a strategy that is aimed at getting the communication message across to the target group through multiple channels at multiple points in time, in perfect congruence with each other. Strategies of this sort are very useful in marketing communication. A campaign such as the one pursued by Albert Heijn involves massive budgets.

Still, the essence of it can also be applied very well on a smaller scale. It all begins with a good target group analysis: know your target group! If you know where people come from, what they like and how they tend to communicate, you can align your communication strategy with that and thus maximize the effect of your marketing campaigns. And what is more, you can try to influence the knowledge, attitude and behaviour of the members of your target group. The following example will make clear that it is important to formulate knowledge, attitude and behaviour objectives – based on your knowledge of the target group – after which you opt for the right means.

Events as a Marketing Communication Tool: Giving Substance to the Message

As you have already seen, events are an important means to achieve communication objectives. By opting for a certain concept and theme, the event already communicates part of its contents. By opting for a theme in connection with the organization of a conference by a sector organization, for instance, the organization already communicates what is currently considered an important topic in the industry. The programming and the choice of certain speakers also convey a certain impression of what is all the rage today within the industry or field of study. In this case, the conference is the tool to enter into dialogue with fellow professionals, to explain trends

---

Box 5.5. Charity event

Suppose you were commissioned to organize a new charity event for a charity in Scotland. The geographical boundaries for your target group have already been set. Later on, you can identify other, smaller target groups within the main target group. The event does not yet exist in Scotland, but people are aware of the concept, which has been marketed successfully in other regions. This means that there is zero name recognition in Scotland. So, you will have to work hard on your knowledge objective. At that point, you are thinking about the communication channels. It is important to know which channels the people in Scotland generally use: you will need to find out which regional papers, news channels, websites and free local papers are read and/or visited. To find out what is the best way to engage the people in Scotland, you will have to do an analysis. What will work and what will not work in this particular region? What images and what message will be the most likely to enthuse Scotland about the charity event?

Once you have made your choice for the channels, means and visualization, the question remains of how you are actually going to get people to visit the event and support the charity. You will have to look for ways to achieve this. This will be relatively easy for a certain part of the target group. If your programming is good, some people will come on their own volition. Just announcing the event will be enough. But, there will always be a group that is more difficult to persuade. Having detailed information on your target group and knowing when (in which phase) to target them actively will help you make a choice for a communication strategy.

and developments, to identify consequences for the discipline, and so on. The conference is a meaningful tool that has the potential to lift the discipline to a higher plane. Before, during and after the conference, there will be reason for certain communities to communicate. The annual trade show, IMEX, for instance, recently decided on the theme of 'Still at the heart of the meeting business', which gave substance and meaning not only to the various seminars and workshops, but also to the layout and decor of the location. The IMEX vision delivers a packed education programme and initiatives committed to showcasing innovation in the meetings industry. It brings to IMEX a range of education sessions, streamed into eight *easy-to-find* topic tracks, a host of venues on the show floor to explore latest trends and exciting fun and new activities to the programme (www.imex-frankfurt.com, accessed May 2019).

Events as News

In the previous sections, we have shown that events can influence knowledge, behaviour and attitude. Events often have such a great impact that they are reported on by various news media. This may involve news for internal as well as external media, depending on the size of the event, the public or private character of the event, the number of potential visitors, and so on. By organizing an event, a company creates something newsworthy by definition. The geographical scope of the newsworthiness of an event varies; the event may be local, regional, national or even international. It is good to be aware that events have newsworthiness. You can use this fact to your advantage by generating as much free publicity as possible. Free publicity is editorial attention in online and offline media, such as print, radio and television. It involves a news item that is made by the editors of a media outlet. You do not have to pay anything for this, but the downside is that you have nothing to say about the way in which and the degree to which the item is covered. The great advantage of free publicity is that readers, viewers and listeners usually find the information more reliable and credible than communication messages that are spread via commercial channels.

What is news? What makes something news? There is no general answer to these questions. Nevertheless, a number of criteria can be given (Sterk and Kuppenveld, 2007, adapted by the authors). News is news if:

- it is different;
- it comes from or relates to a celebrity;
- it generates a high degree of involvement; and
- it has many consequences for many people.

An item that meets all these criteria is bigger news than an item that meets only one criterion, and as one criterion increases in applicability, the news is bigger, too. An example is when someone from a big city is living it up at a dance event on a Saturday night; this is not news. When a Member of Parliament (MP) is spotted partying at that same dance event, this is relatively big news with national coverage. After all, it is different, unexpected. The general image of an MP is that of a man or woman in a suit engaging in political debate. That is their national reputation. You do not expect someone like that to go to a dance party at the weekend. The second criterion also applies here: it concerns someone who has been elected democratically to represent the people. In other words, it is an important person, and in that sense, a celebrity.

Creating news value through events

The criteria for news value as mentioned above suggest that companies can also create news themselves. Events, to begin with, are news because something is about to happen that is out of the ordinary: something that is going to take place in a certain area or at a specific location, clearly visible to the people living in the surrounding area and attracting a lot of people. There will be signs in the city directing people to the event, perhaps even diversion routes: more than enough subject matter for news stories. The trick is to give events as much news value as possible by playing with the criteria. Launching new products at a trade show, for instance, is a common practice to increase the trade show's attractiveness for visitors. As a result, you will enhance involvement and your trade show will be different. You can also arrange for a celebrity to open your event: this can be the general manager in the case of a personnel event or the Minister of Education in the case of a conference on educational innovation.

Personal interaction at events will ensure that people talk and write about the event, which is indicative of the significance of the event for society. A process of image and opinion formation will occur among people. Events can also be used to make a point; for example, demonstrations, silent marches and protest marches. When you manage to mobilize lots of people, you get to express your points of view and your organization will make an impression. Events are news by definition.

New Media

Developments in the field of new media have gained momentum and have a huge impact on the choice for media and tools, on the possibilities available to the sender to get his message across. Old or traditional media include print media (newspapers, journals, special interest magazines, trade show representation), television and radio. New media comprise the Internet (websites, blogs, YouTube channels, Facebook, and so on), applications for mobile telephones, new audio-visual techniques (LED lights, holograms) and online and offline gaming. Our definition of new media is 'interactive digital media or new developments in existing media' (see Fig. 5.3).

Radio, television and print media (newspapers, magazines) used to enjoy a relatively high degree of attention. The entire marketing and communication budget was allocated to these media. New media have given companies far greater choice in terms of reaching out to their target markets. Over the past few years, communication and advertising firms have extended their range of services to incorporate the entire spectrum of media, beyond traditional television commercials and newspaper advertisements. Budgets are being directed to more media outlets and tools. There are many reasons for this, but the main reason is that almost everyone has access to one communication channel or another, regardless of time and place. As an organization, you will have to employ a carefully balanced and integrated media mix.

Traditional	New
Radio / Television / Print	Radio, television, print
	Telemarketing
	Sponsoring
	Sampling
	Website
Telemarketing	Smartphone
Event	Event
Sponsoring	Games
Sampling	YouTube
And so on	And so on

Fig. 5.3. Shift in media attention. (Source: Van der Poel, November 2008, presentation, unpublished, adapted by the authors.)

- Media commissions have declined because advertisers (companies/brands) buy and organize media space, thus pocketing the commissions themselves.
- The social media are on the rise, providing alternative advertising platforms.
- Today's consumers are characterized by zapping behaviour.
- There is a tendency from target group thinking towards community thinking.
- It is becoming increasingly difficult to reach the recipients you want to reach, because of communication overload. The catchment range of traditional media alone is no longer sufficient.
- Radio, television and print media are less suited to modern experience communication.

Table 5.2 presents the differences between old and new media.

Below, we will provide a brief description of the four categories of new media.

Internet

The Internet has developed rapidly in recent decades: from a collection of websites to a complete platform for interactive web applications. The Internet is characterized by the interaction between users and the sharing of information. It is personal and social, and also free of charge. Technically, it is an open source, which means that it provides free access to the source materials, it has open standards, and it has data collection and programming possibilities. Examples are Wikipedia (knowledge), social networks (sharing contacts and information), weblogs, chatting, YouTube, Twitter and Facebook. Webcasting is the live broadcasting of an event via the Internet. On-demand streaming means that pre-recorded material is broadcast via a portable device. Online ticketing involves buying and selling entrance tickets via the Internet. With the web, it is possible to make things – that are actually the same for everyone – seem personal; this is also referred to as mass individualization. Consumers can personalize products or services easily and cheaply by designing their own calendar or photo bag.

Mobile applications

Personalized and interactive messages can be sent to any target audience at any time via a mobile device (smartphone, iPad, and so on). Mobile marketing is making its entrance, or put differently: marketing via the mobile channel. The well-known text messaging system (short message service) is part of this, but also WhatsApp, mobile Internet (thanks to a special format, websites can now also be accessed on mobile devices such as telephones), mobile television, Bluetooth (wireless communication), Twitter (exchanging quick and short messages with other users via the computer or mobile telephone) and mobile coupling (barcodes in a mobile telephone serve as entrance tickets). Developments have not yet come to an end; more possibilities will appear in the future. Technology currently focuses on virtual reality, holograms, and so on. Various companies specialize in ticketing, for example, by making smart use of mobile ticketing. A well-known example is Paylogic, which has managed to attract partners such as ID&T (Tomorrowland), André Rieu and RAI (Rijwiel- en Automobiel-Industrie) by offering a good online (and offline) infrastructure as well as data management and mobile ticketing services.

Table 5.2. Old and new media. (source: IDEA Project Group, 2007, unpublished, adapted by the authors.)

Old media	New media
Closed	Open
Specific audience	Users
Supply driven	Demand driven
Mainly based on text	Mainly based on images

Audio-visual means

The impact of events, and also the communicative message, will increase accordingly; just think of laser shows, applications of light, virtual reality and sound effects. Projections of previously recorded three-dimensional material can be displayed by means of a digital projector or flat screen on a foil screen, to create a hologram.

Video gaming

Video gaming involves games via the Internet; for instance, the Nintendo Wii. Through networks, the games can be played together by people all over the world.

New media and the role of events

New media are frequently applied within the events sector. In order for these applications to be effective, they must comply with the following requirements:

1. The applications of new media must contain interactive and personal content.
2. The applications of new media must be based on cross-media approaches, throughout all stages of the event. The message for this purpose must be communicated via various new media platforms at various points in time.
3. The application must be extremely user-friendly.
4. The applications of new media must be consistent with the wishes and needs of the target group, as this will expand the catchment range.

It is also crucial for new media not to become a goal in itself; after all, they are subservient to the strategic objectives of the event itself and have a supporting function. The wonderful thing about new media is, of course, that they have brought countless new possibilities to get in touch with visitors before, during and after the event. In terms of content, as well as in terms of the various services, new media have become indispensable as tools to intensify the experience, the level of involvement and the provision of services to the visitor.

In Practice: Translating the Communication Message into the Event

In order to attain the objectives of the marketing communication message, they have to be translated to practice in concrete terms. Below, you will find a couple of practical examples in a nutshell; they are by no means exhaustive.

In order to give real substance to communication, event organization agencies often work together with businesses that specialize in a certain discipline; in some cases, this involves 'full-service agencies'. Many organization agencies (including event organization agencies) team up with external businesses, which are called in because of a certain area of expertise, specific experience and know-how. A wide range of businesses offer support to event organizers in many different ways; for example, designing and building sets, developing promotional material, designing websites, arranging audio-visual equipment. When the partnership starts, it is crucial for the external businesses to have been briefed accurately on the assignment concerned. Communication is a very important aspect throughout the completion of the assignment. There must be continuous communication between all persons and/or parties involved. Everyone must be well informed about the proceedings with regard to the event. Good communication will ensure that everything goes smoothly. The message that the event is supposed to convey should obviously be discussed extensively in advance. If the external business has not been informed well in advance, it may happen that the sets or props are out of character with the message.

Cooperation with external businesses is often necessary because few event organization agencies have set-building facilities of their own. Some agencies have their own designers, and subsequently have their sets created by specialist set-building companies or freelancers, or – in the case of participation in a trade show – by a standard design company.

The example of the World Expo in Shanghai (Box 5.6) shows how the stands for the World Expo were designed, based on the objectives of the various clients of the Dutch event agency, Hypsos.

Printed matter

An event will only be successful if it attracts enough visitors. That is why it is very important to ensure potential visitors are enthused and informed prior to the event. It all starts with the invitation. An invitation is an important weapon in the competition for the recipient's attention. The invitation should arouse interest and spark the imagination but, above all, it should communicate the goals and intentions of the event.

Digital and print

As a business, you may decide to have your corporate identity reflected in all printed communication relating to the event. You may also choose to design a separate logo especially for the event. When this happens, all stationery, envelopes, business cards and brochures will be adjusted accordingly. The general advice is to start your preparations at an early stage.

When you decide to outsource this component, you can engage a designer who will take charge of the entire process. The designer will request quotations from printing firms and will oversee the entire print production process, from design to distribution. Together with your designer, you can choose your own colours, style, typeface and type of paper. The designer will present his sketches and working drawings to you for review and modification (if necessary), after which he will format the final version.

Box 5.6. AutoRAI

Kubik was commissioned to revitalize one of the oldest car shows in the world: the AutoRAI in Amsterdam. The target group consists of Dutch people with a more than average interest in cars as well as professionals from the automotive industry. Kubik's assignment was to create a setting that allowed consumers to see and experience all car brands under one roof, with emphasis on the enjoyment aspect of cars, based on an all-in exhibition concept to meet the desire of Dutch car importers to be able to show their models in an efficient way.

The new design of the AutoRAI was based on a playing field with various levels where all car makes enjoy the same facilities and branding possibilities. To make the exhibition floor attractive to visitors, the traditional set-up was changed: large background displays of the car show were moved to the corners of the halls. A gallery setting was created with a large red carpet. Kubik created a tailor-made design for each brand, based on the brand identity and the overall concept, making it all cheaper. This ensured maximum exposure for the brands and at the same time it was cost-effective. The concept followed the theme of the AutoRAI: 'Discover your drive'. Visitors had the opportunity to discover their favourite cars by meandering past all the stands. Special side events were organized to underline the position of the event: the largest automotive show in the Netherlands.

Source: Best of Events Awards, beaworldfestival.com

Every piece of communication must reflect the same consistent identity. The colour scheme, the design and the overall look of all communication media must be the same, so that the connection with the event is clear at all times. In a time where visual messages are becoming increasingly important, a special event logo – as mentioned above – may fulfil a crucial role.

Fig. 5.4. Olympic Games logo.

Box 5.7. EETAFOOR!

The concept of EETAFOOR! is based on the starting point that eating means communication and fun. Food stimulates people. And food is emotion. Everything that EETAFOOR! serves is an edible metaphor. The concept 'sells' flavours to go with communication objectives. The EETAFOOR! tour bus is available for events, lunches and dinners on location. The organization also provides customized company training based on the philosophy that snacks with meaning enrich an event and support a message. Specially trained staff (Eetaforistas), who are briefed extensively on the meaning of the Eetaforen and thus the objectives of the event, ensure that the essence of a party, conference or event is discussed in a tasteful manner. What does a new mission taste like, for example, or how do the annual figures taste and what is the taste of development?

Source: www.eetafoor.nl

Instant recognizability is not the only purpose of logos: they actually evoke certain feelings and emotions, such as memories of an experience or an event; the logo stirs something in people. This is an aspect of communication that certainly must not be underestimated.

Turning strategy into action is a key component. The brand image, logo and typeface, as well as typographical standards, are all protected and registered with official bodies especially set up to this end. There is, of course, a very good reason for this. Research has shown, for instance, that the McDonald's logo enjoys 100% recognition among children in Western countries.

Almost everyone who sees the logo in Fig. 5.4 knows that it is the Olympic Games logo.

The AutoRAI example demonstrated the importance of brand identity and corporate identity. Sometimes, having your corporate identity reflected in each and every piece of communication uses up just too big a chunk of the available budget. In a concept like the one created by Kubik, both objectives – showcasing one's own brand identity and optimizing the visitor experience of each car brand – were achieved, for the car show as a whole as well as for the individual car brands.

Location

The location has a considerable influence on the character and ambiance of the event. It affects the visitor experience of the event. Nowadays, it is no longer self-evident that events are held in party centres or theatres. The possibilities are endless: from old factory halls transformed into hip and trendy event locations to classy listed buildings that have had several uses. Whatever a company wishes to communicate through the event obviously affects the choice of location. The location in itself already communicates some of the experience (see also the experience tools in Chapter 8).

Catering

The culinary aspects of an event are often very important, if not critical. Eating together has a strong experiential aspect and therefore has a direct influence on the total experience. The composition and quality of the catering offerings must match the target group and the objective of the event and give the event a certain character. An important development in this respect is that caterers have discovered the market of events. They are focusing increasingly on all-in-one concepts for events, in which catering obviously plays a leading role.

Summary

What is typical of communication is that sender and recipient switch roles all the time. Not only is the message itself important but also the communication channels. An event is a medium and a platform at the same time; it is the place where people meet, as well as the communication channel. Live communication is the key; it allows the recipient to decode and respond to the message immediately. As for the message itself, four aspects are important: the business aspect, the expressive aspect, the relational aspect and the appealing aspect. The four modalities of communication are information, PR, advertising and propaganda – the latter modality usually involves one-way communication.

Good communication is characterized by efficient coordination among goal, message, means/tool, target group and timing. Events facilitate interpersonal communication and can be used to generate changes in knowledge, attitude and behaviour. Understanding the process of communication, the various means/tools and their advantages and disadvantages, and old and new media is important in this respect. Multi-channel strategies can be applied in this process as well, so as to get the communication message across to the target group via multiple channels at several points in time. Because an event often has news value in itself, free publicity is a welcome side effect.

6 Events and Branding

Thomas van Velthoven, Ronald van Olderen and Dorothé Gerritsen

© Dorothé Gerritsen and Ronald van Olderen 2020. *Events as a Strategic Marketing Tool*, 2nd Edition (D. Gerritsen and R. van Olderen)

This chapter describes the role of events in relation to branding. First, we will look at what a brand is and what its attributes are. Then, we will discuss the significance of brands for building a brand from the perspective of the producer as well as that of the consumer. This will be followed by a discussion of the building of brands. Finally, the phenomenon of *brand events* will be dealt with and attention will be drawn to the connection between strategies of brand building and the types of events dealt with earlier.

Learning Targets

After studying this chapter, you will have learnt:

- what a brand is;
- what the two meanings of branding are and events that can be distinguished;
- how brands are built;
- which brand strategies can be used at events;
- how the principles of brand building and image transfer can be used at events; and
- what the role is of events within the framework of internal branding.

The Magic of Brands

Brands are an almost inescapable facet of our daily existence. Inner cities and shopping malls would present quite a different view if brands could not be displayed. It is virtually impossible to imagine the Internet, television and the print media without brand communication. Schoolyards and open-plan offices would be quite different scenes without the phenomenon of designer clothing, either admired or reviled, in which people dress to distinguish themselves from others.

It is true that a product can play a part in fulfilling a need, but a branded article goes beyond this; it fulfils the longing for certainty and alleviates the dilemma of choice. Perhaps a brand can best, and most powerfully, be defined as something that offers a promise – a promise of healthy relationships, of being seen, of feeling happy. Or that of a real party! After all, you do not uncork just a bottle of bubbly but a genuine Moët & Chandon. The creators of such a brand are like modern magicians in our society: they know how to enchant; they are the masters of the suggestive power to arouse emotions. Not through trickery or force, but by recognizing and using latent feelings and needs, and leading people to what they themselves find of importance. It is, after all, impossible to mislead people all the time. A company develops a brand in the long term by gaining the public's trust and never disappointing people.

With regard to events, the building of a brand must provide an answer to two questions:

1. Is it possible to turn recurring events into a real brand?
2. Can the event make a contribution to completing a brand proposition or creating closer ties with a particular brand?

Events as a product brand or a corporate brand

Although we come across brand names that are the names of companies in the world of events, names such as the Eurovision Song Contest and the Dance for Life, it is likely that on hearing those names the consumer thinks first of the event in question. So, this is about a product brand as a brand name, and what crosses the minds of buyers or consumers first is the products and/or services to which the event is linked, while they do not know the company behind it. There are plenty of examples to illustrate this: the North Sea Jazz Festival, the New York Marathon, the Roskilde Festival in Denmark or Rock Werchter in Belgium – well-known brand names, but the general public does not know by which company the event in question is organized.

In the case of corporate brands, buyers or consumers think primarily of the company. ID&T and Mojo Concerts, for example, are to some extent recognized names. But the number of people that can mention the products of these organizers spontaneously is certainly much smaller. Besides, not much is known in general about the brand proposition (the result of the way in which the companies model their position and profile) (Verhage, 2009), so people do not know what the companies concerned stand for.

Events as brand or image transfer (brand event)

In relation to events and branding, we can distinguish two types. On the one hand, we distinguish events that are used to turn them into strong brand names. Events are then both the source and the objective. On the other hand, there are events as tools to reinforce brands, as mentioned earlier in this chapter. When an event is used as a tool for brand building, it will always involve the phenomenon of image transfer (see Fig. 6.1).

A concept like brand management suggests a certain expertise or strategy, but building a brand is much more than taking a series of premeditated steps. As a magician, you should be focused on particular rituals and incantations, be able to put yourself in the shoes of your audience, engage with your audience, manage your audience, but also detach yourself from it at the right time, and you should do it all with a passionate belief in what you are doing. This does not alter the fact that there are several practical principles that can be used in brand building. They provide no guarantees, but they do offer a better prospect of success. We will illustrate those principles by using the example of the Black Cross, a motocross event

Fig. 6.1. Events and branding.

Events as Brands?

Motocross, stunts, music, theatre, quite a spectacle and a great atmosphere, all mixed together: that is the Black Cross Festival; a unique and bizarre combination that in 2018 (the 20th edition) drew even bigger crowds. The 3-day festival has now become the biggest and most spectacular motocross event in Western Europe, and is famous for the friendliness that is so characteristic of the region where it is held. From 2017 onwards, the motocross festival has even hosted the official Open Dutch Motocross Championships (see boxed text on p. 91). The focal point of the festival is the spectacular motocross in which real world champions compete for the coveted Golden Helmet, but in addition, there are bizarre types of mopeds, self-made vehicles, heavy vehicles and sidecars, and for these it is the fun, not the speed, that counts. With more than 100 bands on 30 different stages, the entire festival grounds are throbbing with music. Besides, the whole area is brimming with activity, with more than 1000 theatre artists and many bloodcurdling and hilarious stunts.

Box 6.1. Black Cross: good luck with the weather for once

The Black Cross Festival in Lichtenvoorde (Dutch province of Gelderland) was a success, according to the organizers. Since Thursday, visitors were entertained by a mix of motocross, theatre, spectacle and music. The 31 stages featured more than 150 music acts.

'The weather was beautiful every day. In previous years, we have had our share of bad luck with the weather,' the organizers reported on Sunday. On the last day, there were performances by Jovink, Direct, and Yentl en De Boer. SP (Socialist Party) leader and music fan Emile Roemer attracted a lot of people with a genuine heavy metal set. (…)

Due to safety considerations, the main stunt of this edition was cancelled. 'An American stuntman was supposed to be catapulted into the air, 30 metres high and 80 metres away, to land in a huge pile of cardboard boxes. However, when testing the stunt in the floodplains of the river IJssel, the massive structure got damaged by the water.' If it is up to the organizers, they will have another try next year.

With 220,000 visitors, the Black Cross Festival was sold out on Friday. That was a first in the festival's twenty-year history. What's more, the visitor number was a record: last year, 197,450 people came to the event in the Achterhoek region.

Source: www.nu.nl

Box 6.2. Black Cross to become the biggest sports event of the Netherlands

The Black Cross Festival and the Royal Dutch Motorcyclists Association (KNMV) have joined forces. The finals of the KNMV Dutch Masters of Motocross competition will be held in 2017 at the Black Cross Festival. As a result, the Black Cross will be the biggest official sports event of the Netherlands (a designation currently held by the TT motor-racing event in Assen) and the biggest official motocross event in the world.

Source: www.zwartecross.nl

With 220,000 paying visitors and lasting for several days, the Black Cross is the biggest outdoor musical event in the Netherlands. But does that mean that it is a brand as well? Or, to phrase it differently: does the Black Cross also behave as a brand?

What is a brand?

This is a simple question, but simple questions often do not have ready-made answers. In popular terms, a brand stands for quality, for a particular aura, 'a good feeling', for the promise of a supposed quality or the perception of a particular product.

Chernatony and McDonald have come up with the following definition:

> A brand is a product, service, person or place to which, with the buyer or consumer in mind, relevant, unique, symbolic values have been added that are closely related to the needs of the consumer. (Chernatony and McDonald, 1992)

A brand is successful if it is able to uphold these added values in spite of the pressure exerted by the competition.

Brands are not tangible, but a construct: a network of associations that has found a place in our brains. This makes them subjective, but also dynamic. And although brands are the legal and economic property of the producer in modern economies, it is the consumer who really *owns* them. What a brand statement invokes in us is, in fact, 'our thing'. The power of branding lies in the strategic efforts of producers to create in the minds of many people a network of associations related to the brand with a large degree of similarity in its structure and elements.

Anyone who googles 'Black Cross' will be shown features of this event, such as merriment, lasting several days, camping, outdoors, music and beer. These are not very distinctive features and they may apply to the Roskilde Festival in Denmark and the Glastonbury Festival in the UK as well. But, there are also characterizations that are specific to the Black Cross: more or less unconventionally constructed vehicles take part in races at a motocross venue and the public is presented with displays, including many stunts; vehicles that have often taken clubs or groups of friends many months to build. Figure 6.2 shows the brand attributes of the Black Cross.

The Black Cross distinguishes itself clearly from other events. Moreover, many visitors attribute more or less similar characteristics to the festival. So, Black Cross matches our most elementary definition of a brand: for many, the festival fulfils the promise of specific needs. That makes the Black Cross indisputably a distinctive event and it also displays the characteristics of a brand. Does the festival behave like a brand as well: in other words, can you imagine that there is a magician who animates the brand?

Fig. 6.2. Brand characteristics of Black Cross.

Does the producer of the Black Cross, Feestfabriek Alles Komt Goed BV, handle its event as a brand? From a producer's perspective, it is essential to know what elements make up the construct, what the desired associations are, how to invoke them and which elements are preferably not seen or heard. The moment when this 'branding game' is performed consistently and successfully, Black Cross can be called a brand. All employees are proud to work at the Feestfabriek and to be part of the Black Cross. They feel at home here and fit in well with the company. Core values mentioned by the employees themselves are 'diversity', 'accessibility', 'conviviality' and, most importantly, 'humour'. It should be noted that it was difficult for them to express these words. The core values are felt intuitively, but never or hardly ever explicitly expressed, which is probably the strength and magic of this festival brand (Projectgroep NHTV, 2014).

Brand thinking

Brand thinking is traditionally based on two principles:

- provide a competitive advantage; and
- create brand-added value.

The continual struggle of companies to distinguish themselves from their competitors shows that each product or service can be differentiated. This occurs in phases: from a generic to an expected to an augmented to a potential product (Levitt, 1980). Eggs are packed in batches of six or ten, in protective carton boxes. This means that the producer meets the consumer's minimum need of convenient transport. Further differentiation is then possible by producing a cholesterol-lowering egg by using special chicken feed. Such an adaptation goes beyond the minimum need of the consumer. To call something a potential product requires an addition that ties the consumer to the product. Through a code stamped on the egg, it will ultimately be possible to pay a virtual visit to the farm that has produced the egg. Pine and Gilmore (2000, 2011) distinguish several phases in which economies are transmuted into ever new forms; in which companies make a new attempt to gain the favour of the consumer. A society in which the exchange of primary raw materials was the focal point was replaced by a product-oriented society in which, due to mechanization and economies of scale, the added value came under such pressure that the card of additional services had to be played. This phase was succeeded by the lifestyle phase, which was then followed by that of the experience market. The consumer does not merely buy a product with added services but a total and memorable experience. In this last phase, Pine and Gilmore can see the emergence of a new commodity for the experience market: companies will become producers, or co-producers, of experiences that lead to a meaningful change in the consumer (see also Chapter 2).

The mutation of the Western exchange economy into an experience economy takes us straight to the heart of the leisure domain. The emergence of event producers, dating agencies or brokers in the creative industry is then a logical consequence. Marketing and branding have been linked to products for years, but it was not until recently that the service and experience industry started using the achievements of those fields of study. And the event and dating agencies in turn require differentiation to which brand thinking is one thing that can make a contribution. Building the brands of product and service providers and embracing a phenomenon like experiences, which is new to them, indeed places the leisure and event managers in the vanguard of strategic thinking in their original domain: theatres, museums, the worlds of sports and travel have been selling nothing but experiences for years. Therefore, it is an essential task for leisure and event managers to create a strong position for experience within the strategic brand policy of product and service providers, for example, through a live form of communication such as an event.

The Significance of Brands

Meaning is attached to brands from two sides: the demand side is called brand-added value; the supply side is called brand equity.

The demand side: brand-added value

Brands have a so-called brand-added value. This concept, introduced by Riezebos (1995), has been further operationalized by Franzen (1996) as the added price a consumer is willing to pay on the basis of the difference in preference when a choice is made between the branded article *with* a brand name and the same article *without* a brand name. Using this concept, it is, for example, possible to find out how much more a student is willing to pay for a glass of Heineken or Bavaria beer than for an unbranded beer. A brand like Apple can offer its laptops at prices that are 30–65% higher than those of, for example, Acer or Dell.

It is a common misunderstanding that brand building and brand-added value are related to Maslow's theory of needs. Consumers were supposed to be prepared to pay much more to providers of products or services when pursuing the fulfilment of needs at higher levels; needs like appreciation, recognition and self-actualization. Even if this is indeed the case in times of plenty, it does not tell you anything about brand-added value, because this concerns the comparison of those who provide a brand and those who do not. The question of when consumers are willing to pay a premium in the form of brand-added value is then essential.

Over the past few years, an increasing number of researchers have come to share the point of view that brand-added values can be realized at all levels. Even in the case of a commodity like petrol (Shell Vpower), a brand can link symbolic, expressive and identity-affirming qualities. Whenever consumers find it hard to guess which expectations they are allowed to have with regard to the purchase of a product or service, and can derive a certain identity from a product category, building a brand is useful.

According to Chernatony and McDonald (1992), the functions of brands can affect consumers at different moments. The function of a brand can be that of identification, it can be related to assurance or it can be symbolic. During the orientation and purchasing stage, the identification or signalling function, as well as the assurance function, play a role. In the stage after the purchase, it is the symbolic function, that of owning something, that plays a role. These functions cannot be strictly separated. Moreover, the possessor function can affect the functions before or after the purchase.

Identification function

The identification function simplifies the process of choice for the consumer. How would we ever be able to make a quick choice from a shelf full of toothpastes if a brand name did not provide information to make identification possible? Without too much effort, the consumer recognizes the product, the product varieties, the intrinsic product attributes and the extrinsic product values. Colour, image, logo, design and holograms are cues that help recognition, so that, as a consumer, you know that you really have Signal toothpaste or an FC Barcelona shirt in your hands.

Assurance function

The assurance function offers a kind of guarantee of quality, but in addition it makes it possible for the consumer not to feel directly responsible in the case of failure. When one of the attractions at Disneyland is a disappointment, you do not have to think that it would have been better to take the children to another amusement park. In that case, you will look for emotional redress from the Disney brand, so that, as a parent, you do not cut a sorry figure. That makes the Disney brand risk averse.

Symbolic function

The symbolic function is an extra that comes with the brand after the purchase. Brands can add meaning to the lives of consumers. The symbolic function can be divided into an expressive function, a socio-adaptive function or an impressive function. The expressive function indicates that people show what they find important in life. Brands are an extension of someone's personality; they accentuate what a person stands for and what he finds important. The socio-adaptive function allows people to become part of a group. Brands give off the correct signals to subcultures and make it clear that someone wants to conform to the subculture concerned. In the case of the impressive function, it is not so much the environment that has an impact but the consumer's own feelings. If a visit to Sensation White makes someone feel great because of the special and paradisiacal decor of this dance event, the impressive function has been fulfilled. For a visitor who is focused on meeting the right people and being accepted by the group in question, the socio-adaptive function applies. This example shows that the efficacy of brands is dependent on the arguments of consumers.

The supply side: brand equity

Brand equity is the financial value that a brand represents for an organization or producer. Brand-added value offers the consumer something extra due to the added value of the brand, but the producer can also look forward to a healthier balance sheet as a result of brand building. The financial value of a brand is often many times higher than that of the fixed assets on the balance sheet. After The Entertainment Group (TEG) went bankrupt in 2009, Mojo was able to take over the Symphonica in Rosso concept, for instance, for €1, which prevented the 70,000 visitors from becoming creditors. Outside the context of a bankruptcy, however, the concept would have yielded up to many times the value of the set props, the website and the printed matter.

Brand equity is based on a series of certainties. A strong brand, for instance, has a group of purchasers and visitors who are loyal and who also propagate it to others. Nothing in this world is certain, but a brand offers some guarantee of potential buyers. Naturally, due to the preferential position taken by the consumer, a higher price can be asked for the products and services of a brand than for those that are unbranded. Besides, there is less price elasticity. From experiences in the retail sector, it is known that higher discounts can be obtained for strong brands when they are purchased. Even for the so-called A-brands, Spar (a strong brand with more than 12,000 shops in 30 countries) pays a lower purchasing price than the weaker Lidl. Such an effect can also be expected when strong event providers are involved, both on the purchasing side and in the process of acquiring sponsor contributions. To build a strong brand requires consumer insights, good marketing knowledge and excellent marketing and communication skills, but also the competence to carry out the strategic control of internal and external processes, consistently and over the years. This makes a strong brand an expression of high-level management as well; something that is much appreciated in the financial world.

Building a Brand

A brand contains the promise of an experience. A brand manager consciously determines how he would like to see his brand manifested in the minds of buyers.

Positioning is about creating a congruent relationship between what the brand is, what is relevant to buyers and what distinguishes it from the brands of competitors. Sometimes, a brand builder is very free in building up brand identity; for example, when a completely new brand concept is being developed. Mostly, however, there already is an existing brand with features from its history or a strong link to the identity of the founder or founders. Positioning in the case of the Black Cross can be referred to as inside-out positioning. This means that the values and personality of the brand are a given, strongly linked to its founders. So, acquiring a better understanding of the internal aspect of a brand is an essential requirement for positioning. There are many methods of getting to the bottom of what a brand is. The methods that we will discuss in the following sections have been chosen for their orientation on values as well as their attention to external physical features. Accommodation, decor and multi-sensory stimulation can be utilized as distinguishing features with regard to events as brands as well as brand events.

Brand associations

In Fig. 6.2, we presented a number of brand attributes connected with the Black Cross Festival. They have been obtained from a survey among a small target group. It is relatively easy to organize such a survey. For example, people can be asked for their associations exclusively on the basis of the words 'Black Cross' or the logo. Naturally, a survey like this can only be conducted among people who have experience with the brand.

Biel (1999) has mapped out possible moments when consumers come into contact with a brand (contacts) and on the basis of which they make associations (see Fig. 6.3 and Chapter 9 on touchpoints).

According to Lane (1993), building a strong brand image is dependent on three factors:

- the degree to which a consumer makes positive associations with the brand;
- the intensity of the associations; and
- how unique those associations are.

Positive associations

Farquhar (1989) asserts that consumers assess a brand in three ways: from an emotional context, from observable characteristics and from intended behaviour. The degree to which consumers make positive associations with a brand is influenced strongly by the question of whether they expect that the product or service will meet their needs. The quality of the product offered will be a key element of the consumers' assessment, besides the question of whether or not it is of added value to them. On delivery of the product or service, the company then has to prove that the

Fig. 6.3. Contacts. (Source: Biel, 1999.)

association comes up to the expectations of the consumers. In their assessment, the consumers will, of course, take into account what the relevant features are in the context in which they will use the product or service. It is harder to make positive associations with product features that are relatively unimportant in the context concerned.

Intensity of the associations
The intensity of brand associations depends on the way in which the information reaches the consumer and how that information supports the existing brand image. It is a function of both the quantity and the quality of the information. The more attention is paid to the contents of the information, the stronger will be the associations that ensue from it. There are two factors that will boost intensity: the personal relevance of the information to the consumer and the consistency of the information presented. The intensity of the brand association determines the speed and ease with which a consumer recalls the brand and the associations belonging to it. Another factor is the situation in which the consumer finds himself and the number of links to the brand in that situation. An attitude arising from behaviour-related experiences will be remembered more easily than an attitude based on indirect experiences that are not behaviour related. The degree to which the consumer is exposed to the information can also make it more likely that the information is remembered.

Unicity of the associations
The degree of uniqueness of brand associations is important because the brand must try to distinguish itself from other brands in the same product category. These unique associations should include superiority over other brands. This is an essential feature of the success of a brand. It is vital to focus consistently on this unique aspect, so that it is fixed in the mind of the consumer. Consistency in this context refers to the degree in which a particular association shows similarities to other associations of the same brand. Positioning of the brand is then used to obtain a sustainable competitive advantage or a unique sales proposition, so that the consumer has a convincing reason to buy the branded product. Unique brand associations can be based on features or advantages that are, or are not, product related. In many cases, the features that are not product related, like user type or user situation, will be the source of unique associations. Associations with a brand can be shared with all brands in a product category. This usually concerns product-related features that are relevant to the consumer, and these features may also be a decisive factor in the response of consumers. Some of those features will be considered typical of or essential to all brands in a product category. In this way, shared associations make categorization possible, and the extent of the competition with other products and services can be determined. However, a disadvantage of shared associations is possible brand confusion.

Brand associative system
The aggregate of associatively linked brand attributes in a person's memory is called the brand associative system by Franzen and Bouwman (1999). This system is the residue of all brand observations and experiences that a consumer has absorbed in the course of time. Such brand observations and experiences in combination with the associations of the users of a brand (user image) can develop into a brand personality. People have a tendency, after all, to project human traits on to inanimate objects like a brand.

Separate brand attributes are mutually connected, but they can be ordered into a lower, higher or intermediary category. Building a structure requires an insight into the elements of an association's network. Reynolds and Gutman (1984) have come up with a means–end analysis, a method to determine how: (i) concrete attributes of a product or service can be abstracted to brand values; and (ii) how brand values in turn can be translated into concrete customer contacts.

Chapter 6

The underlying model of the meaning structure analysis is the so-called means–end chain. Figure 6.4 shows the meaning structure of the means–end chain; a structure consisting of three levels, each with two sublevels.

1. Values or goals:
    a) Terminal values and fundamental values: the values that people find it important to pursue in their lives.
    b) Instrumental values: the way in which people try to realize terminal values in their lives.
2. Meanings/consequences:
    a) Psychosocial consequences: the way in which certain attributes of the product or service can be used by the consumer in a psychosocial context.
    b) Functional consquences: the consequences for the consumer of the use of a product or service.
3. Attributes of the product or service:
    a) Abstract attributes or benefits of the use of a product or service.
    b) Concrete attributes of a product or service.

In practice, it is certainly not always possible to distinguish three levels with regard to a product or service. The term 'meaning structure' refers to the fact that we lend meaning to everything that we see, hear and observe and that we, often unconsciously, place those meanings in a mental structure. We not only apply this to the people we meet (a form of stereotyping or pigeonholing) but also to products and brands as well.

Using the research technique referred to as laddering, Fig. 6.5 presents the means–end chain of the Black Cross (see also the section on quantitative measurement in Chapter 10). The 'cross' label is a concrete attribute. But, phrases like 'all is possible' and 'a fat lot I care' are connected with a terminal value, freedom.

So, the method of laddering is not only helpful in finding the connection between the various types of associations but also it presents us with the probable terminal values from which

Fig. 6.4. Brand meanings.

associations can be distilled. Events are generally experienced as entertainment products, and that is the reason why the more emotional attributes are also important when the client, the company, wants to develop a recurrent event into a strong brand.

The significance of the functional attributes of sensual brands should certainly not be overlooked. Indeed, they often affect the desired associations at other levels. The fact that the Gergiev Festival is organized in De Doelen in Rotterdam in a hall that is praised for its acoustics undoubtedly contributes to its popularity. And the enormous amount of attention that is traditionally paid to the decor of Sensation White in the USA is, in the eyes of the public, a distinguishing feature that will certainly contribute to how the festival is experienced and to the significance it has for individual visitors. Figure 6.5 shows that the elements of motocross, mopeds and stunts are connected strongly with the terminal values of 'a fat lot I care' and 'everything is possible'.

Value patterns

Value patterns are very important in the positioning of brands and in giving them meaning. Since 'sensual brands' are sold on the basis of the need for happiness or identity that they can fulfil, values are clearly essential in the development of brands in the fields of leisure and events. Vyncke (2002) refers to values as happiness criteria. The degree in which someone can realize their values determines their happiness. But, values are also the central element of the formation of a self-image. So, that makes values criteria of identity as well. People are searching for something new that is worth the trouble of identifying with. In clubs and, to a lesser extent, in churches, the role of brands is emerging as one that is of significance as a determinant of identity. Something that started as a joke with the magicians, Hendrik Jan Lovink and Gijs Jolink, and manager, Ronny Degen, when they first organized the Black Cross has turned out to be a very strong product, to say the least, with all the right ingredients for making it even stronger. The associations are related strongly to what the Achterhoek region stands for: an independent life, lived in your own way, living it up, a little rebelliousness expressed in words like 'nobody tells me what to do', averse to 'moaning and groaning'. Aunt Rikie, the queen of the festival, personifies those characteristics to perfection. But the other elements of the festival, such as stunts, cross and mopeds, are strong attributes that under the banner of 'everything is possible' and 'a fat lot I care' lead to an experience of freedom.

The Trendbox research agency has mapped out the value pattern of the Dutch people (see Fig. 6.6). The figure displays four value segments on the basis of the dimensions of collective versus

Fig. 6.5. Structure of meaning analysis with reference to the Black Cross Festival.

Fig. 6.6. Value pattern of the Dutch. (Source: Kralingen, 1999.)

individual and order versus freedom. These segments are a representation of what people find important. The strong feeling of freedom is fed by instrumental values such as independence and broad-mindedness. In the eyes of its founders, the starting point of the Black Cross Festival was the idea for a nice party. It could be said that the Black Cross reflects the identity of its founders.

On the basis of the grouping of Fig. 6.6, Trendbox has come up with a refined grouping of eight segments (see Fig. 6.7) in which groups can be recognized with a more or less similar orientation on values, and thus on behaviour. The idea here is that a brand with an equivalent orientation will establish a natural relationship with groups of people in the segment in question.

The value of such groupings does not really lie in the absolute segments, because a population does not only change in its composition but also in its orientation. Continuous monitoring is necessary. And although an environment-conscious event manager will now and then see new groupings drift across his desk, they are only presented here to show that as a brand builder you can reach more or less like-minded people in a society by using value patterns.

The relevance of features

Finally, a closer study of brand associations can also give rise to questions about the relevance of features. From the meaning structure analysis presented earlier, it appears that in contrast to the Achterhoek region, the element of 'countryside' has no link to other elements. Franzen and van den Berg (2002) distinguish brand associations, the key concept and mental assets. They claim that brand associations are relevant in so far as they lead to higher appreciation and/or persuade a consumer to buy something. Part of the brand associations of consumers is covered by the core concept. This concerns all associations that are relevant to the positioning of the brand in a

Fig. 6.7. Refinement of the value pattern. (Source: Kralingen, 1999.)

person's memory (brain positioning). Associations that are related to buying behaviour belong to mental assets. Those associations have a positive effect on the competitive position and the power of a brand. 'Stunts' and 'cross' are extremely relevant to the positioning of the Black Cross. As a consequence, these attributes merit the full attention of the brand builder.

Identity prism

Another method to discover what a brand stands for is the brand-identity prism developed by Kapferer (1992) and shown in Fig. 6.8.

Fig. 6.8. Brand-identity prism. (Source: Kapferer, 1992.)

The prism displays six aspects of brand identity: physical, personality, culture, relationship, reflection and self-image. Additionally, a distinction is made between the image of the sender and that of the receiver. What makes the prism such a powerful tool is that it makes it possible to analyse an existing brand carefully, but it can also be used to find out what the brand could or should be and what the brand or event manager must organize externally to convey the desired image.

The description of a strong brand should be like that of a person in terms of physical and personal characteristics, but it should also include elements of the stereotypical user denoted by the terms 'reflection' and 'self-image'. A brand has aspects that determine its inner side: personality, culture and self-image. But, on the basis of this inner side, it also displays an outer side that is in harmony with it through physical aspects, relationship and reflection.

What all strong brands share is that all those aspects are attuned to each other properly or logically. We will discuss the six aspects of brand identity next.

The physical aspect

The physical aspect concerns everything that a person links to a brand name in terms of physical aspects. How does the consumer recognize the brand? Is there a recognizable image or design style? What, in fact, does the brand look like? Although Kapferer does not include a multi-sensory function in his prism, questions could be asked, such as: what does the brand taste, smell or feel like? Aunt Rikie's logo, for example, is a recognizable expression of the Black Cross Festival. The importance of design as a physical signature reflecting personality is being accepted more and more widely with regard to brands.

Personality

Personality points to the character of a brand. By the way it is displayed or presented in the physical world a brand shows that it has a distinct character. This can go to great lengths; for example, a brand that consciously uses a *personal endorser*: a person representing the brand. Aunt Rikie is the personification of the Black Cross. Aunt Rikie interprets this as just being yourself and an attitude of 'a fat lot I care'. Mark and Pearson (2001) have described archetypes that, in practice, can be recognized in brands as well (Table 6.1).

Table 6.1. Archetypes and brands. (Mark and Pearson, 2001.)

Archetype	Helps people	Brand example
Creator	Craft something new	Williams-Sonora
Caregiver	Care for others	Zwitsal
Ruler	Exert control	American Express
Jester	Have a good time	Pepsi
Regular guy/gal	Be OK just as they are	Dirk van den Broek
Lover	Find and give love	Hallmark
Hero	Act courageously	Nike
Outlaw	Break the rules	Harley-Davidson
Magician	Affect transformation	Calgon
Innocent	Retain or renew faith	Oil of Olay
Explorer	Maintain independence	Levi's
Sage	Understand their world	Oprah's Book Club

Culture
Brand culture is the system of values and basic principles; it is what guides a brand. It is culture that provides a direct link between the brand and the organization. An example is fun in the style of the Achterhoek region: this is the culture, do not dress things up.

Relationship
The relationship shows how the brand is related to the buyer. In the case of the Black Cross, the relationship can be described as 'my best friend who is always up for a good party'.

Reflection
Reflection refers to the stereotypical user of the brand. Thus, the Black Cross Festival appeals to a young, non-urban person who wants to have a few days of uninterrupted fun. The actual target group of the Black Cross is much broader: from young families to the over-50s, everyone who feels the appeal of the same set of values – fun, independence and freedom. The biggest mistake a company can make with respect to a brand is to present a portrait of a person in its communication who is an actual mirror of the target group. The trick is finding representatives of the value patterns in question.

Self-image
Self-image refers to the mirror that the target group holds up to itself. If the brand knows about the image that the target group likes to create of itself with the help of the brand, powerful information will be available for communication purposes. As the mother visiting the Black Cross with her son says, it is all about a setting in which he, as well as she, are free to do their own thing, letting their hair down: a carnival of the East. To obtain more information about self-image, researchers should be able to hear what is not actually said. After all, a male consumer will not say out loud that he buys Axe body spray to compensate for his inferiority complex towards women.

Brand Events: Using the Principles of Brand Building

As we said at the beginning of this chapter, there are events that are, or have become, a brand, or want to become one, and events that are used by companies to load their brands in the sense of giving it meaning. There are plenty of examples in the field of events of those that have developed into a brand, or have the potential of doing so, such as the Sziget Festival in Budapest, Hungary, the Rock in Rio in Lisbon, Portugal, and Tomorrowland in Boom, Belgium. Still, the number of providers consciously using a marketing strategy remains limited. But, in relation to events, the role of branding is more than merely helping an event to develop into a strong brand. The event as a brand has earlier been discussed extensively; here, we focus on the role of events connected with a strong brand.

Companies use events to explicate or accentuate their brand positioning. There are various strategies to do so. We compare those strategies with types of events and, with the help of concrete examples, we will show how an image transfer is created.

Red Bull, with its proposition of 'giving you wings', has several brand-specific and -sponsored events that the company uses to make its own brand positioning absolutely clear (think of the Red Bull Air Race World Series and the Formula 1 teams, Red Bull Racing and Scuderia Toro Rosso). This makes Red Bull a good example of a company that is willing to make a big investment in order to load its own brand positioning through the strategic use of events. The firm became actively involved in Formula 1 by buying up Jaguar Racing and the Minardi team. Moreover, the company owns three soccer teams: Red Bull Salzburg, playing in Austria's top league, MetroStars, an American club whose name is now Red Bull New York, and SSV Markranstädt (Red Bull Leipzig), which plays in a minor league.

> **Box 6.3. Red Bull**
>
> The Red Bull Air Race World Series started at Abu Dhabi in the United Arab Emirates at the beginning of April and flew on to the American cities of San Diego and Detroit. In the Red Bull Air Race World Series, 12 pilots vie with each other to decide who is the best. Speed, precision and skills are crucial. After Rotterdam, the daredevils will go to London, Budapest, Porto and Perth, among other cities. As the races are about flying low at top-speed and extremely hard manoeuvres involving high G forces, only very experienced participants will perform in this spectacle.
>
> (Source: RTL 7, 19 July 2008.)

Figure 6.9 shows where brands use events as a branding and marketing tool. The objectives of brand building are presented in the dark green part. This concerns stand-alone brand building and has not been discussed so far. The light green part covers brand building via the phenomenon of image transfer.

Image transfer

Image transfer is the transfer of valuable associations on the part of the consumer, or visitor, from one brand to another brand, product or activity. From all the impressions and experiences that people have with a brand, they create an image for themselves (Keller, 1993). People create an image of a phenomenon through chains, or networks, of associations. This produces a mosaic of impressions, the totality of which is the image (van Riel, 1996). At least two parties are required for an image transfer: a source and a target. The target, the public or a visitor or consumer, must have certain associations at a source, because otherwise there is nothing to transfer. There are three chief categories of associations: content, polarity and power.

The content says something about the *what* of the associations. Sensation White, for instance, can be associated with dance, paradisiacal, beautiful, out of this world. Polarity refers to the labelling

As product: an event is a product
The event often has a more generic product name (ICT trade fair, Rotterdam Marathon) and more or less specific product attributes but does not behave like a brand

EVENT

The event is a brand
(example: Zwarte Cross, Pinkpop)
The event has its own strong brand association

Co-branding
(example: BrabantStad as a candidate for Capital of Culture = co-branding strategy)

Business-to-business event Extension strategy

Business-to-consumer event Extension strategy

Brand event
The event is used by a brand to realize a desired association network

Brand-owned event
(example: Red Bull Air Race = extension strategy)

Business-to-employee event Internal branding strategy

Business-to-business event Ingredient strategy (supplier is ingredient)

Sponsored event
(example: Ski World Cup – Audi Quattro = endorsement strategy)

Business-to-business event Endorsement strategy

Sponsored (side) event
(example: Oxfam Novib lounge and coffee corner at Lowlands = ingredient strategy)

Business-to-employee event Endorsement strategy

Business-to-business event Internal branding strategy

Fig. 6.9. Events as a branding and marketing tool.

of the content: positive or negative. 'Out of this world' may then be seen as the taking of 'pills'. Power, finally, is an indication of the intensity of the associations linked to a brand.

Brand strategies

Brand image transfer is a part of several brand strategies: ingredient branding, extension strategy, co-branding strategy and endorsement strategy. Though internal branding as such is not a brand strategy, it is true to say that image transfer is indeed used in developing an internal brand. That is the reason why internal branding is incorporated into Fig. 6.10 and is discussed in detail in the section on internal branding events.

Events Based on Image Transfer

Below, we will deal with various events, each of which utilizes image transfer. In addition, a connection is made to the types of events (see also the section on types of event marketing in Chapter 3).

Brand-specific events

Brand-specific events are events totally controlled by the organizer, who is also the financier. At a brand-specific event, the aim is to convey as precisely as possible those associations that are valuable to and desired by the consumer. The source can invoke a very clear association network that is channelled to a different setting and a different product form, and which can even grow into a cash cow on its own. Heineken beer uses the Holland Heineken House at the Olympic Games to try to channel associations and an experience to a new product form. Holland Heineken House could be seen as an extension, an extended product of Heineken, the flagship. Anyhow, this is about multi-channelling the Heineken experience.

Fig. 6.10. Branding strategies connected with image transfer.

Fig. 6.11. Meaning structure analysis of Red Bull.

Red Bull profits because the Red Bull Air Race enables the company to get across to a much wider public the meaning of 'giving wings to' and to boost the appreciation of the brand among potential buyers, generally young people. As a result, it is a successful example of a business-to-consumer event. With the air race also being a VIP event for stakeholders, distributors and retail chains, the moment has arrived that a business-to-business event has been linked to the brand-specific event. In that particular setting, the gives-you-wings experience can acquire an extra dimension with an appropriate decor and catering.

The wings can be regarded as a concrete attribute and the power of the bull as an abstract one. This is how Red Bull adds something extra to the idea of flying, in dizzying stunts, feats performed by stunt pilots flying between pylons and under bridges. The pilots are the embodiment of what is expressed by 'getting everything out of life'. And of course, they themselves need a boost from time to time to be able to sustain life on the edge.

Brand extension is a strategy that involves an extension of the brand to new markets, target groups and user moments, while preserving the brand name. The magazine of the same name as the Black

Cross, for example, provides the possibility to entertain a relationship with the brand outside the actual event, in the pre- and post-exposure phases. Other examples are Nozem Oil (an energy drink developed for the Black Cross especially), a children's book in Achterhoek dialect and special Black Cross Grolsch beer cans. The core values of the Black Cross are carried through to other product concepts. This opens the door to other advertisers (such as Grolsch) as well. The more value-oriented a brand is, the greater the potential for extending it, as is shown in Fig. 6.12. It even opens up possibilities for new event concepts; in the case of the Black Cross this involves its little 'brother' Mañana Mañana (see Box 6.4).

Brand extensions are an attractive way to innovate. The brand has already been established among buyers, which makes it very likely that new logical products will be accepted. The marketing and communication costs involved in launching the new product do not have to be very high, and the risks are limited. Besides, the extension can clarify the positioning of the brand. Thus, it is also a strategy to increase brand equity, a strategy that may be so attractive to brands that there is a danger of overstretching. The Harley-Davidson wine coolers and Bic underwear are examples of overstretching. The extensions failed because the products were too far removed from the core of the brand.

Sponsored events

An event is referred to as a sponsored event when a brand, the endorsed brand, attempts to link up to an already existing event: the endorser, because the naming company sees opportunities to strengthen its brand image. The naming company is a co-financier, but does not have complete control. Because the firm sees possibilities to reinforce its brand image, it joins an event organized by another party with its own brand.

> **Box 6.4. Mañana Mañana**
>
> Mañana Mañana is the most relaxed festival of the Netherlands in a stunning location set in the natural beauty of the Achterhoek region. This party at Landgoed Enghuizen in Hummelo is a beautiful and increasingly poorly kept secret of young rockers, old hippies, tough girls, handsome boys, happy families and local residents.
>
> Ever since its first edition in 2013, Mañana Mañana has been known for its extremely relaxed atmosphere among the visitors of this amazing party. Camping and partying festival fans spread a unique festival vibe across the stunning site by the pond and in the ancient forest. Jamming, dancing, drinking, making campfires and basically having fun until the early hours of the morning at the secret after party.
>
> Source: www.mananamanana.eu

Fig. 6.12. Possibilities for brand extension.

Box 6.5. Quattro

The World Cup ski races provided the Audi brand with an excellent chance to build a clearer image of the Quattro, a sub-brand in fact, in an original way. Originally, Quattro was the label of Audi's four-wheel-drive vehicles, but it developed more and more into a sub-brand: a sub-brand is one that shares features with the parent brand, but, in addition, it has its own association network that translates the brand value of 'independence' into 'control under all conditions'.

The meaning structure analysis in Fig. 6.13 displays the general build-up of Quattro. If ever there was an activity that could be used to bring out the performance element of grip, it is skiing on a knife edge: the World Cup is held in wintry conditions in the most famous ski resorts in the world. In addition to its efforts aimed at the public, Audi can now organize hospitality events as part of the travelling circus of the World Cup that are aimed at suppliers and the bigger buyers of the brand, like fleet managers. Moreover, Audi has invested money in a facility of its own in Finland, where you can join the ice-drive experience for a week.

Audi also organizes 1-day training events, skid courses, provided in the Netherlands by Gijs van Lennep, to gain the 'responsible' Quattro experience.

Furthermore, Audi has been sponsoring the Dutch Design Awards for several years now, an event aimed primarily at the Dutch market and meant to highlight design coupled with boldness. The Dutch Design Awards have been organized for some time and have become famous for the presentation of the best that up-and-coming designers have to offer. Audi is reinforcing its position as a leading stimulator of design. Audi has a long-term sponsor contract to make the renovation of the Stedelijk Museum in Amsterdam possible, and also organizes events of a smaller scale at the museum. The collaboration with this leading museum in the field of modern art underlines the importance of design to Audi. The selected events have extra value because Audi uses innovative digital technology not only in the design of brochures, showrooms, commercials and its website but also in its cars.

> **Box 6.5.** Continued.
>
> In the case of Quattro, the strategy concerned is an endorsement strategy. Audi, the owner, feeds Quattro, the sub-brand. The upper value areas of the analysis are also valid for the Quattro brand. Quattro probably also adds something to the endorser, something like unbridled sporting achievements, but also responsibility. Thus, an almost perfect situation has come about in which both brands share and increase their power.
>
> **Fig. 6.13.** Meaning structure analysis and the events within it.

Sponsored side events are a subcategory of sponsored events. A brand does not lend its name to the entire event but to a specific part, because it is that part that conveys exactly what the brand wants to achieve. That is why Oxfam Novib, for instance, has set up an easily accessible coffee corner at festivals to reach young people with its not-only-aid-but-fair-trade message, and to acquire a young image: delicious sandwiches, lemon coolers and good coffee (www.oxfamnovib.nl).

Ingredient branding event

Sometimes, it is attractive to the host of an event to advertise prominently a partner (ingredient) who is part of the total event. The reason may be that the partner has a very high-quality profile among the target group, often due to patents. Thus, a musical event at which superior sound is important can obtain added value if a partner like Bose contributes to it. A mountain-biking event powered by Shimano can gain in strength. It is also possible that the chief host has a profile without much differentiation and needs the ingredients to convey particular clear signals. A relatively unknown women-only event, for example, can suddenly achieve a distinct profile by linking it to Moët & Chandon, Illy or Nespresso, and when powered by Omo, it will be a different kind of event altogether. Finally, an event may be new and unknown, and vague as well, because it belongs to a new category. A business event at which ingredients like Oxfam Novib, the International Red Cross, Yacht and Yer are displayed gives off a signal that it has something to do with recruitment in the charity market.

Co-branding

When two brands put a new product on the market under a shared name, this is referred to as co-branding. In the world of events, co-branding is common as a means of branding a destination, a city, region or country. Lafferty and Chalip (2006) have shown that the degree to which the combination of brands is suitable is related to the strength of the association between the two brands. With regard to the connection between the event and a place, city or region, the rule applies that the host should organize only those events that are linked to the associations of the destination in question. Another essential condition is that both brands are known to some extent.

The link between the 2015 Tour de France and the city of Utrecht, where the start of the race took place, was all about the Tour de France as a sportive and dynamic event and Utrecht as a sportive, healthy and cultural city and also as the centre of a region with a strong economy. With its enormous media reach (estimated media values of €15 million), Utrecht saw this as an opportunity to show itself to the world as a city with tremendous creativity and organizational ability. Moreover, the opportunity was seized to put Utrecht on the map as a cycling city.

The idea behind the coupling of the Capital of Culture and BrabantStad 2018 is also based on the principles of co-branding. BrabantStad is the urban network of the five big cities in Brabant: Breda, Eindhoven, Helmond, 's-Hertogenbosch and Tilburg *and* the province of Noord-Brabant. BrabantStad is an enthusiastic and professional network with an investment programme of €1.4 billion and concrete projects that are carried out together. BrabantStad is the A-brand of this collaboration. The link to the brand of Capital of Culture opens up possibilities for stakeholders in the region for the self-examination of distinctive cultural attributes. It is then essential to create a faithful image on the basis of the attributes that link this region to mutual projects that can be undertaken to utilize those attributes better, and make them come across well. Just as in the world of co-branding of product brands – Philips and Douwe Egberts with Senseo – this will lead ultimately to innovative insights, projects and attractions among certain target groups like international investors in employment. Unfortunately, this collaboration did not result in the ultimate awarding of the title of Cultural Capital 2018 – which went to Leeuwarden (see also the introduction of Chapter 10).

Internal Branding Events

When a company focuses an event on its own staff, this is referred to as internal branding. In her book, Barendse-Schijvens (2009) describes that a brand image is also formed by the employees, who act in accordance with the values of the brand. Ideally, the image of a company is built up from the inside, and not the other way round. Employees act in accordance with the brand values, either consciously or unconsciously. Each experience a customer has with the organization confirms the image of the service or product. Conveying the correct brand associations to the internal branding event will be most successful if it is controlled by the company itself. Another option is hiring a specialized event agency to make the link to the brand.

Some organizations have been value driven from the moment they were founded: the founder has a very clear picture of what the principles of the company are and what it wants to achieve. He makes a business model and selects staff on the basis of those principles, or moulds them to fit the desired profile. As has become clear in practice, it is not always simple in the longer term to make a company fit the original mould. As a result of the growth of the company, the absence of the original owner, or mergers and takeovers, the original principles may be watered down. In addition, changes in the market may require a reconsideration and reappraisal of the way in which the values have been worked out in the business model, the positioning of the brand and communication. When this moment has come, the organization can discover, or rediscover, its positioning, or confirm it and accentuate it again through the process of internal branding. Internal branding events can be a vital part of a campaign to attain that goal. Internal branding is a matter of aligning the external brand (marketing) with the employees (HRM) and the identity of the organization (internal communication). Examples of internal branding events are presented in Table 6.2.

Aim of internal branding

Internal branding has a dual purpose. The primary objective of internal branding is the optimization of the consumer or visitor experience. A brand is reinforced externally when this brand is supported internally and is reflected in the conduct of the employees. The second objective concerns greater commitment on the part of the employees; employees feel more involved with the organization and the brand. Internal branding goes beyond internal communication. Internal communication is mainly a matter of getting a message across to the employees, knowledge. According to Ind (2007), there is a general misconception on the part of management that internal communication is something that always comes across. If it does not, it must simply be a matter of more communication. But, it should be realized that besides top-down communication, it is vital to create facilities for bottom-up and horizontal communication. Culture and style are then more important than a set of procedures. To achieve identification with the principles of the organization, an activity is often much more important than communication.

When a brand involves direct contact with a customer, it is an essential requirement that the experience as propagated by the brand is in accordance with the experience at the moment of direct contact with the employees. Internal branding is not limited to customer departments. It is a fact that its effect will be strongest if the entire organization and all its employees forge the brand, internally and externally, by the way they act, think and do things.

Corporate identity

If the original principles of the organization have been watered down, it will be necessary to polish up its identity. In addition to the methods that we mentioned of describing a brand, there is a model of the corporate identity of a brand. Groenendijk *et al.* (2000) have defined corporate identity as follows:

> The corporate identity is the strategically planned and operationally instituted self-presentation and conduct of an enterprise, internally and externally, on the basis of a prescribed entrepreneurial philosophy, a long-term business objective and a specific desired image, with the intention to make all functional elements of an enterprise operational as one entity, both internally and externally.

The model presented in Fig. 6.14 is a tool to describe identity in practice. From the communication, symbolism and conduct of the enterprise, a personality crystallizes as a fourth dimension of corporate identity. The benefit of the model lies in the fact that it tells managers that practice-what-you-preach is relevant to their conduct, communication and applied symbolism. Moreover, the model offers something to go on when the three external manifestations of the identity of the organization and the desired aura of the event have to be brought into alignment. The major weakness of the model is, however, its focus on the outer skin of identity. What determines the identity and what is found to be of vital importance within the organization receives no mention.

Table 6.2. Examples of internal branding events. (Liebregts, 2007.)

Cause	Objective	Keywords programme	Communication
A merger event integrating two companies into one, official kick-off	After this meeting, employees of both organizations should be totally committed to the new organization and convey the correct message externally	Informative, pleased, proud, clear, collaboration, new, feeling at home in new organization	Prior exploratory year with new organization, recurring continually in communication. During event, explicit use should be made of values and feelings. Afterwards, at place of work, again form of communication by new organization
A kick-off leadership event, new identity, organization turned into separate company split into two different departments	Trust in management, understanding of corporate culture, challenge to think along, altering awareness, positive feeling, minimizing distance between management and employees	Surprising, understanding/open trust, feedback, challenge, cooperation, confidence, respect, ambition	Prior involvement in event because of assigned task. Very direct communication during event via management, open! Afterwards, employees receive card with summary of the day
Improving and anchoring internal branding process, reinforcing attachment to brand. Generally applicable concept	Gaining insight by experience. The relationship among employees and the commitment they have to the original organization is becoming visible and palpable again	Transparency, trust, ambition, understanding, respect, together, warmth	During this event, communication is live to a large extent. This is continued afterwards, during a period in which focus is on communication of values for 3 months
Staff meeting to express thanks and pride after year of reorganization	Personal commitment to company and employees reconfirmed by managing director. Employees experience moment of pride, for themselves and pride of the organization	Personal/open, gratitude, pride, surprising, social, 'me' feeling, together	Personal invitations mailed to home address because of target group: mechanics. Very direct communication on part of managing director during event. Afterwards, report by employee in house magazine
An annually recurring leadership event during which information is given about internal matters	Following internal branding process, informing and mobilizing managers with respect to organization now and in the future	Information, fun, networking, trust, ambition, together, open	E-mail with invitation sent by management itself. After event management will make tour of all outlets to create openness. This is also an annually recurring event
A short trip with integrated event together with entire organization, to live the brand	Reinforcing internal branding process, receiving and giving feedback, experiencing 'me' feeling within organization. Experiencing brand, working with brand	'Me' feeling, cooperating, breaking down walls, trust, personal, enterprising, self-willed	Teaser campaign followed by extra information on intranet. Task assigned beforehand. Dealt with during event and assigned new task on conclusion of event

Bernstein's spiderweb method

Bernstein's spiderweb method has been described extensively by Cees van Riel in *Identiteit en imago* (*Identity and Image*) (van Riel, 1996). This effective method – to identify an organization's core values – involves people being invited in groups of a maximum of ten persons (sometimes selected randomly, sometimes purposefully) to define the core values of the organization. Subsequently, the participants indicate on a five- or ten-point scale the degree to which the organization propagates those values. By setting out those figures in a diagram, a spiderweb emerges that shows the core values and the degree of importance. The scores are displayed on the axes of the various values in Fig. 6.15: the higher the score, the closer the line gets to the value.

Other stakeholders can be invited to do the same thing, which makes it possible to map out the differences in the internal and external experience of the brand.

On the basis of the information obtained internally, and possibly externally, a vision can be formulated. And from this, the brand promise that describes what the organization/the brand promises its customers can ultimately be distilled.

From the insights thus acquired, innovative ideas and new stories emerge within the brand created by the employees, and are passed on. The new ideas lead to a new way of organizing different processes and systems that are given shape by those involved, among others, and there is further encouragement for management and employees to continue on the path they have taken. The realization of the regenerating organization leads, internally and externally, to the first success stories, and they in turn will feed new storytelling (see Fig. 6.16).

Fig. 6.14. Model of corporate identity. (Source: Groenendijk *et al.*, 2000.)

Fig. 6.15. Spiderweb method. (Source: van Riel, 1996)

Fig. 6.16. The relationship between new insights and involvement in an organization.

Events are a unique way of loading brands and filling them with emotion. The following example of Deloitte Nederland (Box 6.6) clearly shows how an event conveys the essence of a brand and strategy with the help of emotions.

Box 6.6. Deloitte Nederland

Key data
Project management: Deloitte Nederland (Communication Department)
Creative concept and material and technical production: Otter creators BV
Location: de Efteling, the Netherlands
Date: 1 July 2010
Number of guests: 700

As a consequence of several developments, Deloitte has honed its services and branding. The world of its clients is becoming increasingly complex in the field of tax advice. Standard solutions no longer suffice and clients want not only tailor-made advice but also advice in a broader context. Advice *and* implementation ensure maximum added value. The mission of Deloitte has been adapted to this changed requirement and is now 'We know how': deciding together with the client not only what should be done but also how it should be done. The driving values behind this are: think *and* do, passion, understanding what the client wants and a no-nonsense attitude.

Deloitte's strategy for the following years was adapted as well. The launch of the strategy was supported by a multimedia internal campaign. In addition to newsletters, a plenary webcast, decentralized team meetings and, at the end, a central live kick-off were organized to introduce the strategy. It was in particular the plenary closing event that was essential as the official starting point of the strategy. Deloitte asked event marketing specialists, de Otter creators, to develop the optimum creative and emotional

> **Box 6.6. Continued.**
> programme. Their primary goals were: meaningfully communicating the renewed Deloitte and 'loading' motivation for the new strategy. An infotainment programme with various items was developed in a theatrical setting (the Efteling Theatre in the Netherlands), and after the programme, there was time for relaxation with a visit to the park and a concert to conclude the day. The choice of the theatre was a conscious one: a setting in which aids such as light, projection, music, cabaret, the presentation of formats and stage props were used to get the message across in an emotional way. Variation was the keyword that applied to everything. In spite of the relatively long official programme of 2.5 h, it turned out afterwards that the 700 guests had not felt it was very long at all! As a result of the different formats and the short attention spans required for various parts of the programme, a large amount of information was communicated to the audience in bite-sized, emotional chunks. Other features of the programme were interaction and a logical structure. For example, before the interval, various stakeholders and other participants were given the floor to explain why the new strategy was necessary. There were contributions from all over the world, to give substance to the 'as one' feeling. In addition, the strategy was clarified by the optimum use of visual aids, and it assumed an identity because several of those responsible had been given a role in the programme. The use of voting equipment made interaction with the audience possible; the feedback thus obtained was in turn used as input for the programme.
>
> After the interval, there was only one item on the programme: the concrete question of 'what's in it for me?' For individual staff in the audience, what are the implications of the Deloitte organization's new global strategy in the Netherlands? Three initiatives were dealt with in more detail, and by using humour, fascinating images and interaction, the consequences were made explicit to those present. Afterwards, the audience used keywords like 'proud', 'essential' and 'motivated' to characterize the meeting: absolute proof that an event can have an optimum effect as a tool to build and load a brand.

Summary

A brand should be in alignment with the needs of the consumer. In this respect, brand attributes are of vital importance. On the demand side, brand functions include identification, assurance and symbolic functions. On the supply side, there is a role for brand building with the related brand associations and values. Some events have become brands themselves. The Black Cross is an example of this.

Companies use events to load their brands, to accentuate their positioning. Think of the air races organized by Red Bull. Among other things, the process of image transfer and co-branding is used in this context.

A company uses internal branding events to address its own employees, in which optimization of the customer or visitor experience is the main objective.

7 Events and City Marketing: The Role of Events in Cities

Jacco van Mierlo

© Dorothé Gerritsen and Ronald van Olderen 2020. *Events as a Strategic Marketing Tool*, 2nd Edition (D. Gerritsen and R. van Olderen)

City marketing is a form of marketing that utilizes events, among other things, to make a city pleasant to live in and attractive for inhabitants, companies and visitors, and to do this in a sustainable way. This chapter covers the emergence of city marketing and city branding, and the relevant developments in these fields.

Learning Targets

After studying this chapter, you will have learnt:

- how city marketing has developed;
- what is meant by city marketing and city branding;
- the role events play in city marketing policy;
- the role of events in how a city functions;
- what an events policy is;
- what the impact is of city marketing and events on the major target groups of a city;
- what an eventful city is; and
- how a city can utilize events successfully as a strategic tool.

This chapter is about the role of events in a city. Such events take place in a broad context; therefore, we have opted for a broad approach. After a discussion of the emergence of city marketing, we will describe the development of the role of the city and city marketing in the past century. We will also provide a definition of city marketing. Next, a link will be made to the core of this chapter; the role that events play or may play within the framework of how a city functions. We will deal with the role of events from various angles.

The Emergence of City Marketing

These days, it is hard to find any city that is not familiar with city marketing or is not yet consciously involved in it. Cities try to distinguish themselves from their competitors by positioning themselves as an attractive proposition. This has not come out of the blue. To understand contemporary city marketing, a bit of history is useful.

Industrialization and the emergence of the service sector

During the Industrial Revolution of the 19th century, factories were set up in the cities and the workers settled near those factories in the cities. The attractiveness of the city was mainly determined by location factors from then on. The proximity of raw materials and transport routes were decisive factors for a manufacturer who had to choose a city to set up a factory. Because of the money they could earn there workers were lured to the city.

The second half of the 20th century saw the emergence of the service sector and factories were shut down. Increasing prosperity also enabled the employees to live outside the city where they worked. This gave rise to the building of dormitory towns outside the historic and industrial cities. This led to depopulation of the inner cities, because in the evenings and during the weekends the employees working in commercial or municipal jobs were watching TV in their dormitory towns. The inner cities turned into ghostly rows of houses from which all life seemed to have gone.

Source: Noordman, 2004

City promotion

City promotion was already being used in the 1940s in an attempt to retain the city for its inhabitants, or to get them to return to it. The following text is from a brochure issued in Amsterdam in 1939:

> **Amsterdam is not expensive!**
>
> Amsterdam is a city to live in. Amsterdam is not expensive! Live where you work! Cheap necessities of life! Fifteen museums, eight theatres, 34 cinemas!!
>
> Each year thousands of families return! If you move outside the city, you will be poorer by hundreds of guilders due to expenditure on removal, furnishing, laying out a garden, and so on, but you will at least have one positive experience: Amsterdam is not expensive!!!
>
> Source: Buursink, 1991

This is a clear example of promoting cities over the countryside, whereas these days, there is much competition between cities.

In those days, the municipal authorities saw that their duties went beyond the mere provision of information to the inhabitants; promoting their city was now part of the communication package. It was, however, not until the 1980s that this was referred to as city promotion. The aim of promotion was not only to attract residents to the city or to retain them (residential city promotion). Cities also aimed their promotion at tourists, and for that purpose the 'Verenigingen voor Vreemdelingenverkeer', tourist offices, were set up at the end of the 19th century (Buursink, 1991).

Although city officials made great efforts to retain residents in the city and to attract tourists by using city promotion, the period up to the beginning of the 1980s was dominated by discussions about urban decline and urban problems, in which the focus was on poverty, unemployment, criminality and poor housing. Cities had to contend with a bad image, well-to-do residents moved to the quieter and greener adjoining towns, and many cities were in financial trouble.

The emergence of city marketing

Although urban problems have not disappeared, the image of the city had taken a positive turn by the end of the 1980s. Opportunities and plans for development were now predominant, and at the same time a positive view of cities was emerging. Ashworth *et al.* (2004) claim that social and cultural causes are the reasons for the increasing competition among cities. They mention, for example, changes in society, such as the individual relationship with work, the structure of households, consumption patterns, the choice of where to live, and so on. In addition, major policy changes have occurred on the part of the government: central government allows cities more latitude and is stimulating and supportive. These changes have encouraged local governments to become players in the world of city marketing. As a result, cities work on a new future under their own steam, with a clear focus on strengthening the local economy. Later in this chapter, we will discuss the importance of the increased autonomy of cities and their task to provide other activities for the city's users, in addition to boosting the local economy. We will then also deal with the role of events.

City Marketing

The developments that we described in the section above have, over the years, led to a situation in which cities have to compete with other cities in order to sustain the local economy. The city has to put together a profile of itself, to distinguish itself and to excel. After all, attracting inhabitants, firms and visitors, the primary target groups of city marketing, translates into tax revenues, employment and income for small businesses. This will also generate more and diverse cultural activities, of which events, as the bearers of culture, are a major component. The city should be sold as a place in which to live, work, go out and invest. City promotion by itself is no longer enough; city marketing is hailed as the new policy tool.

Market-oriented thinking

Cities increasingly regard themselves as a kind of company. It is true that cities distinguish themselves from their competitors on the urban market, but city marketing is different from marketing in commercial business. A market is a situation in which supply and demand are tuned to each other via the price mechanism. In that sense, a non-profit organization like a municipality is not a player in the market, and is less dependent on the market, too. Municipalities exert a more indirect influence on the market through their expenditure and investments. The point is rather that this involves a market-oriented way of thinking on the part of cities that is manifested by ties to business, the sense of competition and reflection on the ever-changing environment. The market-oriented way of thinking alluded to here may make government policy much more effective. Attracting the right target groups to come and settle in a city or use what a city has to offer leads to a healthy financial organization that is strong enough to create a place where it is good to live, work and spend your free time, today and in the future. Properly speaking, it is not a profit in financial terms that is the starting point for cities but the aspiration to achieve an optimum level of well-being. This is not to deny the importance of a healthy balance sheet. Through the strategic use of events, and by facilitating and stimulating them, the level of well-being can be raised.

The seven Ps of city marketing

By taking a look at the traditional marketing mix, we can make it clear that there are similarities and differences when you compare the marketing of a product with that of a city. Figure 7.1 shows the marketing mix for city marketing (the seven Ps).

It will be clear that, after what was said in the previous section, the city *product*, in contrast to the usual marketing products, is very complicated and diverse.

Place is all about getting the buyer (resident, visitor, firm) to the product; this means that the city should be accessible in a physical as well as a communicative sense. *Promotion* is often wrongly identified with city marketing in all respects, though it is only a part of it. Another important point to make is that you cannot simply put a *price* tag on a city as a complete package. The price is generally determined by the various components of the package, but if there are too many components, the municipal authorities can only act as initiators and facilitators to make

Fig. 7.1. Marketing mix for city marketing (the seven Ps). (Source: Kotler *et al.*, 1993, adapted by the authors.)

the city more attractive as a total package, or with respect to certain components. The P of *politics* refers to the fact that a municipal organization is set up differently to an enterprise that has to make a profit, and its objectives are also different. Well-being, not profit, is the starting point. City marketing is affected strongly by politics, and the political climate has an impact on the profile of a city. The *personnel* employed by the municipal organization must learn how to operate in a market-oriented and customer-friendly way. If a city wants to propagate a marketing strategy, it is essential that this strategy will first be ingrained in the minds of municipal staff. Moreover, the inhabitants of a city function as its ambassadors, but they cannot be instructed in the way that an employee of a profit organization is. Aura and image are of vital importance to the *presentation* of a city and should be in alignment with the other Ps. The presentation of a city features things like infrastructure, setting, facilities, neatness, decor and security.

Consuming and producing

City marketing is not only a matter that concerns the municipal authorities but also something that involves all the parties that make up a city. Companies play a vital part because, as heavy users of the city, they benefit from a city that is attractive to both their employees and their customers. This affects their image in a positive way. The inhabitants are, as it were, the ambassadors of a city and make their satisfaction known by word of mouth. They largely determine to what extent a city comes across as a hospitable one. Visitors also determine a city's image, and they take that image home and tell people about it.

Companies, inhabitants and visitors can be regarded as both consumers and products. There is a relationship between city marketing and business, because firms, too, try to involve consumers as much as possible in the realization of their own products and bind them through an optimum experience (co-creation). There is an automatic involvement of consumers and interested parties within a city marketing policy; it is essential to confirm that involvement and, preferably, to reinforce it.

An attractive city

Florida (2002) mentions 'the role of the creative class' in making a city attractive. According to him, the industrial economy is developing into a creative economy. Creative people are the engine of this new economy. Younger generations are mobile and increasingly opt for places that give them energy, where they are challenged. As a consequence of the increasing importance of this critical creative class, the members of which can find a place anywhere, cities are forced to devise strategies to lure creative talent. But, even though a city may do the best it can to be attractive, history shows that *the* attractive city does not exist. The development of cities has always been somewhat unpredictable, so that not everything can be planned, much to the regret of policy makers. In spite of this unpredictability, there are factors that can increase the chances of a city becoming attractive: enough interaction and a variety of things on offer.

Interaction

First, there should be enough interaction. It is the inhabitants of a city who create a situation that invites interaction, and the way a city is laid out may be helpful. The point here is not the number of persons, but rather the number of contacts, the density of the interaction. Meeting places such as parks, pubs, bars, restaurants and squares can have a stimulating effect, of course. In addition, events are temporary and flexible occasions where large numbers of people meet. Thus, they make a big contribution to creating meeting places in a city.

Diverse supply

In the development of a creative city, a vital role is played by a diverse supply of knowledge and technology, as well as the willingness of creative people to make use of this supply. Interesting new combinations arise from the communication between people of different backgrounds.

A city with a diverse population mix can benefit from an equally varied knowledge and expertise. Diversity breaks through 'people like us' notions, makes room for creativity and attracts talented people from outside.

An attractive city is not only unpredictable but also densely populated, interactive, knowledge-intensive and diverse. Many cities, including those in the Netherlands, meet these criteria, but the attractiveness of a city should also be known to others. Its image is the decisive factor for a city to be regarded as attractive. Just like products, cities have a brand value and that is the reason why they invest in city branding.

City Branding

City branding is a trend in city marketing that focuses on putting a city on the map in a distinctive way. City branding can be used to build a clear city identity on the basis of well-defined core values, and is aimed at entering into relationships with target groups. According to Berci *et al.* (2002), the emergence of city branding is related to the increasing need for individuality in society. The public wants an ever-increasing number of possibilities to choose from, diversity, distinctiveness and profundity to enhance its own individuality and to be able to connect emotionally with its natural habitat, while what is supplied is becoming more and more monotonous and predictable. In cities, too, uniformity is on the rise. Inner cities resemble each other more and more, with the same retail chains, but this is certainly also due to a tendency by the cities to copy each other for fear of missing something. The world is getting very close to a monoculture. The *global village* is arriving. It appears as if cities are losing the ability to distinguish themselves; they generate little or no emotion, attachment and involvement, and are in danger of becoming impersonal, anonymous and, ultimately, uninhabitable. Cities must do something to escape this vicious circle. It is no longer enough merely to adopt and transform successful ideas and formulas from elsewhere. Urban renewal is required to fulfil the desire for diversity.

Increasing individualization and globalization are the starting points from which to shape urban development from a new tradition. Thanks to individualization, people have more freedom than ever to fulfil their own aspirations and enter into relationships all over the world.

Self-expression as a marketing tool

According to Berci *et al.* (2002), self-expression is the marketing tool of the future. This creates a new framework to shape the city from within, based on its culture and its character and the chemistry between its inhabitants. Therefore, a city will have to reflect on the factors that can reinforce the emotions and chemistry between people in a specific place. City renewal involves the creation of an identity with its own experiential value, profoundly original and non-reproducible, with the aim of enhancing the current market position of a city and making it more distinctive, as a result of which that unique position can be claimed even more convincingly in the future. Cities need a soul, and that soul emanates from its inhabitants. But, allowing something to arise spontaneously without interference from the top should certainly not be interpreted as *laissez-faire*. The renewal is realized in consultation with various parties, and policy is shaped by what is going on in society. Moreover, this policy offers scope for initiatives from society and facilitates these initiatives.

Urban development and creativity

People make a city; a city leadership that focuses on its citizens and is concerned with their happiness and well-being is doing all right. Contented inhabitants are, after all, the best spokespersons for a city. So, policy makers could do worse than putting out feelers in society. Ideas can be found anywhere. The trick is, starting from the insights of citizens, to find the correct key to urban development. A policy maker needs to have an open mind to be able to track down the hidden gems in a city. It is not only the creative class that plays a role in this context; each resident can be creative. What this is all about is creating the broadest support for an attractive city. Urban development is an art, not a formula. Compartmentalization is a feature of many cities and the distance between policy makers and everyday life in the city is too great. So, it should not come as a surprise that cities find it hard to be distinctive. The key to success is to ensure that renewal in a society is given shape by imaginative, daring and properly coordinated policy measures, investments and innovations. In this respect, it is more important to make good on promises than having an impressive campaign and a catchy slogan. A good example of this is Rotterdam, which not only has an innovative new central station, but also the impressive Markthal, which was opened in 2014 by Queen Máxima amid great interest from the public.

The digi-panel is a frequently used tool to enable the city leadership to keep in touch with what is going on in their city. It is a digital citizens' panel in which residents of 16 years and older can make their opinion known on a particular subject by filling out a questionnaire on the Internet.

Advantages of a city as a brand

The advantages of an attractive city are often connected with the economically driven desire to position cities more strongly in the midst of a scaled up, mobile and abundant market of locations and destinations (Berci *et al.*, 2002). City marketing and city branding, used as strategies, can provide cities or districts within cities with an image, a cultural content, a soul, a brand. The brand can function as a source of symbolism and lead to added value in economic terms. A simple example is the historic market in the centre of the city, where a cup of coffee is more expensive than outside the centre. The urban brand is an indication of the status of cities as a tourist destination or as a residential or business location.

Within city branding, it is not only economic functionality that plays a role with respect to the attractiveness of a city. The sociocultural effects are relevant as well. Brands bring a certain degree of order or coherence to the pluriformity of contemporary society to make it possible to read each other and our surroundings better. The brand provides people, things and events with a sign and, as a result, they can be recognized as a part of the whole. This makes brands not merely a source of distinction but also of identification, recognition, continuity and a sense of community. Used in this way, brands can then also be economically successful. According to Berci *et al.* (2002), city brands appear to be more successful, as they are better able to penetrate the latent and tactical level of sentiments and affinities in or around a city. In this respect, the main question is to what extent they can provide direction and coherence to them. In other words: as a resident or a visitor, you do not love a city for its sights but because it fulfils your specific needs.

A Definition of City Marketing

In this chapter, we use the following definition of city marketing:

> City marketing is acquiring a distinctive relevant position to be able to attract the right enterprises, visitors and residents, and retain them, by establishing core values for the creation of a clear city identity from the inside out, and based on the culture and character of a city, utilizing the commitment of the parties involved and aligned to city policy, which leads to involvement with and a willingness to do something for a city in such a way that reality matches the image created.

City marketing has the following implicit assumptions as its starting point (Landuyt and Ummels, 2008):

- Attracting and retaining the right inhabitants, companies and visitors leads to more economic and sociocultural activity in a city.
- As a result of the increased mobility of residents and companies, the city enters into competition with other cities in the fields of economic and cultural activities to become more attractive. In other words: doing nothing about the image of a city results in a less positive image of it and a possible decline in comparison to other cities (a competitive disadvantage).
- The choice to live in a particular city, to set up a company there or to visit it is determined by what a city has to offer and by subjective emotional considerations. These subjective emotional considerations come together in the word 'image': the image people have of a city.
- The image of a city can be created and, with the use of strategic interventions, can be intensified, enhanced or adjusted.
- A positive image is not sufficient; the image should also correspond to reality. A city should deliver what has been promised. That is the reason why organized activities to realize the image should be an integrated part of a good city marketing strategy and a good city marketing plan.

City brands are loaded by a wide diversity of resources. This is also clear from the definition at the beginning of this section. According to Kotler *et al.* (1993), four elements are involved in making a city more attractive. They are:

- *Urban design*: this refers to the design that reveals the character of a place and shows how it has been transformed in the course of time.
- *Infrastructural improvement*: infrastructure enables urban design.
- *Basic services*: good public services are a given in the competitive struggle between places, or cities.
- *Attractions*: this concerns physical features and events in which residents, visitors, companies and investors play a part.

In this chapter, we will discuss this last element, attractions, in more detail. Events in a city have a strategic role in loading a city as a brand. This may involve not only public events but also business-to-consumer events (see the Red Bull Air Race in Chapter 6), (international) trade fairs and conferences.

Events Policy

With regard to events within the city limits, public or otherwise, municipalities are becoming more and more professionalized. Nearly all municipalities have now formulated an events policy, which is revised every few years. First, the municipal authorities want to have a good and clear picture of everything concerning an event; and second, there is a growing understanding of the importance of events for the urban economy, the quality of life and the attractiveness of a city. It cannot come as a surprise, then, that an increasing number of cities put a lot of work into drawing up a clear and transparent events policy aligned to a city marketing policy.

The objectives for writing a memorandum of events, as the policy document is called, differ between municipalities. A municipality is free to formulate an events policy according to its own views. Still, there are many similarities. Here is a list of a number of aspects that often can be found in a memorandum of events in connection with an events policy. In this respect, it is noteworthy that, due to recent events in the field of terrorism and other calamities, increasing emphasis is placed on safety. Risk analyses are an ever more important part of event requests. Additionally, the municipal consultations on event safety (in which an event's safety risks are assessed by representatives of emergency services, such as police, fire service and medical assistance organizations) have led to a considerable tightening of the criteria with regard to maintaining safety at events.

An events policy:

- describes what is meant by an event, including a division into subcategories;
- comprises a vision on the development of events in the municipality;
- is aligned with the integrated city policy (also city marketing);
- discusses the desirability of events and the criteria used to assess them;
- includes quality assurance with respect to events;
- describes the conditions that an application should fulfil;
- describes what to do if an event crosses the city limits;
- comprises the process of applying for a licence and subsidy;
- describes the organizational structure of the municipality that deals with events; for example, cooperation with an events organizer or an events coordinator or committee;
- describes how events are facilitated;
- describes the financial resources available for events; and
- comprises evaluation procedures.

> **Box 7.1. The ambitions of Rotterdam Festivals: deeper into the city, further into the world**
>
> Rotterdam is a good example of a city with a well-thought-out policy on events. In this process, the city has deliberately opted for fewer but stronger, high-end events, impacting the city at a deeper level. The strategic objectives, the critical success factors and the explicitly articulated key performance indicators for the 2013–2016 period can be summarized as follows. The strategic objectives focus on a large and wide audience, but are based on an events programme that matches the city's character and identity. Furthermore, these objectives relate to strengthening Rotterdam's profile as an events city, both nationally and internationally, and Rotterdam wants to contribute to a strong events sector in the city itself. The critical success factors have been described in great detail and include factors such as public awareness of the events on offer and prioritizing events contributing to themes related to the city. Finally, the key performance indicators are measurable so that the results can actually be measured. Examples of this are: events in Rotterdam are in the international news at least six times a year, and in the summer period the city offers 13 consecutive weeks of programmed events that are accessible free of charge.
>
> Source: Rotterdam Festivals, Culture Plan 2013–2016 (2012)

The Role of Events in the City

Events play an increasingly important role in our society, and cities acknowledge this more and more. What was the role of events in a city in earlier days? And what is their real role in today's cities? These are the questions we will deal with in this section.

The role of events in the city in the past

Events have played an essential role in cities for thousands of years. Think, for instance, of the markets of pre-industrial society, like the Greek agora and the Roman forum, places that were brimming with life. Events were a vital diversion from the harshness of existence and were used by rulers to strengthen their position.

In the industrial city, events played a significant role in strengthening new urban traditions, such as parades and travelling musicians. They were even becoming a threat to privileged religious and royal events; the Church and the Crown came up with new events to keep in touch with the population. Examples are the building of royal concert halls and also the Dutch King's birthday, which is celebrated in the Netherlands.

During the period of industrialization, when cities introduced more regulation, 'arts and culture festivals' (or fringe festivals, as they were referred to) were organized as a kind of marginal phenomenon in an ordered society. There are still arts and culture festivals today that test cultural boundaries, and in view of the sameness of various cities, this is no bad thing at all.

Festivals and events expanded into indispensable bearers of culture in the modern city and they were generally organized in or around the city centre. Events made money, contributed considerably to putting a destination on the map, advanced the commercialization of tourism, contributed heavily to the image of a city and were used to relieve the pressure on cities by spreading activities.

The contemporary role of events in a city

Even in times of economic crisis and declining industries, the authorities exploit the creation and marketization of cities as cultural centres in an attempt to create a new business climate. As culture and creativity gained a position of central importance on the public agenda and entered the intercity competition, cultural events were assigned a new function, that of *generators of meaning*. There is a strong interaction between culture, economics and place in our cities. Events are used consciously as strategic, meaningful tools of experience to contribute to objectives formulated previously. In other words, events are powerful tools that make a vital contribution to the implementation of the objectives of city marketing. The role of self-expression in all this is an important one, and this applies to organizers, residents and visitors. Thanks to events, a suitable identity can be created and supported, and this is done from the inside out, from the culture and character of the city. This holds good both for events that have been organized in a city for decades and for new events that give voice to the character of the city, develop it and support it. In the way they promote character, events can be regarded as crucial counterparts of the monoculture of an increasingly globalized world.

Events contribute to the *symbolic added value* of cities and create a certain order and coherence in today's pluriform society. They allow cities to distinguish themselves, increasing their recognizability to residents and visitors alike. They also give people something to hold on to and enable them to understand better the world around them. However, events also provide a city with *points of identification that contribute to the emergence of a fresh identity of the city* that is outside the mainstream. Events reinforce subcultures and create togetherness. Thus, events have developed into important tools for urban development and the revitalization of the city; they add to the rhythm of a city. They bring out the various seasons: Christmas markets in winter, races in spring, outdoor performances and flower parades in summer, and film festivals in autumn. Incidental mega-events are mixed in and create their own new rhythm, thus highlighting the non-cyclical special happenings in the city. There are, in fact, various urban rhythms that

> A city without events is a city without a beating heart.

flow and blend together. They produce an atmosphere of excitement, a buzz, in the city. This sense of things starting to hum affects the way in which people look at a city; the image of a city improves and the inhabitants are (again) proud of their city.

'Eventful Cities'

Many contemporary cities have been transformed into festival and events cities. Richards and Palmer (2010) call them eventful cities. They refer to cities where cultural festivals are used in a harmonious way to achieve the following:

- improvement of the quality of life in the city;
- creative activity;
- an increase in public groups;
- new forms of cooperation;
- possibilities for recreation and education;
- economic and social advantages;
- improvement of image; and
- contribution to social objectives.

So, distinction is based not only on landmark buildings and imposing museums; it is often events that create a pleasant atmosphere and environment. Events give cities their appeal. Events have the following advantages over physical, infrastructural objects.

- Events are more flexible than physical infrastructural objects.
- Events can help physically flat surroundings to stand out.

- Events add something intangible to the physical culture of a city.
- Events can give meaning to place and time.
- Events are an element of the rhythm of a city.
- Events offer a better opportunity to create spectacle and atmosphere.
- Events generally create an atmosphere that draws people to the events; they want to be part of them.
- Events involve fewer expenses and can have a bigger impact in the short term.

Looking at the statements above, it is as if events are a universal remedy, but this is not what they will automatically turn out to be. In many cities, there is room for improvement in the events programme, and it is hard to realize the desired situation in practice. Furthermore, cities should realize that there might be positive as well as negative effects. In the latter case, there will, of course, be negative consequences for the image of a city, and the impact will be bigger than that of positive effects; as a result, it takes more time to polish up a damaged image. The recent terrorist attacks in France – targeting, for example, Stade de France and concert venue Bataclan in Paris and the fireworks show in Nice during the French national public holiday – are not helpful in terms of the positive image of these cities or even the whole country for that matter, and may lead to potential visitors preferring to avoid these destinations (see also Chapter 10).

Box 7.2. The magic of Bosch: old painter, new city marketing

The old Dutch Masters Rembrandt and Van Gogh are hugely popular abroad. These national icons contribute to the cultural profile of the Netherlands, while the museum collections are an important reason for visiting our country.

In 's-Hertogenbosch, a memorial year was glimmering on the horizon: 500 years of Jheronimus (Jeroen) Bosch in 2016. The mission was twofold. In addition to Jeroen Bosch being permanently connected to the city of 's-Hertogenbosch, the painter would also have to acquire a position in the 'premier league' of painters originating from the Netherlands. From the outset it was clear that in 2016 a substantial part of the works would have to be returned to the city of Bosch for a major exhibition. The exhibition formed the anchor point for a large-scale, multiple-year event called 'Jheronimus Bosch 500'. It was a huge challenge, because the city no longer owned a single one of Bosch' works. Nevertheless, in 2016, the city succeeded in organizing the largest Bosch exhibition ('Visions of a Genius') ever. The exhibition attracted some 400,000 visitors, approximately one third of whom came from abroad.

Source: Duif, 2016

The Role of Events within the Main Target Groups of City Marketing

Events contribute greatly to the realization of the desired situation as described in the broad definition of city marketing. Ultimately, it is really about a positive positioning of a city with respect to other cities, about a city where it is nice to live, work and play. What does this mean for the main target groups? This section will discuss residents, visitors and companies in the city.

Residents

Public events contribute to the quality of life and well-being of the inhabitants of a city. Events generate a merry and lively atmosphere and provide relaxation and recreation. Additionally, they contribute to social cohesion within a community. Thus, events in a certain area can put the residents in touch with each other and promote more understanding between various cultures.

The more successful public events are at accentuating the values of a community, the greater will be the contribution to social bonding. The better the event is able to appeal to the values of the community, the prouder the community will be of the event, making the contribution of the event to city marketing even greater. Moreover, this feeling of togetherness makes people more willing to participate in the event, so that the inhabitants make a positive contribution to the positioning of their city. In the end, this active participation will lead to more cultural diversity and sociocultural activities in a city. Besides, inhabitants who are content and proud are the best ambassadors: they care about their borough, are open and hospitable, speak in positive terms about their city and invite friends to visit events, public or not, in the city.

A good example of an event that brings the members of a community together is the Zundert Flower Parade in the Netherlands (Box 7.3).

Visitors

Attracting (large numbers of) visitors to an event generates much income for a municipality and thus contributes considerably to the local economy. Visitors not only spend their money on the event itself but also on additional activities like shopping, going to other attractions, a museum for example, and an overnight stay in a hotel, to mention only a few possibilities.

Public events are not only good for a local source of revenue but also they play an important role in transferring the desired identity and core values of the community in question. The profiles of Rotterdam and Eindhoven, for example, are clearly those of sports cities as a result of organizing and landing major sports events.

Each public event has a particular content. If this content is aligned to how a municipality wants its profile to be, the event acts as a city marketing tool. And, of course, if an event attracts much attention from the media and many visitors, this will ensure great exposure.

Visitors to an event take their image and memory of everything that has happened home, into the world, which makes them in their own modest way ambassadors of the municipality, and they may return to a city for a repeat visit. Without realizing it, visitors play a vital role in enhancing the attractiveness of a city. Visitors from out of town bring new insights and different cultures to the city; thanks to events, an intercultural dialogue and exchange can have a good or better start.

Companies

Companies play an essential role in city marketing. As top users of a city, they benefit from an attractive city, with respect to both their employees and their customers. Moreover, an attractive city will boost the corporate image. Public events can also make a contribution to the customer relationship management of companies. Events are often used to pamper relations, presenting them with an unforgettable experience to underline the importance of business and personal relationships. Cities, in their turn, use events to tie companies to them. Companies in municipalities with the same core values will be willing to sponsor events. The result is a win–win situation that is good for the company, the city, its residents and its visitors.

Box 7.3. Zundert Flower Parade – meeting the sun!

In Zundert (hometown of Vincent van Gogh), they are mad about their flower parade. Even their grannies were mad about it. The flower parade was organized for the first time in 1936. By the first Sunday of September, flower parade fever has taken hold of all the inhabitants of Zundert. Will the floats be finished in time? Are there enough dahlias? And who is going to win? Everybody should go to Zundert to experience it!

The Zundert Flower Parade is not just an event; it is an event that preoccupies the inhabitants of Zundert all year round. The parade bonds them together and is their cultural heritage. Young and old are involved, and several clubs even link their jubilees to the parade.

The four parade seasons

The day of the flower parade is New Year's Day in Zundert. Everything happens before or after the parade. When, on the Tuesday after the parade, the floats and construction tents have been dismantled and the builders, still tired of all the exertions, have stored away the undercarriages, the preparations for the next parade will start immediately. The next parade is in 363 days, after all!

Box 7.3. Continued.

Autumn

So, the new parade year starts right after the parade, and the first season of the new parade year is the parade autumn. This is a time of sadness, of retrospection, during which Zundert looks back on the latest parade filled with feelings of melancholy. Did the right contestant win the first prize? And what way does the jury seem to lean? Dahlias intended for other parades are picked from the fields into the month of October. November is the start of the winter period, during which the dahlia bulbs are stored in holes or barns. Zundert concludes the autumn period by looking back at the latest parade by means of photographs and videos. This retrospective moment is the end of autumn and the beginning of winter.

Winter

The parade winter is the season in which it seems as if nothing much is happening in relation to the parade. But, appearances are deceptive; the parade winter is the period in which the executive committee and various subcommittees of the Zundert Flower Parade Foundation are fully engaged in making plans for the next parade. And the long, dark winter nights are the ideal moments for the designers to brood on new ideas. The parade winter is concluded by a special tradition: the presentation of the standard. The winning neighbourhood makes a standard of honour in the style of the winning design. The unveiling of the standard is part of a fascinating piece of drama that is attended by the entire parade community. The presentation of the standard is the close of winter and the start of the next parade season, spring.

Spring

The parade spring begins right after the presentation of the standard on the second Saturday of January. Neighbourhoods start preparing the construction site: designers make their models. The dahlia fields are waking up from their winter sleep, as well. In April, the dahlia bulbs are planted. And all of a sudden, parade fever strikes again. The parade spring is concluded by a model festival, a weekend in June, when models of the floats for the next parade are displayed to the public. The entire population of Zundert turns out and speculates vehemently on the likely winners. During the model festival, the chairman of the winning neighbourhood of the previous year hands in the challenge cup.

Summer

The model festival heralds the parade summer. Construction tents are put up, the undercarriage is wheeled in and the main frame is welded. As soon as the main frame is ready, it will be getting increasingly busy in the tents. There is work for more and more people, and parade fever is taking hold of the entire village.

Everything not related to the parade is postponed until after it. There is just one priority: the parade float. People work hard and feverishly during the warm summer nights. The colossal floats are slowly taking on their final appearance. The flower fields are busier too. The fields are harvested twice a week from the beginning of August.

The highlight of the parade summer is, of course, the parade itself. The greatest day, the day everyone has been working towards for four seasons. On the first Sunday of September, you can watch the fruits of a year's labour.

> **Box 7.3.** Continued.
>
> The Zundert Flower Parade wants UNESCO [the United Nations Educational, Scientific and Cultural Organization] to recognize its parade as a protected, intangible cultural heritage. This again underlines the position of the parade within the community of Zundert. The definition of intangible cultural heritage in the UNESCO convention is:
>
> > This intangible cultural heritage, transmitted from generation to generation, is always recreated by communities and groups in response to their environment, their interaction with nature and their history, and gives them a sense of identity and continuity, thus promoting the respect for cultural diversity and human creativity.
>
> The float builder from Zundert who manages to get through the somewhat woolly formulation will at once say: 'That's us'.
>
> Source: www.bloemencorsozundert.nl, accessed January 2011, adapted by the authors.

Critical Success Factors for the Events Programme

In their book, *Eventful Cities* (Richards and Palmer, 2010), the authors mention several domains that determine the success factors for event programmes (see Fig. 7.2). These domains are:

- culture (content);
- place (context);
- power (leadership, political support);
- relationships (involvement, forms of cooperation, independence/freedom);
- resources (financial and human resources); and
- planning (long-term vision, clear objectives).

To these domains is added sustainability, as an umbrella principle. The fact is that cities are also unique and have their own relationship with the supply of events. So, the various factors involved should always be seen in the light of a specific situation.

Culture

In an 'eventful city', culture in its broadest sense always comes first. There are events that are organized mainly to expose people to an experience, to bring about economic growth or to polish up a city. However, the primary goal of city marketing should be: ensuring a broad cultural base in relation to events, so that the cultural landscape of a city becomes part of the events programme. This means recognizing the diversity of a city as well as attuning the event to a specific environment.

Due to the greater mobility of the past few decades, cultural diversity has grown. This provides new intercultural and transcultural opportunities for the substance of the cultural supply, which can mix the old with the new. All urban programmes and policies should be viewed through an intercultural lens. Intercultural cities provide new challenges for culture management and cultural festivals; they have the potential to stimulate intercultural dialogue and exchange. Cultural diversity in the events programme should not be allowed to result in different events for all groups. This would put the emphasis on differences instead of on the integration of groups. The focus should be on sharing and exchanging experiences. The events programme should also be innovative, a source of inspiration, provocation and critical reflection on the relationship between culture, including events, and a city. This will ensure that the cultural supply remains up to date, challenging and distinctive. To achieve this, unorthodox approaches

Fig. 7.2. Key areas with respect to an 'eventful city'.

to devising an events programme will often be required to give new initiatives a chance and to be able to anticipate with flexibility the ever-changing needs of public groups. Attention should then be paid not only to highbrow elitist culture but also to popular expressions of culture in a city. This means that a creative director with the necessary knowledge and a good feeling for the situation can take on a guiding role when choices have to be made. It is more important to invest in quality than in quantity. This may lead to a reduction in the number of events, so that the focus will be on the desired outcomes with a well-balanced events programme. New events will then always be assessed critically to see if they are aligned to the values and objectives of a city, and the chief question in this context should be what they add to cultural life and what their meaning is to the inhabitants.

Place

Place refers to the local context in which cities can distinguish themselves. Each city has unique physical elements and must create spaces where people can meet and exchange ideas. Policy makers should pay careful attention to how those spaces should be laid out. This raises the problem of a city being required to be distinctive on the one hand and being recognizable on the other. Naturally, the atmosphere of the city is an essential factor as well. Events can play a big part in creating atmosphere, so that people feel at home and are proud of their city. Events utilize physical meeting places in a city and create their own meeting places that are transformed into places with their own magnetism as a result of special experiences and moods. This unique potential makes it possible to connect different meeting places in a city to an event and stimulate visitors to move from the familiar meeting places in the centre to new, unknown places on the periphery, which may give new meaning to those places in day-to-day life as well.

If events in different cities have a similar content or theme, embedding the event in a particular environment may be the key to distinction. As an event, the Edinburgh Military Tattoo in Scotland, for example, cannot be compared to other tattoos: it is a breathtaking experience against the backdrop of a brilliantly illuminated castle, giving you the feeling that Edinburgh is the one and only place for this event. This example shows that desperately shielding a place-bound event is completely unnecessary. Indeed, copies of place-bound events make the desire of the visitors for the only real event even stronger, because that is experienced as something authentic.

As well as place, time is an essential element of the event programme. Time refers here to the phase in which a city finds itself at a certain moment. Every city is in a particular developmental phase, historically, culturally, socially and economically. This context should be subject to assessment in an events policy.

Power

The public sector is the one that is responsible primarily for supporting the development of an event structure; it is ultimately answerable for the lasting effects of events. This must be organized within the municipal structure and aligned with the various policy areas. Though public participation in the decision process is necessary, it should be realized that many sustainable events could not take place without strong political leadership coupled to a long-term vision. Politics must devise a framework for the residents and the event professionals. This is not the same as a totally *laissez-faire* approach; there must be some kind of structure. To give broad sections of the residents the opportunity to participate in the events programme, political leaders must draw up transparent evaluation and selection procedures, so that everyone can play his own role in the events programme, whether it is an existing programme or one that is being developed. In the end, choices will have to be made on the basis of programming qualities enhanced by intuition, experience and pragmatism. A professional, a creative director with autonomous powers of decision, can make such choices.

Business relationships and partnerships

The bond that an event manages to create between the various parties involved in an event that is going to be organized contributes to its total impact. Consider, for example, a situation in which the various cultural parties in a city think about the content of the event and involve visitors in the programming at an early stage. This is much like a partnership.

Trust is the basis of all relationships and partnerships, and should be supported by policy and responsibilities. This concerns not only the trust between, for example, the stakeholders of the event programme of a city but also the mutual trust between cities and regions. Against the background of global competition, successful cities realize that they are required to work together. In the long run, the advantages of cooperation outweigh the short-term advantages of a competitive approach of regional cities towards each other. In more and more regions, partnerships are established, especially where it concerns the positioning of cities, or regions, in an international context.

Relationship with the media

The relationship with the media is of vital importance. To a large extent, the media determines the success of a city and its events programme. According to Rennen (2007), city events without extensive media coverage are not very likely to be successful (see also the box on p. 134). An increasing number of organizers opt for setting up their own media networks. Thus, they try to reduce the dependence on independent (critical) media and present themselves in a way that appears to be journalistic.

Due to the strong emergence of live news coverage, many events, while in progress, develop into historic events. The organization often plays the hand of good memories, because wonderful memories ensure that cities, media and companies can profit from the event for quite some time, even when it is over.

The impact of media attention on the visitors of events decreases as the media attention ebbs away. So, this forces cities to offer a variety of events with which the target groups in a city can be served. Besides, activities must be spread over the year and take place in sequence to hold the

> **Box 7.4. Positive media impact**
>
> Events have an impact on place image, mainly through media coverage. That is the statement tested empirically by Fatingan *et al.* (2009) and that has led to the following conclusion: by hosting events, places can attract positive media coverage. The Football World Champion Tournament in Germany is a good illustration.
>
> Research has shown that by organizing that tournament in 2006, Germany managed to attract much media attention. The aim of the organization was to change the negative image of Germany, place image, into a positive one. Media analysis has shown that organizing the World Championship has, indeed, had a positive effect on Germany's image. After the championship, media coverage decreased quickly, but the tone was still more positive than prior to the championship. The conclusion is that organizing an event can generate positive media attention.
>
> Source: Fatingan *et al.*, 2009, adapted by the authors.

attention of the consumer and improve or preserve the image. It is true that events are not the only way to achieve this, but they can be important eye-catchers within the total policy concerned with the image building of a city.

The media can also encourage artists to come, because the aura of a city fits their own image or because they would like very much to perform in a particular city, which can keep the cost down to a considerable extent. Moreover, positive media attention will generate extra demand from local, national and international markets.

Positive media attention does not have to be very expensive, as is shown by the use of free publicity, among other things. Press bulletins are disseminated and journalists are invited, but awards can also help a city to distinguish itself. The best-known examples in the Dutch context are The Event City of the Netherlands Award and the City Marketing Award.

Resources

In order to realize good events programming, resources must be made available. This requires a good physical events structure. Think of indoor and outdoor locations in a city, provision of information, transport and visitor information. Financial resources are partly provided by the government, which sets the conditions and is responsible for the events infrastructure, but businesses will have to make a contribution as well.

The organizers of events should wean themselves off subsidies as much as possible in the future and organize events like a business. This approach requires them to remain astute and discerning. Of course, the aim of the event and the role it plays in society determines the financial dependence on the government. In the case of an event that is focused strongly on social cohesion within a borough and is in alignment with the objectives of the city, that dependence will be greater. The discussion about resources for events is inseparable from the issue of quality versus quantity. A serious attempt should be made to find a good balance in events programming. Less is more, if the quality of events is enhanced and the burden on the city is reduced to acceptable proportions. The discussion about resources is not limited to money; the commitment and involvement of people, human resources, play a vital part as well. Think of volunteers, for example, who complement the contribution of the professionals responsible for the events programme. Because of their large commitment, volunteers are willing to invest in a successful

> **Box 7.5. Collaboration between Tilburg and Brabant in Spoorzone**
>
> In this example, two perspectives are described with regard to the redevelopment of the Spoorzone area (railway zone) in Tilburg as a cultural events venue, illustrating the role of government and business. It is an example of a merger between non-profit and profit organizations to make an area profitable in various respects.
>
> The municipality of Tilburg and the province of Noord-Brabant are together exploring and working out the options for the redevelopment and restructuring of Spoorzone. This has been laid down in a cooperation agreement covering a 10-year period. The province already decided at an earlier stage to grant subsidies worth €3.5 million for the restoration and redevelopment of the 'NS Werkplaats' (workshop of the Dutch railway company). Henri Swinkels, member of the Provincial Executive (for Liveability and Culture) mentioned the value of the heritage in this area as the most important reason behind the collaboration. The backbone of the new heritage policy is called 'the stories of Brabant', narrating the history of the province and allowing for a new future focusing on re-use and redevelopment.
>
> With the Spoorzone project, Tilburg is showing its worth and its core values. Proud and open-minded. This was our past and it is a wonderful foundation for our future. The industrial activities of the past can still be clearly felt around the large factory halls of the former NS Werkplaats. This is where generations of Tilburg residents worked on trains and locomotives, but also on the first 'Puk and Muk' children's book at Zwijsen publishing company. Thanks to the typical Tilburg vigour and roll-up-your-sleeves mentality, one special initiative after the other is now born here. All the activities have created a breeding ground for knowledge and innovation in Spoorzone. And because of the unique cultural and catering facilities, Spoorzone has grown into the place in Tilburg to explore for private individuals, entrepreneurs, or hospitality operators. Those who think innovatively, dare to be different and lead the way with love, will feel at home in the Spoorzone area.
>
> Source: www.spoorzone013.nl

event. They are the links to the residents and foster involvement and support in the community. That does not alter the fact that briefing, training and supervising volunteers takes time and energy. Therefore, it is crucial, especially in the case of recurring events, that volunteers are inducted properly and that the organizer invests in their commitment to the event, so that trained volunteers with all their knowledge and specific skills are saved for the event as well as the city.

Planning

The events policy of a city requires the formulation of a clear vision containing the strategic starting points for individual events and a description of how events contribute to the objectives of the city. This policy must be laid down for at least 5 years, but a multiple of this period may be required in the case of large-scale infrastructural improvements and tactical changes in the environment. Planning should be integrated into other policy areas within the municipal organization, so that synergy is generated and events are made part of the entire cultural context of a city.

It is essential that planning includes procedures for monitoring and evaluation, both of the separate events and the events programme as a whole. The evaluation comprises various items and, ideally, deals with various aspects: economic, social, cultural and environmental. The results of the evaluation can be used for feedback and, if necessary, must lead to tightening up the current events policy.

Sustainability

Sustainability used to be a neglected issue in the events sector, but that has changed over the past decade. The success factors discussed earlier, such as culture, place, power, relationships, resources and planning, must be placed in a sustainable framework.

In the past, it was usually only the economic effects of events that were detailed and not enough attention was paid to social and cultural values and the pollution of the environment. The 'green' production of events has been on the rise, even if it is a marketing objective in many cases and the event is not produced CO_2 neutral. Sustainability comprises more than just the environment and has various components. Approaches like *people, planet, profit* and 'socially responsible entrepreneurship' clearly show that sustainability, in its broadest sense, is the issue that will make a difference in the future. Organizations that are capable of sustainable production will be more profitable than those that are not. The people component refers chiefly to social equality and is thus linked directly to the cultural component. Think, for example, of fair working conditions and wages, intercultural respect, the participation of residents and other involved stakeholders in the decision-making process, and ensuring a broad cultural approach. The planet component comes down mainly to the CO_2 neutral production of events by using green energy, durable and/or easily degradable materials, reduction of waste production and separation of waste.

So sustainability concerns a broad objective that includes sustainable growth, equal working conditions, taking responsibility for nature and the environment, and social well-being. Getz (2009) sums up a number of points in connection with sustainability at events and relates them to the six domains of events programmes:

- minimizing negative effects with respect to economic, social, cultural and environmental aspects;
- generating more economic benefits for local residents and fostering the well-being of communities;
- improving working conditions and creating employment;
- involving the local population and other stakeholders in the decision-making process;
- striving for cultural diversity and contributing to the conservation of natural and cultural heritage;
- creating valuable experiences by connecting visitors and residents in a meaningful way;
- taking into account people with a handicap; and
- being culturally sensitive – fostering respect between visitors and residents, strengthening local pride and confidence.

To be able to attain results, the parties involved must collectively introduce sustainability in the events sector, and implement it. First, the provider and suppliers involved will have to search their own hearts. Initiatives like '10,000 hours' and 'Green Events' – a platform for making events more sustainable with activities such as 'Green Deal' – demonstrate that the sector itself is taking responsibility for this issue.

The first cautious steps are being taken. Support from politics, in the form of rules and regulations, is needed to develop sustainability to the full. Besides issuing new guidelines for production, the government can help make adjustments through the use of subsidies, and facilitate events that meet the guidelines. At the moment, the government (local government primarily) does not yet pay much attention to event sustainability. This has to change in the future, especially when taking into account that events are meaningful instruments for visitors. Events can be an example of the sustainability of a city.

> **Box 7.6. Green Deal**
>
> Together with a number of event industry leaders (Amsterdam Open Air, DGTL, Extrema Outdoor, Into The Great Wide Open, Mysteryland, Solar Weekend, Welcome to the Future, Black Cross, NederlandSchoon, the Ministry of Infrastructure and the Environment, and the Ministry of Economic Affairs) Green Events has been working on the Green Deal 'waste-free festivals' since October 2015. The main goal of Green Deal is to reduce the amount of waste per visitor, to separate waste, and to increase and improve recycling. Festivals are also supposed to become cleaner by the amount of waste on the ground being reduced. Together with the industry and experts, Green Events looks for effective solutions to prevent waste or to have waste collected and processed in such a way that useful raw materials are produced again. Over a period of 3 years, various pilot projects will be conducted together with leaders in the festival world and the best solutions will be tested. These will then be shared with other interested parties in the sector. The project groups are involved in testing the following pilot solutions: hard cups; composting of green waste; camping waste and litter; and plastic recycling.
>
> Source: www.greenevents.nl

> **Box 7.7. 10,000 hours mission**
>
> WE'RE ON A MISSION…
> To give the dance floor's positive energy back to the world.
> To share our togetherness with the people who need it the most.
> To take care of our planet so we can dance on it with dignity.
>
> WE BELIEVE…
> That volunteering makes us happy.
> That our festival community can help local communities.
> That when doing something meaningful, every hour counts.
>
> Source: www.10000hours.nl

On this issue, the government and the visitors are a powerful force. If visitors are convinced that events should be produced sustainably, the market will do the rest.

But, taking the actual steps on the road to sustainability, as described in this chapter, is more easily said than done. It is a long-term matter. Still, the following steps can be taken in the short run:

- A (sustainable) network can be set up, the members of which inform each other, and that initiates actions.
- Local government can draw up guidelines for the sustainable production of events. This can be a model with stages spread over several years. On the basis of detailed cases at the local level, national politics can be involved at a later date.
- A study can be done of the (sustainable) effects of events, with a focus that shifts from economic to social, cultural and environmental effects. Educational institutes can play a vital role here. An additional advantage is that the new generation of event managers will gain an

- Sector organizations can play an important role by informing individual companies of the potential of sustainability in the area in which they are active. This does not concern merely sector organizations linked to an event, but also the Chamber of Commerce, for example.
- Proceeding from the idea that sustainable events can be good for the corporate image, the sponsors of events should be more aware of the fact that they can make demands where sustainability is concerned. This can be done via networks or information sessions, for instance. Thus, sponsors will become more mindful of their new role.
- A quality mark for sustainability can be introduced for which companies can register on a voluntary basis. Getting awarded such a quality mark will deliver much positive publicity. If the quality mark is refused, the company concerned will have a clear picture of the areas where work still has to be done. The funding of this quality mark should come from all parties involved, government, sector organizations, business, schools and even the public.
- Events can be organized with a focus on sustainability as a strategically meaningful experience. This can be initiated by the various parties involved.

Summary

For thousands of years now, events have played an important role in cities. Just think of town markets and 'bread and games for the people', which can be traced back to the ancient Greeks and Romans. All cities have by now become very much aware of city marketing. City promotion was exercised as early as in the 1940s. The traditional marketing mix of the original four Ps – product, price, place and promotion – is extended by presentation, politics and personnel in the field of city marketing.

City branding is a trend within city marketing. City branding involves a city working on a distinctive identity on the basis of core values. In this connection, self-expression is one of the marketing tools, and creativity, too, is an essential component of making a city attractive. City branding is about the city as a brand, and its starting point is the needs of residents, companies and (potential) visitors.

The events policy of a city should be in alignment with the city marketing policy, and must result in a well-balanced events programme. Culture, place, power, relationships, resources and planning are all success factors with regard to events programmes. Sustainability is something that affects everything and deserves a central place in urban events policies.

Part II Do

In Part II, we discuss the 'do' phase of the strategic use of events, so the central part of the EVENTS model.

We start with the translation of strategy into concept, and then we deal in more detail with touchpoints: the points of contact between the initiator of an event and the visitor.

8. The Translation of Strategy into Concept
9. Touchpoints

Appendices to Chapter 9: Touchpoint Models for Trade Fairs and Corporate Events

Appendix 1. Touchpoint Model for Trade Fairs

Appendix 2. Touchpoint Model for Corporate Events

8. The Translation of Strategy into Concept

Dorothé Gerritsen and Ronald van Olderen

The concept and design of an event should be developed from the strategic objectives following from the four strategies of relationship marketing, marketing communication, branding and city marketing. The concept should be based on the values of visitor groups and on the values, vision and mission of the initiator of an event. This chapter is about how that can be achieved.

Learning Targets

After studying this chapter, you will have learnt:

- how you translate strategic objectives into a concept and design for an event;
- what values are in relation to an event;
- how the experience model is made up;
- what the concept of experience is;
- how to develop a concept of experience based on strategic objectives; and
- how to make a concept of experience specific.

To be able to translate a strategy into a concept, you first need an analysis of demand and supply, the environment and the values of visitors, among other things. You must also know what requirements a good concept has to meet. A further important question is what happens to visitors when they attend an event. It is not until those questions have been answered that it is possible to stage the experience of an event by utilizing content, form and tools in such a way that they touch the visitor and the message comes across. This is perfectly illustrated by the events organized by the Possibilize Foundation.

Values of the Target Group

If event developers succeed in linking values to their events, the emotional involvement of the target group will be much greater. From that involvement with an event, it is possible for emotional ties to arise with an organization and/or brand, enabling the organization to distinguish itself from its competitors as well. A good translation of an objective into a concept or design of an event is then within easy reach.

The concept of value can refer to tangible items, such as a DVD, a signed photograph or a jewel, but it can also refer to intangible matters such as religion, health, happiness, relationships and entertainment. So, attending an event may also have an immaterial value, which also involves individual opinions of what is desirable or good. If you attribute value to something, you find it important. Emotional value is linked inextricably to material things. A ticket to a concert or a signed photograph of a pop star will then stand for the one and only time in your life that you have seen your idol. Through that ticket or photograph, you enjoy that moment again and relive that emotional event.

The translation of strategy into concept

Values are an essential component of our cognitive system and they determine our expectations of people and things. Values affect how people think and act and handle information, and how they collect, store and use that information. In that sense, values are criteria that people use to test information, of whatever nature. We will explore this subject in more detail in the section on values.

Analysis of Supply and Demand

Apart from the visitor, the initiator of the event also has values. The city or brand wants to transfer certain values to the visitor. What are those values? What is the vision? To what extent do those values correspond to those of the visitors? The answers to these questions are essential to the successful exploitation of events. Through events, the values of an organization can converge with those of the visitors, on the condition that the provider makes a proper analysis of the client or initiator of an event to arrive at a good event concept.

Box 8.1. Possibilize turns apparent impossibilities into possibilities

Possibilize is an international platform offering young people the opportunity to push their boundaries. Through regional training programmes, the foundation offers them a chance to organize groundbreaking projects. The following slogan is central to this process: 'The Art of Possibilizing: thinking and acting in possibilities, in every situation'.

The Possibilize Foundation stimulates, motivates and supports groups of people to participate in activities on their own that, to them, seem impossible to perform at first sight. It organizes groundbreaking events that inspire the participation of the target group in our society. The foundation's work is based on the values of purity, passion and open-mindedness.

Possibilize is a player in the events business that stands out because the event is used to get a message across. That by itself is not unique: the Live Aid Concert is another example. But Possibilize specializes in events that seem impossible: music festivals for the deaf and photography projects for the blind.

Possibilize sees what is regarded as impossible by a target group or an individual person as a source of inspiration; as a challenge to find out how something that is impossible can still be done. From this attitude, Possibilize developed several innovative applications that stimulated the senses, so that deaf youngsters and those hard of hearing could still pick up the emotion of music.

Research has shown that emotions in music can be transformed into vibrations (through the specially designed sense floor and the feel-the-music suit), in scents (through the aroma jockey), in taste sensations (through the food jockey and/or ice jockey) and image (through video projection, text jockeys, sign dancers and sign interpreters, who vividly translate the emotion on the stage).

These events, which go under the name of Sencity, enable deaf people and those hard of hearing to enjoy music. People who can hear also appreciate these events very much because of the innovative experience. For those who want to receive it, there is an underlying message as well: if you really go for something, you can do it, you can even make the impossible possible. This message is not actively communicated during the events in order to remove any barriers to attending it.

Possibilize also takes up personal challenges in its own organization. All employees are asked what they consider impossible for themselves and would like to realize within Skyway. The organization works as a platform to support people to deal with their own challenges. What is required to access that platform is enormous ambition and the conviction that often people can do more than they think. Possibilize's own policy plans are drawn up with a challenge in mind as well. After the first event, the next step was setting up a musical event for deaf people in a local community on every continent. Possibilize is now active all over the world. Events have been organized in São Paulo, Capetown, Johannesburg, Sydney, Miami, Mexico, Finland, London, Berlin and Madrid. In the Benelux countries, the concept has been extended by adding SENS11: musical events that provide sensory stimulations for people with and without a mental handicap. And with increasing frequency, Skyway is asked to apply its knowledge and skills to organizations facing a challenge.

Setting grand, seemingly impossible goals with an uncompromising ambition to attain those goals brings the talents of their employees to the surface, enabling them to develop those things to which they want to apply themselves, whether this is graphic design, dancing, organizing or bookkeeping.

> **Box 8.1.** Continued.
> The energy thus generated in employees can be seen at the events, characterized as they are by an enthusiastic, open atmosphere with a high experience value. Visitors have an intense experience, a so-called transformational experience that will not be soon forgotten, and which may even change them permanently.
> Source: Molenaar, 2019, not published; www.stichtingskyway.nl; www.your-sencity.com, adapted by the authors.

So, in order to bridge objectives and event, it is important to make a proper analysis of the demand and supply sides. A target group analysis focused on values and an analysis of the vision and mission of the initiator of the event provide the necessary basis for the next step of emotional bonding. To make this clear, we will first have a look at the effect of an event as a staged experience.

Staged Experience and True Experience

Clearly, events are all about producing an effect on the visitors. How individual visitors experience an event is dependent on many factors. Here, we explain what the difference is between a staged experience and a true experience, and which factors affect the individual experience of an event.

The Experience Economy by Pine and Gilmore (2000, 2011) was certainly not the first text to cover the economic value of experiences. But, as a result of their book, the idea that people wanted to be touched personally in the first place received widespread attention. Pine and Gilmore define experience as follows:

> An experience occurs when consumers get involved in something in such a way that they will gain a lasting impression. The event is memorable and very personal. The consumer is touched emotionally, physically, intellectually, indeed spiritually.

In contrast to English, which has only the one word for 'experience', Germanic languages like Dutch and German distinguish between 'erleben' and 'erfahren'/'beleven' and 'ervaren'. 'Erfahren' and 'ervaren' refer to the placement of an experience in a mental framework. From the Dutch verb 'beleven', two nouns can be derived that mean 'staged experience' and 'true experience', respectively.

We define 'staged experience' and 'true experience' as follows:

> The staged experience is the (more or less delineated) event as it can be staged, put on, by a provider. It is the stimulus that can trigger a true experience on the part of a consumer.
> The true experience is the inner, personal, emotional response to a stimulus. The true experience can transcend the staged experience in time and space.

The staged experience is the event itself; it is about something that can be staged, a stimulus that should trigger something specific. The true experience is the result of the staged experience. Not every staged experience will lead to a true experience. Depending on the psychosocial frame of reference (see the section on the psychosocial framework), a true experience will, or will not, occur, or will be more or less intense. For example, when watching a football match, one person will have a strong experience, while the person next to him is not affected at all by the same stimulus.

Levels of True Experience

Three levels of true experience can be distinguished when looking at the intensity of the emotion and the extent to which it is retained in the memory (Lier and van Wijngaarden, 2015). With the help of the experience model in Fig. 8.1, we explain how you can arrive at a concept of an event starting from strategic objectives. We will refer to this model several times in the course of this chapter.

The staged experience in this model can be regarded as the event; the stimulus that you try to give its proper shape and staging to the best of your ability in order to attain certain objectives.

The Translation of Strategy into Concept

Fig. 8.1. Experience model. (Source: Lier and van Wijngaarden, 2015.)

It is impossible to predict exactly how that stimulus, the event, affects the individual person. There is a kind of black box, the psychosocial framework, containing a wide variety of factors that can have an effect on the way in which a visitor experiences the event. The outcome is a true experience that can vary from visitor to visitor. The three levels of true experience are:

1. The basic experience coincides with (exposure to) the stimulus. An emotional response occurs, but the experience has not enough impact to be retained in the memory for a longer period of time.
2. The memorable experience is at a higher level and results in memory value. This does not concern merely memory at a cognitive level but especially the ability to recall the emotion later.
3. The transforming experience causes a lasting change in the individual at the behavioural or attitudinal level.

Transformation is not an easy concept. And what is the meaning of 'lasting' in this context? When does transformation become manipulation? Transformation is not the automatic result of every intense, memorable experience. In a study conducted in three war museums, the respondents described the experience of their visit in an experience report 2 weeks after their visit as emotionally charged: their experience was an intensely memorable one. However, their answer to the question of whether their visit had changed their attitude towards the subject was negative.

Their involvement, and the underlying values, was perpetuated by their visit (van Buuren, 2006).

It is possible for an event to become a life-changing experience, provided that, thanks to the event, the person involved can express dormant values, as a result of which the experience has taken on a more profound meaning.

As has been said before, the level of experience attained can differ from person to person. Those differences can be explained with the help of the psychosocial framework. The same stimulus that triggers only a basic experience in one individual can trigger one that will remain in the memory of another for a longer time. In another person again, the experience may be the cause of a transformation. Figure 8.2 provides a visual display of the process from staged experience to true experience.

The Psychosocial Framework

Nobody can say with any degree of certainty what the factors are that are crucial to the realization of the experience. As a consequence, the effects of the event are uncertain as well. But, with the knowledge available to you, you can try to control the factors and design the event in such a way that the objectives with regard to the target group are attained. The following factors are involved: knowledge, expectations and past experiences, motives, mood, involvement, social context, personality and competencies, and values (see Fig. 8.1).

The first six factors are connected to the specific experience that the visitor to an event undergoes. We will explain them in order. After this, we will deal with the final two factors, those that transcend the experience: personality and competencies, and values.

Knowledge

At first sight, knowledge and a true experience seem to be two contradictory concepts. However, knowledge, or background knowledge, can have an effect on the experience and, in some cases, lead to enhancement of the experience. A lack of knowledge, on the other hand, may be a barrier to the experience. Modern, abstract art can often be appreciated only with background knowledge so that you can give a work of art its place.

Due to the Internet, access to knowledge and information has expanded enormously in the past few years. The visitor to an event can obtain all possible background information. A supplier should be well aware of the fact that visitors will come fully prepared, because they can obtain all the necessary information.

Expectations and past experiences

The second factor that has an impact on a true experience concerns earlier experiences and the expectations arising from them. If an experience is stored in a mental frame of reference, it will become an experience. The memory of the experience is carried over to the next experience in the form of an expectation. An expectation, too, is often coloured by emotions; it is very much like an extension of the true experience. Fulfilling expectations is important, but surpassing them is better still. Naturally, expectations that are not fulfilled will be fatal to a positive experience.

Fig. 8.2. Visualization of staged experience and true experience. (Source: Moniek Hover.)

Experiences do not have to be of a strictly personal nature for them to lead to particular expectations. The experiences of others can have a strong impact on an expectation. Digital media provide computer users with much scope to share experiences. People feel an increasing need to send their experiences and emotions into the digital world; witness all social media like Twitter, Facebook, Slideshare, Snapchat, weblogs and discussion forums. Spontaneous virtual communities of people who share the same values and interests arise around events. Many suppliers in the events sector increasingly regard these developments as an opportunity to gain a better understanding and knowledge about what really is important to people. Sometimes, however, they are also regarded as a threat. Chapter 2 presented a detailed exploration of the future scenarios within the live communication sector in the light of current trends and developments, including technological ones.

The focus of events should not merely be on the direct exposure phase (the moment when an event actually takes place), but indeed on the pre- and post-exposure phases as well, because it is there where the experience is extended in the form of an expectation and pleasurable anticipation; and when the event is over, there is the enjoyment of the memory and afterglow. This is well illustrated by the example of a Coldplay concert (Box 8.2).

Box 8.2. Coldplay

'Coldplay is going to give a concert!' This is the introduction to the story the fan is going to experience. This is the start of the pre-exposure phase of the experience. The moment when a fan has managed to obtain a ticket for that concert (the trigger within the story), the onset of pleasant suspense can be felt: the anticipation, counting the days, visiting websites, Facebook pages, and so on to share those feelings with like-minded people. The arrival at the venue where the concert is given is the critical moment, the 'crisis': just a few more moments! Coldplay enters the stage and start their gig. This is the climax. When the concert is over, the post-exposure phase begins; the rundown of the storyline, with everything falling into place. The fan reads reviews, shares photos and videos, visits websites and buys a CD or DVD to experience the concert again, and invoke the emotion again.

For an individual, each experience is, as it were, a personal story that unfolds around the actual experience, and comprises the following components (see Fig. 8.3):

- the introduction;
- the trigger moment;
- growing suspense;
- the crisis;
- the climax; and
- the rundown.

A supplier must try to imagine the story of the experience in the hearts and minds of the visitors and feed this story in each of its phases. Of course, several climaxes is not unheard of (see Chapter 9).

Motives

According to Neulinger, two things are of essential importance for the emergence of a leisure experience in an individual person (Beunders and Boers, 1997). First of all is the type of motivation. Intrinsic motivation is about the pleasure someone expects to have when kicking a ball, for example. In the case of extrinsic motivation, the reward is important: playing football to win. There is often a mix of the two.

What is also relevant is the degree of perceived freedom when an activity is performed: not every leisure activity is done voluntarily. Sometimes there is an element of social obligation involved in an activity, which is bound to obstruct the experience even before it takes place.

Moods

There is a difference between moods and emotions. Emotions are usually linked to an occurrence or object; moods are not. Generally, moods last longer than emotions. They are often the result of earlier emotions. Moreover, they may make it easier for the emotions involved to arise, or indeed they may reinforce them. Therefore, moods have a great effect on how an experience is formed. The behaviour associated with a mood is aimed at ending an unpleasant mood and the continuation of a pleasant mood (Boom, 2006). A supplier can certainly exert an influence on moods.

Involvement

Moments of optimum involvement during an activity occur in a flow. A flow can also arise during events when a visitor feels completely immersed in an experience. This can be seen clearly in

Fig. 8.3. Storytelling. (Source: Laurel, 1993, adapted by the authors.)

photographs of the visitors to Glastonbury Festival during one of the performances. However, involvement as a factor within the psychosocial framework is about the involvement that someone already feels, the way someone enters the experience. It may then be a matter of enduring involvement or one of situational involvement. In the case of situational involvement, someone is deeply involved in a particular activity for a very short time, but this involvement disappears when the activity is over. Think, for example, of booking a holiday. After everything has been organized and the trip has been made, there is no longer any involvement.

Enduring involvement does not have to coincide with a concrete activity or experience, but it certainly is often the result of one or more memorable, even transformative, experiences. Enduring involvement will not always be expressed in specific behaviour at a certain moment. Someone who is mad about sailing may be unable to do it for a while due to circumstances in his life. That does not mean, however, that the involvement has gone.

Research has shown that the higher the level of enduring involvement in an activity, the more likely it is that the person in question will get into a flow during the activity (Havitz and Mannell, 2005). Someone with a feeling of enduring involvement with the Rolling Stones, a true fan, is much more likely to get into a flow during one of their gigs than someone without it. From additional research, it has become clear that there is a reverse relationship as well: if someone undergoes an intense experience and gets into a flow, this will lead to stronger enduring involvement in relation to the activity.

Social context

The social context is of crucial importance to the experience. This applies first and foremost to the company with which someone undertakes an activity. The effect on the level of experience of a visit to an event together with colleagues can be totally different from that of a visit to the same event with the family. The impression formed of other visitors has an impact as well. What one person experiences as a jolly nice crowd, another may regard as irritatingly crowded.

The social context goes beyond the bounds of time of an event. As has been mentioned earlier, virtual communities have created new social contexts that have an effect on an experience, certainly also in the pre- and post-exposure phase. The role of staff is often regarded as part of the social context. This is a vital touchpoint, as will be demonstrated in Chapter 9.

Two factors of the psychosocial framework are not connected directly to a specific experience. As such, they can be said to be of a more transcending, more stable nature: that is, personality and values.

Personality and competencies

There are certain human traits that can have an effect on experience. Csikszentmihaly, the American-Hungarian psychologist, sees a relationship between creativity and getting into a flow, or being able to get into a flow. Open-minded people see something new and uncertain as a challenge that appeals to them (Nijs and Peters, 2011). A surprise will often be experienced as positive by this group. People with a closed mind, on the other hand, will find the uncertain and the unexpected stressful; this will have a negative effect on their experience.

Fantasy is something else that seems to be important to the ability to enter into an experience. Someone who, during an experience, does not stop thinking 'this is fake' or 'it will all be over soon' will have an experience that is less strong than that of someone who totally surrenders to it. In this sense, fantasy is not a distortion, but an enhancement of reality. 'Fantasy is liberating.'

At first sight, it may seem hard for a supplier to take people's personality into account: after all, a personality cannot be changed. But, a supplier can always make use of certain traits of the visitors to an event.

Chapter 8

Values

It is becoming increasingly hard for companies, cities and organizations to distinguish themselves from their competitors on the basis of product attributes or quality. Therefore, the focus is shifting to values as a possibility to do so. Rokeach was one of the first to conduct a study of values in the 1970s (Rokeach, 1973; Boom and Weber, 2001). He distinguishes two types of values: terminal values as the desired end goals and instrumental values as a means of achieving those end goals (see Fig. 8.4).

Many festivals have or are looking for distinctive core values. In this age when festivals are enjoying huge popularity and growth, the importance of this is becoming more and more apparent. How do you connect the right target groups, fans or community to your festival or brand? Events such as Burning Man, SFWX and Lowlands – an established festival brand for more than 20 years – have turned out to be quite capable of forging a bond with their communities.

Franzen elaborates on earlier research on values and distinguishes three types of values (Nijs and Peters, 2011):

1. *Functional values*: these are qualities, attributes and achievements of the product itself. They are usually referred to as product benefits in day-to-day advertising practice.
2. *Symbolic values*: there are three subcategories:
    2a *Expressive values*: these concern our relationship to others and how we want others to see us.

Social harmony
- Peace
- Equality
- Freedom
- National security
- Salvation (eternal life)

Personal fulfilment
- Social recognition
- Comfortable life
- Pleasure
- Accomplishment

Personal contentment
- Happiness (being content)

Competence
- Ambitious
- Independent
- Creative
- Capable
- Logical (rational)

Compassion
- Forgiving
- Helpful
- Cheerful
- Loving

Self-actualization
- Beauty (nature and art)
- Wisdom
- Inner harmony
- Self-respect
- Accomplishment
- Security
- Family care
- Salvation (eternal life)

Love and affection
- Mature love (sexual and mature intimacy)
- Real friendship

Social attitude
- Polite
- Obedient
- Tidy (clean)

Integrity
- Responsible
- Honest
- Self-control

Fig. 8.4. Rokeach's value model. (Source: Rokeach, 1973; Boom and Weber, 2001.)

The Translation of Strategy into Concept

    2b *Impressive values*: these are focused on our self-perception (feeling good about yourself, inner harmony, thrift, and so on).
    2c *Terminal values*: these are the idealized pictures of life as we would ultimately prefer to live it. In fact, they are the highest ideals we aspire to (see also Chapter 6).

3. *Social values*: these are the ideals that we cherish in relation to our direct environment and society as a whole (e.g. peace on earth, conservation of nature and national freedom).

Figure 8.5 shows an example of this.

Box 8.3. Lowlands

Based on the factual description, you would not stand a chance of selling it: nobody gets excited about the term 'crossover festival'. Particularly if you cannot say in advance who will be performing. And what about the location? In the middle of bumblefuck nowhere. Nevertheless, the 55,000 tickets to 'A Campingflight to Lowlands Paradise' invariably sell out within next to no time. Lowlands is a brand, but also more than a brand. It is a community, a movement, perhaps even a cult. Too big to fail. The Lowlands programme features music, literature, politics and science. An important success factor is the 'epic scale', the heroic story. In the past, the need for an epic scale was mainly filled by churches, governments, sports associations and, for example, broadcasting corporations. The democratization of the media has brought this scale size within reach of others too. The origin of Lowlands is unsuspicious and free from ulterior motives. The festival did not originate out of an eccentric businessman's whim, a political movement, a broadcasting corporation or a magazine title. The breadth of Lowlands gives visitors the feeling of being part of a greater whole. If something has meaning, it is not only valuable and important to ourselves and our closest friends and relatives, but also to a much larger group. Meaning is something that we are all trying to obtain more of.

Source: www.marketingfacts.nl

Fig. 8.5. Three types of values. (Source: Nijs and Peters, 2011.)

From Strategy to Concept

An event is a staged experience with the aim of attaining a particular goal. Starting from the experience and perception of the visitors and an analysis of the values of the visitor and the initiator of an event, we can take the following step: translating strategy into a concept (see Fig. 8.1 under 'Content').

What's in a Concept?

The word 'concept' is used frequently in the leisure sector, but not always unambiguously. Sometimes, it seems to be a meaningless, catch-all term: anything can be called a concept. Our definition of a concept is as follows.

> A concept (as the elaboration of an idea) is the active principle that creates coherence and gives direction to the realization of one or several goals.

A concept does not disappear the moment when its realization in a product, or products, and place has been achieved. On the contrary, it ensures (permanent) coherence.

Box 8.4. NPO 3FM/Serious Request.

In 1965, the current NPO 3FM (at the time: radio station Hilversum 3) was launched to counterbalance the popular new offshore stations. Much has happened in the 50 years since. A lot of music was discovered, many new DJs started at NPO 3FM and a lot of major events were reported on. There were highs and lows. In short, history was written. In 2000 a difficult period started for radio station 3FM when Edwin Evers switched to a commercial station. With Florent Luyckx as the station manager, the radio station embarked on a series of changes. For example, 3FM introduced a new logo and the new slogan of 'Serious Radio'. Various programmes and DJs were replaced and the organization as well as its programming practices were screened and, where necessary, updated.

One of the new initiatives of the radio station is Serious Request. This concept is a collaborative effort of 3FM and the Dutch Red Cross. Every year, awareness and money are raised for a silent disaster somewhere in the world. Serious Request first took place in 2004, when three 3FM DJs had themselves locked up voluntarily in a glass house in the week before Christmas, playing songs requested by listeners and visitors in exchange for donations. During the days that the DJs are locked up in the glass house, they are not allowed to eat solid foods. They inform the public about the necessity of the fundraising campaign, which has evolved over the years into a real ritual in the run-up to Christmas.

Serious Request has meanwhile been organized in a range of Dutch cities: Utrecht, Den Haag, Groningen, Eindhoven, Leiden, Enschede, Leeuwarden, Haarlem, Heerlen and Breda. 3FM has set up a platform especially for 3FM Serious Request where fundraising initiatives can be submitted. People can sign up to join or sponsor these events. By submitting an initiative, you will become an ambassador of 3FM Serious Request and you can get media attention during the event in December.

3FM Serious Request ends on Christmas Eve. The event is uppermost in the thoughts of a substantial part of the Dutch population, especially in the campaign month itself. During the other weeks of the year, however, 3FM disappears into the background, and consequently, so too does the possibility of raising awareness and money for charity.

Source: www.3fm.nl

By the term active principle, we mean the way in which something essentially works, something it derives its right to exist from, in other words: what makes it tick.

The active principle within a concept can simply be there, like the cold North Sea extending a more or less cordial welcome to take a dip, but a concept does not emerge until this active principle is consciously exploited for the realization of a goal. To stay with the example: the New Year's Day Dip, with thousands of people taking a dive into the sea, is a concept in this sense.

A person, too, can grow into a concept. Jamie Oliver, for example, has an authentic active principle: a sincere, trendy boy who just happens to like cooking a great meal. The moment when this active principle is recognized and somebody has the idea of exploiting it consciously, Jamie Oliver can become a concept.

So, in the case of a concept, there is an underlying idea; the concept brings order to the various parts or building blocks, such as themes, products, personnel and communication.

The example below describes the development of a concept based on the objective of bringing a 'silent disaster' to the attention of a large audience.

The Experience Concept

We make a distinction between functional concepts and experience concepts. Functional concepts are aimed at functionality. Thus, the active principle of a transport cafeteria is the self-service principle. The physical environment, the staff, the activities: everything is aligned to the functions of 'fast' and 'easy'. A functional concept in the context of an event is, for instance, a meeting or a staff briefing; sharing a message simultaneously with everyone via live communication. Questions can be asked at once, participants can respond to each other, and so on.

The aim of the experience concept is realizing an experience on the part of the visitor. All choices, including those related to functional aspects, are in this case aligned to the concept of staging the planned event. An event aimed at realizing an experience is, of course, about an experience concept, so the functional concept does not have to be discussed here.

Criteria for a strong experience concept

A strong experience concept serves its purpose when the goal has been realized and the experience actually occurs. We provide five criteria for a strong experience concept. A strong concept:

- Is meaningful, it contains a sort of inner truth. By basing the experience concept on values relevant to the target group, its authenticity can be felt. The point is that it is important to make a connection to what people feel.
- Is distinctive and, ideally, unique. Today's consumers are spoiled: they have seen and experienced much. Uniqueness does not have to be a matter of something completely new; it can also arise from a surprising combination of existing elements.
- Has endurance. A strong experience concept appeals to people over a longer period of time. It also leaves room, however, for regular innovation or extension without losing its power.
- Has several layers. There is more than *one* possible interpretation, for instance, in the case of a concept for an event that is thrilling and interesting for more than one target group. In this sense, a concept has features of a fairy tale. A fairy tale, too, frequently has a core message within a story consisting of various layers. Therefore, storytelling is a key to strong experience concepts (see also Fig. 8.3).
- Is well timed. A concept may be strong on paper, but if it is not realized at the right moment, it will lose its potential value. For this reason, it is vital to keep a close eye on trends and developments, not only from an analytical point of view, but also intuitively.

The Creative Development of an Experience Concept for an Event

We now know what a good concept is, and the conditions that have to be met to make a concept successful. But how do you arrive at a good concept in practice?

There is a key role for the creative development of an experience concept that connects supply and demand. Indeed, by linking the experience to values in an innovative way, a valuable experience will be created for the visitor to an event.

Creativity

Developing an experience concept by using purely analytical methods will not produce a result. Although knowledge and analysis are indispensable, creativity is the crucial ingredient for the process of developing a concept. Creativity has the following important aspects:

- Creativity is related to problem solving.
- Creativity is related to innovation – thinking of solutions that others have not yet thought of. This may be about not only coming up with completely new ideas but also the skilful combination of different areas of knowledge.
- Creativity is related to crossing boundaries; applying the knowledge and ideas of other subject areas will often result in a fresh look at the matter in hand.
- Creativity is not the result of activities that take place exclusively in the right half of the brain; it rather arises through the interaction between the rational, structural left half of the brain and the intuitive right half (Nijs and Peters, 2011).

The creative process always originates in the heart. If there is no heartbeat, there is no movement. It is vital to think from the heart, allow the heart to speak and act with heart and soul. From the heart, you go to the head, to the left half and the right half of the brain.

Left half of the brain: acquisition of knowledge

The left half of the brain is related to the phase of knowledge acquisition: making an analysis of the problem or idea. The point here is to challenge the problem itself, look at it from different angles and map out as many connections as possible: analyse the existing (internal and external) supply, potential networks, trends and developments and target groups.

Target groups can be analysed at the level of values. An existing experience can be analysed as well. Most studies of values and experience are *qualitative* ones that use methods such as depth interviews, group discussions, participatory observation and often (creative) techniques like laddering and visualization (mood boards, for example).

An analysis of values and experience is not enough on its own. Use as many sources as possible. Watch films, read stories, visit locations, look at the world around you and allow everything to inspire you.

Creativity comes into play as soon as switching between the left and right half of the brain occurs.

Right half of the brain: dreaming, experiencing, brooding, brainstorming

The phase of knowledge acquisition becomes a phase of musing over things. This is a chaotic phase during which hope, frustration and new insights alternate. Dreams are visualized and mutually communicated. A clear picture of the intended experience is of primary importance in this phase, and creative sessions are a vital tool. What are the emotions in question? What are the values that play a role and how can they be expressed? What are the images that match? What colours and scents? But, above all: what is the objective, what is the feeling with which a visitor leaves an event?

Developing an experience concept by means of creativity

One method for developing an experience concept is storytelling; you choose a story as the active principle within the concept. This makes it possible to put values and emotions into the experience from the inside out via this story. The story may be the story as the visitor will experience it; an experience often seems to have a storyline in the perception of the consumer. Expressing a concept in a one-liner is a way of narrating the story in its most essential form. This one-liner can also be used as a name or a form of communication (see Fig. 8.3 and the accompanying explanation).

Abdomen: creation of a vision and the experience concept

The abdominal phase (see Fig. 8.6) is about detachment and taking a look at every bit of knowledge and feeling that has arisen from the right half and the left half of the brain in the first phase. This can generate a clear, innovative and fitting vision. A vision is subjective by definition: it is a (personal) opinion or a bundle of opinions, a way of seeing or perceiving, an inner contemplation (Nijs and Peters, 2011). A vision can relate to three levels:

Fig. 8.6. The creative process.

- the world;
- humans in general (and the target group in particular); and
- the 'product'.

Lego's corporate vision is phrased thus:

> We believe that play is the essential ingredient in a child's growth and development. It grows the human spirit. It encourages imagination, conceptual thinking and creation.

This is a vision of humans in general, and the child in particular. The link to the product is in the reference to play.

In line with a vision, a meaningful experience concept can arise that catches the essence of everything that someone knows and feels. This is about a *good feeling*: the concept must feel good, it must add up.

The Lego name says, in fact, what the concept is. Lego is derived from the Danish words 'leg godt', which mean play well. In Latin, Lego means 'I join, collect, gather'. What is clear from this vision of Lego is that dreaming up something for yourself and building something yourself is a good way to play.

Legs: staging the experience

An experience concept must 'land' somewhere sooner or later; it must make contact with the earth. The concept is translated into a concrete experience, but all the related products and means and channels of communication that go with it should ensue from the concept as well (see also Chapter 5).

The Setting of an Event

In a good concept, attention is paid not merely to the content of an event but also to the form: the physical or virtual environment, or setting, in which the event takes place – atmosphere, decor and forms of communication. In this section, we will deal with the physical environment of an event (see the experience model in Fig. 8.1).

The physical environment has a great impact on an experience. Studies have shown that a location has to meet a number of basic conditions before the question of a positive experience even comes up. The Disney company is a classic example in this respect. In fact, Disney Parks have been designed completely in line with those basic conditions. A clean environment is a primary condition. The location of the park may be ever so nice, but dirty toilets or overflowing bins will destroy that beautiful picture at once.

Studies have shown that people are willing to take 21 steps on average to throw something in a rubbish bin. As a consequence, there is a rubbish bin every 20 steps in the Disney Parks.

> **Box 8.5. Empty Chubby Gus**
>
> Empty Chubby Gus has been a familiar figure for decades in the Efteling, a Dutch theme park. The concept of this fairy-tale character has arisen from a reformulation of the question: 'How can we prevent litter lying around all over the place?' The question was changed into: 'How can we make a fun thing of the removal of litter?' (Nijs and Peters, 2011). Empty Chubby Gus is a talking litter bin, who shouts 'Litter here!' If a (young) visitor puts litter into his mouth, he will say: 'Thank you!'

The second basic condition concerns the location of available facilities. It is a given that sanitary facilities near the exit of a museum will shorten the time spent there, whereas providing a resting place and catering halfway will, in fact, prolong the stay (Nijs and Peters, 2011).

Recognizability is the third basic condition. Psychology tells us that people immediately look for points of reference to see how a location is laid out. When a visitor enters a big exhibition hall, he is often overwhelmed by a large number of signs with pictures and texts that try to tell him all sorts of things. This is very confusing. A similar confusion can occur at festival grounds. Several festivals help visitors to find their way by developing applications for smartphones, with the help of which visitors can consult the map and programming of the event interactively (for more about this aspect, see Chapter 9).

A place must hold surprises, but if roaming about means getting lost, the experience is disturbed at once (Hesselmans, 2005). Signposting is important. Basic information can also be cast in a meaningful form, for that matter. Use can be made of stilt walkers, for instance, or other characters at key points of the event location. It is their task to inform the visitor in a way that is felt as an experience.

The Experience Tools

The experience tools are the resources required for staging the event in such a way that the message touches the visitor (see Fig. 8.1). This section will subsequently discuss: thematizing, storytelling, the senses, play, co-creation and staff.

Thematizing

Thematizing is a frequently used tool in the events sector. Think, for example, of the theme, subject, of a congress. A theme as an experience tool is the external, recognizable explicit theme that is carried over into the decor, the details involved and communication.

Themes can be based on:

1. History or epochs, such as the Second World War, the Middle Ages or the Roman era, as a frame for thematic festivals.
2. Culture or (sub)cultures, such as (visual) arts, heritage, music, folklore, countries.
3. Fiction, such as books (*Harry Potter*), films (*SpongeBob*), fairy tales, legends or myths (Robin Hood).
4. Nature: jungle, beach, gardens, animals.
5. Technology, like trains in a railway museum.

This is a broad categorization. A combination of main themes is also possible. A railway museum, for example, can be based on history, heritage and technology.

Themes are aimed at a change in visitors' perception of reality; the point is to immerse them in another world. Ideally, space, time, matter and people (characters) are integrated into a coherent whole (Nijs and Peters, 2011).

According to Pine (International Business Forum, 2003, presentation, unpublished), thematizing is the main ingredient for the creation of a memorable experience: an experience that leaves the visitor of an event with positive memories. As Pine says, it is essential for the theme to be loaded with as many suitable elements as possible, positive cues. Unsuitable elements, negative cues, should, of course, be avoided as much as possible.

Still, thematizing is not always a formula for success. A study of thematizing at leisure locations has shown that thematizing on its own is usually not enough for a memorable experience. Besides, it appears that the role of positive and negative cues depends strongly on the degree to which the visitor is involved in the theme. The lower the involvement, the less value someone attaches to suitable and unsuitable elements.

Storytelling

Storytelling is about narrating stories, which is as old as mankind. It is a perfect way of transferring values and norms (as in fairy tales), arousing emotions, involving people in an event and even bringing about a transformation. Stories can help people understand the world. People are in search of frameworks in order to give meaning to the world in which they live (Rijnja and van der Jagt, 2004). The point of stories lies not in the facts they mention, but in their meaning. Thanks to stories, you, as a listener or reader, can be miles away for a moment, be somewhere else in your thoughts, without losing your head (Gabriel, 2000). Stories activate pride, fantasy and desire (Rijnja and van der Jagt, 2004). These elements are linked closely to an experience.

A vital dimension of storytelling is authenticity, not in the sense of a 'true story' but in the sense of originality and credibility, involving real emotions and meaningful values. From a factual point of view, for example, *The Lord of the Rings* is not very credible, but emotionally it is. In relation to thematizing, contextual authenticity in storytelling plays a role. A story will be better if located in its original environment. Thus, a story about Indians told in a teepee will probably evoke a stronger experience.

Layering is another essential dimension of storytelling. Powerful stories have several layers that can be interpreted at various levels. That is the very reason why children want to hear the same story time and again. They keep discovering new layers in a good story. The continual discovery of new elements in a familiar story is something that may also play an important role in the repetition of leisure activities.

Explicit storytelling means that a story is literally narrated by someone. The narrator can put emotions into the story and involve the audience in it by giving it a role, or through questions and answers.

Implicit storytelling means that a visual representation or object triggers a story in the visitor; he fills it with his own powers of imagination. An object may evoke a nostalgic memory from a personal or collective past. An old cardboard train ticket in a railway museum, for instance, may take visitors back to their own memories in their own personal story, to an experience from the past. An object can also be a metaphor to reduce a (true) story to comprehensible dimensions, like the suitcases with personal belongings in the memorial centre at Auschwitz (Poland) that stand for the personal and human tragedy of deportation.

With respect to the staging of the experience, it is of vital importance to start creating coherence between the experience tools such as storytelling and thematizing already at the concept level.

Stimulating the senses

Sensory perceptions cause emotions (Frijda, 1986), and emotions are the crucial factor for an experience. The stronger the stimulation of the senses, the more intense the experience (Pine and Gilmore, 2000, 2011). But, this is a relative matter. It is also possible for someone to have an intense experience while listening to music or looking at a painting.

In this section, we will discuss colours and scents in more detail. The example below (Box 8.6) shows how a big venue appeals to the senses by developing meeting moods.

Colours

Colours greatly affect the mood of people, and moods, as said earlier, play a vital role in the creation of an experience. Colours can support the structure of a story (Hench, 2003). Colours activate people.

Hench describes the effects of different colours. Red, for example may suggest happiness and put people in a festive mood, but it may also indicate danger and call for alertness. Blue is usually

Box 8.6. Jaarbeurs Utrecht

A convention and meeting centre has developed a unique concept on the basis of the knowledge that colours and other sensory stimulants have an impact on the mood and performance of people. This concept is called *meeting moods*. By using the answers to questions about the objectives and participants of a planned meeting, the client will receive a proposal for the best mood that best fits the meeting, the layout of the room, use of colours, catering, background music, and so on.

The potential target groups for an event are:
- colleagues;
- employees;
- board/committee;
- relations;
- students;
- members/volunteers;
- same-sector colleagues/specialists; and
- partygoers.

When dealing with an event for 'colleagues', for example, the next question will be: 'What is the objective of your event?' Subsequently, several objectives will be presented from which a choice can be made.

- We are going to speed things up with our colleagues. Power is what drives us!
- The important point for us is togetherness. Support, appreciation, but having a good time, too, are the things that are central to us.
- It concerns training sessions, a congress or brainstorming. We share knowledge or ideas.
- We are going to share successes and think of how to propagate them. Thrust out your chest, everybody will be proud!

Suppose that a choice has been made for training sessions, a congress or brainstorming. The final question is then: 'Which of the four fields typifies your organization best?'

1. We believe in long-term relationships on the basis of trust. We respect norms and traditions. We work within frameworks and regulation.
2. We like being inspired by trends. We are proud of who we are and what we do. Positive publicity is very important to us.
3. We decide on the basis of facts and key indicators. As a result of long experience, our name has become established. We accept our social responsibility.
4. We are among the leaders in our sector. The result is what counts. We are original, innovative and dynamic.

Suppose that option 3 fits your organization. The site then presents a film with impressions of a concept for an event. The meeting mood matching this example is 'inspiring'. The colour is blue. The room in which the meeting takes place has blue lighting. The catering is adapted to this: a water bar, a skewer with fruit, and so on. Scents, such as the lemon-like fragrance of flowers, of coffee beans and sweet pastries, are dominant. Subsequently, a mood board can be made that enables the client to prepare a made-to-measure meeting with one of the mood makers of the convention and meeting centre.

Source: www.jaarbeurs.nl/meetup, adapted by the authors.

associated with blue skies, with space and freedom. Brown suggests power, terra firma and deep roots. Green refers to nature, to green trees, abundance, peace and a healthy life. Dark places with cool colours may look threatening but when coloured lights or small pieces of glittering material are installed, they will become attractive and be imbued with a magic, romantic aura (Hench, 2003).

Scents

Experiments have shown that sight is the dominant sense, followed immediately by hearing. Processing scents takes place in the limbic system of our brain. This area also contains the control mechanisms of emotions. A sense of smell is not always recognized as important, in spite of the fact that scents are related strongly to moods, experience and memories (Dekker, 2006).

Increasing use is made of scents at events; there are even aroma jockeys. This requires a subtle approach. If taste and scent clash violently (you smell cinnamon and taste beer), it can be so confusing that the experience is disturbing. Providing too many stimulants simultaneously is not advisable.

Scents can be utilized to divert attention from something that is relatively inconvenient before or during an event: queuing, for instance. Moreover, scents can be used to affect the experience during the pre- and post-exposure phase to increase anticipation or trigger memories.

Elements of play

Is there anyone who has never quarrelled with his best friends in the course of a game of *Risk* or *Settlers of Catan*? Is there anyone who has not felt that feeling of elation at scoring a goal in an insignificant practice match? Computer games, particularly online games, have gained enormous popularity in the past few years. Besides, a parallel, perhaps paradoxical, development can be seen in the strong increase in the sales of board games over the past decade (Hover and Horsten, 2004).

A game is full of surprises, provides scope for creativity and enables the player to develop his cognitive and motor skills, and his emotional side. There are various kinds of games. Sometimes, it is disorganized and spontaneous. This is a setting in which pleasure and development are the primary factors. Computer games are different. They have been designed and organized in time and space. They are focused on the optimization of challenges and tactics (Verhagen, 2006).

Play and sports are closely linked. Though it sometimes seems as if freedom and pleasure are fading into the background in sports, especially in its professional arm, sports has been a popular leisure activity for its practitioners since ancient classical times, and during which emotions can run high.

Play is often associated with children. Yet, play is an important element of the leisure activities of adults as well. A game is the perfect way of involving people in an activity, both as spectators and as participants. When the spectator can actively influence a game, like in *The Voice*, the experience is reinforced.

Play has been utilized successfully for ages during (business) events. It disconnects people from their fixed patterns, carries them along into an experience and offers scope for interaction (the social context). A wonderful example in this context is the real-life escape rooms springing up like mushrooms around the world. An escape room is a room in which participants are locked up and challenged to break free, within a certain amount of time, by solving all sorts of puzzles, riddles and other brain teasers. In De Leerfabriek in Oisterwijk, this is done by means of a theme: the escape room here is a boardroom, decorated in 1960s style, with lots of references to the former factory (https://www.escaperoomsnederland.nl/rooms/escaperoom-kvl-oisterwijk/).

Co-creation

Co-creation means involving the customer in designing the experience that is most in accordance with the meaning that he personally wants to give his life (see also the section on co-creation in Chapter 2).

Consumers are now much better at getting access to information and, as a result, can make decisions that are well founded and better. The role of the consumer is changing. The individual consumer feels a growing need, in interaction with an organization, to create a value proposition that is meaningful for him personally (Prahalad and Ramaswamy, 2004).

It is the ultimate form of driven by demand. Co-creation is often presented as an innovative concept within the experience economy, but it is to a large extent based on the same principles as play. According to Verhagen (2006), the major similarities between play and co-creation are:

- the freedom of choice experienced;
- intrinsic motivation;
- the focus on interaction;
- scope for creativity;
- scope for self-development; and
- the fact that there is no pre-determined result.

It is obvious that co-creation, too, can be exploited as an experience tool. Co-creation between supplier and consumer has played a role in the event as an experience since time immemorial; an example is the battle between gladiators in ancient Rome, where the spectators were one of the parties that could decide the outcome. In the case of an event, the experience does not *really* occur until the spectator participates in it. An artist performing for an empty house is not an experience. The spectators who applaud, sing along or give expression to their involvement in other ways turn an event into an experience: there is interaction between supplier and consumer, and the experience becomes accessible to others. The way in which the fans of different countries dress up and present themselves during a world championship contributes to one's own total experience, but also to that of other people.

By involving a visitor of an event at the level of concept and product development, he becomes part of the co-creation process at an early stage. Digital media like the Internet open up many possibilities. This happens regularly in the context of events. Several big festivals enable consumers, via Facebook and other social media, to vote for their favourite line-up or give their opinions on the various festival acts.

A visitor who enters the co-creation process with the supplier at this level will undoubtedly have a strong personal experience; after all, he can express his creativity, and creativity is linked strongly to experience. Besides, he is involved strongly and personally before, during and, perhaps, after the process, and can share this with other people.

The flipside of co-creation is that a visitor who has been able to define his experience in advance knows exactly what he can expect: there is little room left for surprises, let alone that his expectations will be surpassed. In short, sometimes it is fun to prepare a meal yourself; at other times, it is exciting to have a surprise menu served to you at a restaurant.

The question of whether co-creation is an interesting option for an individual consumer depends very much on the relevance of a specific activity to the person in question (to what extent does he *want* to be involved?). Besides, co-creation requires an effort, and not everyone will have the time and willingness to make that effort. It is a matter of balancing costs and benefits. The competencies of an individual play a part as well. There are people who simply lack the self-confidence, the ability to take the initiative or the creativity to take up the challenge. In this context, too, virtual communities can play the role of a safe 'family' in which individual people can get to work with co-creativity.

Optimum demand control in the form of co-creativity is certainly not the only way to guarantee a strong experience. A profound, meaningful experience can also occur in a supply controlled setting. It is then up to the supplier in the events sector to put himself in the shoes of the visitor, in his position, and whenever possible, arrive at a meaningful experience in consultation with each other (Box 8.7).

Box 8.7. Burning Man

A fine example of co-creation is Burning Man, an annual festival that has been organized in the USA since 1986. More than 48,000 participants travel to the remote Black Rock Desert in Nevada to be part of an experimental community for a week that challenges the participants to express themselves artistically in a huge settlement (Black Rock City) at the bottom of a dry lake.

The organization is carried out by a small group of regular staff and more than 2000 volunteers. Each year, there is a new theme to forge a bond between participants and to encourage them. The participants bring the theme to life in large installations in theme camps on the grounds. People take presents to give to others, and they come with costumes, decorated cars or whatever. Just being there is enough, too. There are no rules telling people how to behave and express themselves, except for rules that protect health, safety and the total experience of the event. Each individual can decide for himself how he wants to contribute and give to the community. Participants share food and drink, for instance. The event is concluded by the burning of the installations. A month after the event, no trace can be found of the city that for many has been the most important city in the country for a short while. Obviously, Burning Man is more than a temporary community. It is a desert city for the ultimate in self-expression and art. The impact of the Burning Man experience is so profound that a culture has formed around it in which people all over the world organize events to rekindle that magical feeling.

Source: www.burningman.org

Personnel

Personnel have a crucial role in shaping an experience, and this has nothing to do with acting out a role. It starts with obvious basic aspects such as kindness, accessibility and a readiness to help, aspects that in practice do not always turn out to be so obvious. As a contribution to the eventual experience, the vital competency required of staff is empathy, the ability to put oneself in the shoes of the visitor and try to surpass expectations.

The perfect example of the role of staff as bearers of the experience can be found in the Disney Parks. Each member of staff, from high to low, is a cast member. Being at work is being on stage, and everyone is part of the show. To many European ears, this sounds like something that is not our style. Still, lessons can be learnt.

Every Disney shop has a budget that is available to an employee to use as he sees fit at a moment when he can create a special, magical event for a visitor. Not only does this enrich the experience of the visitor, but the cast member, too, will derive pleasure from this interaction. *Take five* means: however busy you are, take 5 s or 5 min each day to enjoy the personal interaction with the one visitor you create that magical moment for. Thus, experience cuts both ways. It also fills staff with new energy.

Storytelling is an essential component of the training of Disney's staff. The Disney Traditions programme consists, for a large part, of telling stories.

The staff members engaged for events are often temporary staff, such as volunteers. In such a situation, there is relatively little scope for training programmes. But, it is here that storytelling comes in as an efficient and effective tool to help everyone involved get a feel for the right way to deal with an experience. A fascinating story about how enthralling a staff member was during an earlier event achieves more than a list of 20 instructions.

Summary

The concept of an event should be aligned to the values of the target group. A conversion must be made into a perfectly staged experience. The tools required to do so are an analysis of supply and demand, the values of the target group and the experience model.

The experience model shows how an event will be experienced. In this, the psychosocial framework plays a vital role. There are three levels of experience: basic, memorable and transformative. The factors within the psychosocial framework are knowledge, expectations, motives, mood, involvement, social context, personality and values.

A concept, as the result of an idea, is the active principle that creates coherence and gives direction to the realization of one or more objectives. Clear criteria can be formulated for a strong experience concept, and creativity is indispensable to arrive at a concept that focuses not only on the content of an event but also on the form. Form refers to the setting of an event. The physical environment is part of it and should meet three basic conditions. Finally, the experience tools for an event are thematizing, storytelling, senses, play, co-creation and personnel.

9 Touchpoints

Dorothé Gerritsen and Ronald van Olderen

© Dorothé Gerritsen and Ronald van Olderen 2020. *Events as a Strategic Marketing Tool*, 2nd Edition (D. Gerritsen and R. van Olderen)

In this chapter, we will focus on turning the experience concept into relevant touchpoints: the points of contact that occur during the three phases of pre-exposure, direct exposure and post-exposure. We will discuss two touchpoint models, one from the organization's perspective and the other from the visitor's perspective. The key question is how to create effective touchpoints so as to optimize the visitor or customer experience. In this process, other questions will be dealt with too: What precisely is a touchpoint and which points of contact are there between an organization and its clients or visitors? How can these points of contact be influenced? Which points of contact cannot be influenced? What are the consequences of managing the visitor experience of an organization?

Learning Targets

After studying this chapter, you will have learnt:
- what touchpoints are;
- what the difference is between a staged experience and a customer experience;
- what the customer journey means; and
- how organizations can influence the customer journey of their visitors, in a positive and effective manner, by means of touchpoints.

What Are Touchpoints?

Touchpoints are interaction points between a company or organization and its clients or visitors. Several definitions of touchpoints can be found in the literature on marketing, branding and imagineering (creating experience worlds). Jenkinson formulated the following definition.

> A touchpoint is any time a potential customer or customer comes in contact with your brand – before, during, or after they purchase something from you. (www.surveymonkey.com)

Events appeal to one or more of a visitor's senses in all three phases of pre-experience, direct experience and post-experience: what is there to see, smell, hear, feel and taste? Essentially, it is about the contact between, for instance, a brand, an organization and two or more interest groups. Touchpoints affect perception, satisfaction and loyalty towards an organization.

Whether the touchpoints occur during the organization of a trade fair, a public event or a corporate event, the essence is that every moment of contact, every channel, every contact between visitor and organization is important and deserves careful consideration. After all, every contact has the potential to cause either a positive or a negative experience in the visitor, which has either a positive or a negative effect on the relationship or the experience of the event. Having to wait too long to be able to park one's car, for instance, may have a negative impact on the visitor experience. On the other hand, unexpected surprises may influence customers' opinions in a positive manner. To give an example, handing out umbrellas when it is raining can have a positive effect.

So, it seems that touchpoints occur in many different contexts: websites, registration systems, routing, entrance, facilities including toilets and cloakroom, temperature, product usage, networks, media, means of communication (newsletters, posters, flyers, programme booklets), virtual environments, personnel, artists, format and setting, entertainment, technology, DVDs, location, photographs, catering, audio-visual equipment, goody bags, fittings, decor. It is important to bear in mind that touchpoints go beyond communication. There are just some points of contact you do not have any influence on as an organizer!

Orchestrating touchpoints

As we have shown in the previous chapter, creating an effective event is something that depends on many factors. A good concept alone is not enough. Good planning and communication also

Box 9.1. A warm welcome to cold Iceland

A conference in Iceland has additional experience value purely because of the choice of location alone. This case illustrates how the right mix of experience instruments was used to design the conference, held in the capital of Iceland, as an especially memorable event.

Reykjavik Loves! That's Reykjavik Pure Energy!

Reykjavik is a relatively small city with suburbs, a lively festival and event scene and an artistic climate. Examples include the annual Arts Festival, featuring numerous cultural activities throughout the city, and the construction of a modern conference centre near the old harbour. The city is working hard on its image by means of its brand theme 'Reykjavik Loves', on its infrastructure, efficient air routes with America and the European mainland, and there is talk of building the country's first railway line: in other words, a lot of potential. A European conference like this obviously generates good PR for Iceland in general and Reykjavik in particular. Add to this postmodern people's need for unique experiences and the outcome is a highly interesting case.

From Arts Festival Reykjavik to audience development research

Every spring, artists, as well as a series of photograph exhibitions and a giant marionette called the Little Giant, transform the city into a hotbed of cultural activity. This setting, combined with the workshops on audience development, imagineering and managing creativity, ensured that the first conference day produced interesting insights for us.

The delicious Icelandic food made our Iceland experience complete. We learnt and saw a lot of interesting things in terms of international cultural festivals in Europe, and in Iceland in particular.

The first day of the Iceland experience

Every day was packed with surprising elements, such as the dinner in a power plant, a power station just outside Reykjavik. The delicious meal of lobster soup, salmon, lamb, along with plenty of wine, was a great way to conclude our first conference day. The conference participants were driven back by bus to Hotel Plaza through a vast, desolate and snowy landscape.

Krum, krum, krum: Icelandic songs

The rain songs and lullabies that the participants learnt to sing together in the Arts Museum, led by a famous Icelandic conductor, made them feel all fit and fresh again to listen to the first speaker of the second day. Despite the unusual start to the day, the rest of it was fairly traditional. Plenary sessions were followed by workshops, and then by a plenary panel discussion.

BBC: Electric Proms

A completely different and especially practical story by a speaker from the BBC underlined the enormous variety of speakers and topics presented at the conference. Straight from the heart, she told us how the concept and the actual event of the Electric Proms festival, a combination of classical and pop music, was developed, organized and communicated.

> **Box 9.1.** Continued.
> Good examples and wonderful impressions of the festival by means of both image and sound. What was interesting, for instance, was the way the festival was announced on the various BBC channels: The speaker told us about eight different ways in which the BBC handled the announcement of the festival.
>
> Another lesson that the conference participants learnt was about managing word-of-mouth advertising through the highly targeted use of social websites. An interesting example was the air guitar competition for listeners of BBC Radio 1 to promote Radio 1's Big Weekend. Listeners were asked to make films of themselves playing the air guitar along with their favourite band or artist, and to post these films on YouTube.
>
> Source: 17th IFEA Conference, Reykjavik, Iceland, 2008, adapted by the authors.

are not enough, because events are experienced differently by different visitors, as a consequence of their psychosocial frameworks (see Chapter 8). As an event organizer, understanding psychosocial processes in visitors is not the only thing that matters; you need to go one step further and actually influence these processes. You can deliberately orchestrate important touchpoints in the three phases of exposure, so before, during and after an event. Whether you will achieve your intended objectives will depend partially on the way in which you manage your touchpoints. In this process, you need to be fully aware of the fact that the customer experience goes beyond the experience of the event itself. Engaging your target group is a strategic goal in all cases, and touchpoints play a crucial role in the customer experience (see also Chapter 10 on measuring effects).

From Staged Experiences to Customer Experiences

It is becoming increasingly difficult for businesses to set themselves apart from their competitors by means of products and services (see also Part I of this book). Consumers have access to unlimited information, and products are becoming increasingly alike. Competing successfully requires a different approach, with the perspective shifting from the supplier (organization) to the individual customer. After all, the value of the product or service is no longer the only thing that counts. What is at least equally important is the meaning the individual customer attaches to the product or service. Does the product or service adequately reflect the customer's values or respond to the customer's needs? In this respect, individual customer experiences are extremely important. As a result, event marketing is gaining in importance.

Figure 9.1 shows a continuum of value addition, which starts with the organization and ends with the client. If the focus of value addition lies entirely on the side of the organization, the customer will have a staged experience, orchestrated by the organization. The organization takes the value of the product or service as a guiding principle and builds a perfectly staged experience around it. The *Libelle* Zomerweek (a summer event for readers of *Libelle* – a Dutch women's magazine) is an interesting example in this respect (Box 9.2).

The focus of value addition may also lie entirely on the side of the customer, in which case we speak of customer-created experiences. Value and meaning are created by the customer himself, whereas the organization takes a supporting role. We will also give an example of this side of the continuum (Box 9.3).

Event marketing is about much more than consumer satisfaction. It is about consumer happiness and well-being, giving people a chance to reach their potential and bringing more meaning to their lives (see also Chapter 2).

Fig. 9.1. Continuum of value addition.

Box 9.2. Libelle

Libelle has been the most popular women's magazine of the Netherlands for many years, and it is a strong multimedia brand. The magazine features articles on fashion, interior decorating, beauty, food and drink, tourism and human interest. The main brand extensions are Libelle.nl, the *Libelle* Zomerweek (Summer Week) and the *Libelle* specials. *Libelle* has a strong online community, with a focus on the everyday pleasures of life. A three-dimensional element of the brand is the *Libelle* Summer Week: the biggest outdoor event for women, attracting more than 75,000 visitors. The *Libelle* specials go more deeply into subjects that are important to women, such as interior decorating, life–work balance and travel. The core readers of *Libelle* are women aged between 30 and 55, most of whom are part of multiple-person households, usually families with children. *Libelle* readers represent the average Dutch woman, which is no surprise really, considering the magazine's huge circulation rate. They are contemporary women who put their family first. *Libelle* readers are slightly more highly educated than the average Dutch woman, have a little more money to spend, have an active lifestyle, spend a lot of time on their families and attach great importance to the future of their children. Furthermore, they prefer to undertake things like shopping together with friends or relatives rather than alone, and they are very much interested in make-up and fashion. On average, they have a more than average interest in home decoration and gardening. They also take pleasure in cooking meals (every day), preparing something special from time to time.

All these aspects are represented at the annual event *Libelle* Zomerweek. Not only the various *Libelle* topics but also the atmosphere and values that *Libelle* readers find important are reflected in the concept of the *Libelle* Zomerweek. The concept of the event is entirely consistent with the concept of the magazine; it is, in fact, a three-dimensional variant, which makes visitors feel at home. They experience something that matches their perception of the brand. It may be evident that the organizers of the *Libelle* Zomerweek orchestrate the entire visitor experience by means of programming and atmosphere.

Source: www.libellezomerweek.nl, adapted by the authors.

> **Box 9.3. ING**
>
> ING, a global financial institution, brings together clients (directors and major shareholders) at a dinner, just when some of them are planning to sell their businesses. ING creates an open atmosphere, centred around the personal situations of the guests and allowing them to discuss these situations. In this setting, the guests admit that they are struggling with the idea of selling their businesses, with the sense of emptiness that will undoubtedly be the result of this, and with the question of how to do something useful with their lives again. ING plays a facilitating role in terms of helping its clients deal with this change in their lives. At this particular point, the clients do not derive any value from ING's financial services, but from the experience they undergo in this specific situation. ING will be rewarded with greater loyalty from these clients: the chance of any upcoming important financial transactions being awarded to ING will be increased substantially.
>
> Source: Wiegerink and Peelen, 2013

The importance of physical contact

The process of value addition may be initiated by either the organization or the client. In reality, however, the boundaries are blurred: both parties engage in dialogue with each other and meet each other somewhere in the middle. In this process, there is still a great need for physical contact and non-verbal communication. Despite all the possibilities of Google, Facebook or LinkedIn, we continue to go to every networking party or dinner we can. Attitude and intonation – both difficult to infer from online activities – help you understand better the intentions of your conversation partner. A real conversation can also be steered in the right direction more easily, should any complications arise. What is more, when you see each other in person, you shake hands. This physical contact has a function, as explained earlier. People have a fundamental need to belong, which is equally valid in business interactions.

The value fit

Value fit occurs when organizations and their customers share similar values. This means that the organization's involvement with the visitors of its event must be as great as possible, and that visitors must be given a more active role in the organization of the event (co-creation, see Chapter 8). Without a value fit, the customer will have no interest or use in entering into a relationship with the organization, and the organization will not be able to generate any economic customer value.

That is why event organizers are looking for answers to questions like: What is happening in the lives of our visitors at the moment? What touches them emotionally? Why does a visitor come to an event? What is important to the visitor prior to, during and after the event? Which values occur when, and how can we, as an organization, respond to this as adequately as possible?

The pre- and post-event stages are becoming increasingly important where it concerns the designing of the customer experience. The visitor comes into contact with the organization a long time before the event, but also afterwards, and this will determine in part how this person perceives, values and experiences his journey. The organizer of the event will deploy resources in every phase in order to give the visitor the experience he wants. This is obviously when the touchpoints come into the picture.

The Touchpoint Model

Based on the idea that a good concept based on values has the power to touch people's hearts, you can recognize and specify touchpoints. Remmers specified touchpoints for a theatre, as shown in Fig. 9.2, which could serve as input for a model for events.

The example in Fig. 9.2 serves as input for a model for events (see Figs 9.3 and 9.4). The idea behind this model is that an organization, a theatre in this case, represents a number of values. The main question here involves the degree to which the theatre succeeds in communicating these values to its clients in all points of contact, in order to create an optimal visitor experience. The optimal visitor experience (customer experience) occurs when organization and visitors mostly share the same values: the value fit from the section above.

The organization's values are communicated to the visitors via the second layer in the model. The third layer consists of the back office: the theatre's management and the facilities. The fourth layer concerns the front office: those parts of the organization that are more visible and tangible to clients. These are the 'pillars' for the frameworks to which the specific touchpoints can be attached (the outermost layer). Specific touchpoints to the visitor include parking space and entrance, and booking in advance options. In other words, how the booking and parking systems are organized, and how visitors experience the various facilities.

With regard to events, we can create two models. Figure 9.3 shows the model from the perspective of the organization. This is Remmers' touchpoint model (Fig. 9.2), only without the

Fig. 9.2. Touchpoint model. (Source: presentation by Remmers, 2019, unpublished.)

Fig. 9.3. Touchpoint model for events from the organization's perspective.

touchpoints in the outer layer. The organization finds itself at the core, and in the subsequent layers from the inside to the outside: values, the three phases (before, during and after the event), back office, pillars (front office) and, finally, the actual touchpoints themselves.

The aim of the touchpoint model is to discover marketing and improvement opportunities for the organization. The various channels are identified, in order to optimize the visitor experience, in which the visitor side is obviously the central focus. Let us take a look at, for instance, the touchpoint of websites. Someone who builds a website considers aspects like design and layout. In this process, the client is very important, because the site has to be user-friendly and the design can only be called a success when visitors actually regard the site as user-friendly.

Visitor Perception of Touchpoints

We have already emphasized that organizations need to get under the skin of their customers to find out what really matters to them in the customer experience. In terms of events, organizations need to address the question of what visitors consider important and how the desired experience drives the customer proposition. Which phases does the event visitor go through? In this respect, we are talking about the customer value chain or the aggregate (total) experience.

As we have already shown, the focus should be placed on the visitor's total experience. Suppose that someone has bought a ticket to a concert that is going to take place in a couple of months. Then something happens that forces this future visitor to choose another date to go to this concert. If this client (future visitor) is not adequately assisted by the organization or the

Fig. 9.4. Touchpoint model for events from the visitor's perspective.

ticketing agency in switching the dates – either via the website or by telephone – this will have a major impact on the visitor's experience prior to the event. If an organization takes the customer (and the customer's values) as a guiding principle, and thinks carefully through every interaction that the customer is going to have with the organization, it will be able to create and manage every touchpoint in every phase of the experience, so that the aggregate experience is supportive of the organization's promise to its clients. Even though there will always be aspects outside the organization's range of influence, this is still a solid guiding principle. Or, in other words, every touchpoint matters.

In Fig. 9.4 it is the visitor – along with his values and motives – that makes up the point of departure in which the three phases, before, during and after the event, are critical to the visitor's total experience. The third layer shows that the importance each individual visitor attaches to the touchpoints differs with each phase. Specific touchpoints can be placed in the outer layer, which has not yet been filled in.

Touchpoints for an Optimal Visitor Experience

Organizations can use the layers in both models to check whether the relevant touchpoints are applied in the right phase and in the right manner, so as to build the optimal visitor experience. Figure 9.5 shows that both perspectives need to be connected to each other. The visitor perspective is becoming increasingly important (see also Chapter 2).

In a commercial setting, money will have to be made. So, it is very important to have an accurate understanding of which touchpoints have a high impact and which touchpoints have a

Fig. 9.5. Touchpoint value fit between organization and visitor.

low impact. Nevertheless, regardless of the type of objective, a touchpoint must always be applied effectively in order to arrive at an optimal visitor experience.

When you are organizing an innovative event, for instance, you have to ask yourself the question of just how innovative you have to be in the choice of your touchpoints. Should you offer your visitors innovative catering services? Should you employ the latest hologram technology to add strength to your presentations? Should your room or hall be LED lit? Only when it is clear which aspects add value to the customer experience can well-considered decisions be made with regard to touchpoints – in terms of application and priorities – in which the cost aspect obviously plays a role, too, for the organization as well as the customer. The key question in this respect always concerns the extent to which the touchpoints will contribute to optimizing the visitor experience.

From Events to Experiences

Box 9.4 shows that the visitor experience is absolutely the most important thing to Expoproof. It also serves to show that selecting the right touchpoints is a strong tool for the organizer in creating a positive visitor experience.

Generally speaking, touchpoints may promote a positive visitor experience if they:
- are diversified;
- create a memorable experience;
- focus on values;
- engage several senses;
- inspire emotions;
- are mutually consistent; and
- are chosen purposefully.

These aspects relating to the successful employment of touchpoints will be dealt with in the next subsections.

Satisfiers and dissatisfiers

Touchpoints can be categorized into satisfiers and dissatisfiers. Satisfiers are good touchpoints, surprising the visitor, or even exceeding the visitor's expectations. Dissatisfiers in themselves are

> **Box 9.4. Expoproof**
>
> Expoproof is a company that organizes trade fairs. According to Expoproof's corporate vision, there are always three players involved: organizer, visitor and exhibitor. What you say about one player has a direct influence on the other two players. The visitor experience is the key success factor; the key question being: why does a visitor come to a particular trade fair?
>
> There are several aspects that play a role in this respect, such as:
> - overall quality of the trade fair;
> - the target group of the exhibitors;
> - atmosphere and presentation;
> - catering; and
> - other visitors.
>
> What Expoproof always tries to do is to facilitate networking for its visitors. Fellow professionals should be able to meet up and share ideas. The experience has to be very intense and at the same time relaxed: visitors should be able to find what they are looking for. Addressing a couple of issues at the same time, and organizing and facilitating these issues in an efficient manner, allows you to create the right visitor experience, causing the visitor to come back every year. The experience begins as soon as you spread the first message about the event. The experience is also formed by the exhibitor's communication with the visitors. The experience continues the moment a visitor arrives at the fair. The moment of arrival and the moment of departure may have either a positive or a negative impact on the trade fair visitor (and organizer). If it is raining when the visitor arrives and he is unable to find a place to park his car, there is a real chance that he will decide to turn around and go home. And when entering the trade fair grounds, the way in which visitors are welcomed (with coffee or tea being served?) is obviously important, after which the actual trade fair experience begins. The moment of leaving the grounds is very important, too, because this will be the last thing the visitor remembers.
>
> Source: Van der Zwaag, 2009; www.expoproof.com, adapted by the authors.

good touchpoints, too. Nevertheless, they will not generate any greater appreciation for your organization. If these touchpoints are not positive experiences for the customer, they will be counterproductive. That is why dissatisfiers always represent important preconditions, on which – as it happens – organizations do not always have an influence. An example involving trade fairs, for instance, is catering services. If the price–quality ratio of the catering services is good, visitors will be extremely satisfied, but the organizer of the trade fair will not receive any extra appreciation for it. However, if the price–quality ratio is not good, visitors will mention this on the evaluation form and possibly also spread the word to other visitors, leading to a poorer assessment of the trade fair as a whole. The catering experience compromises the total visitor experience, although the catering services in themselves have nothing to do with the actual theme of the trade fair.

Magical moments

Satisfiers can be used as magical moments. Magical moments are the moments when customers experience a product or service that they had never imagined, that truly surprises them and that shows the organization's commitment to them. The customer experience cannot always be perfect, and it does not need to be so either. There will always be peaks and valleys (see also the section below on the pleasure–pain gap). The relationship between organizer and visitor is a commitment characterized by a certain degree of routine, but also (and this is where the opportunities can be found) by moments of excitement and relaxation!

A magical moment can be created in a very simple manner; for instance, by giving visitors a warm and hospitable welcome – something that organizations fail at regularly. Another example is that of an organizer texting messages to inform conference visitors about a full parking building, along with directions to another car park. On arrival, visitors are welcomed by hostesses: undeniably a satisfier that contributes towards optimizing the total experience.

Some touchpoints are difficult to influence, if they can be influenced at all. Take, for instance, the atmosphere of the location chosen by the client who commissioned the event. To the visitor, this may be a very important touchpoint, whereas the organizer does not have any influence on the visitor's needs or requirements regarding this item. In cases like these, suggesting a new location could be an option.

Peak-end rule

Experiences will be more memorable if the event has the structure of a story, complete with introduction and trigger moment. The story moves towards a climax and, in conclusion, it is brought to an end (see Fig. 8.3).

The announcement of an event in the pre-exposure phase can be seen as the introduction, or in other words, the beginning of the story. Then comes the tension building (including the use of sub-climaxes, if necessary), which will lead to the peak moment (climax). After that, the tension is brought down. The peak moment of the event must be chosen and timed carefully, and it has to ensure a positive ending. In practice, the peak moment is often too early, or the wrong peak moment is chosen. In the first case, it will be difficult for visitors to hold on to the feelings that the peak experience evoked in them until the very end. A wrong peak may be entertainment that is incompatible with the visitor's way of life, as a result of which the visitor will obviously feel little connection. The peak-end rule prescribes that the outcome is always positive (see Fig. 9.6). The last memory of the experience is generally remembered, which influences the experience as a whole.

The post-exposure phase of events is often forgotten. What does the organization do to stay in touch with the visitors? Concert venue and nightclub, Club Vega, in Copenhagen (Denmark) conducted a survey of the post-exposure phase right after a concert, which led to a remarkable outcome. After the live performances in the concert hall, bright white lights were usually switched on rather abruptly. When this happened, the study showed, visitors felt like they were

Fig. 9.6. Peak-end rule. (Source: Gast and Van Moorst, 2009, presentation, unpublished, adapted by the authors.)

torn away from their experience, wanting to make a run for the nearest exit, which is in fact an entirely logical reaction. As a result of this finding, the lighting plan was adjusted, so that the lights went on gradually from faint to bright. Club Vega regularly carries out guest surveys, in a persistent attempt to optimize the visitor experience.

Pleasure–pain gap

The pleasure–pain gap plays an important role in the consumer experience process. The experience must not occur on the same level all the time; there must be peaks. That is why it is important for experiences to be heterogeneous. The distance between a positive pleasure touchpoint and a negative pain touchpoint should be as great as possible. The long queues at the ticket machine – refusing to accept anything but cash – of the brand-new car park after Rihanna's concert in the O2 World Arena in Berlin (Germany), when all people wanted was to go home, is a typical example of a pain touchpoint. This incident made up an integral part of the evening's experience. Positive touchpoints, such as the quality of the music and the concert line-up, are then likely to be experienced as extra-positive, because everything that happens during the evening constitutes the aggregate experience of the individual concert visitor. The aggregate or total experience consists of positive and negative experiences, and everything in between. Due to the fact that negative experiences will always occur too, the positive ones are rated even more positively.

If maximum heterogeneity is achieved in an experience, the visitor will have the best possible experience. This experience may even exceed the peak moment. Obviously, any negative emotions evoked by the pain touchpoint must never exceed the critical limit. This is something of which the organization concerned must be absolutely aware. This gap is clearly depicted in Fig. 9.7. The figure also shows that the most important touchpoints – to the organization (e.g. from a branding perspective) as well as to the customer (customer value) – are applied primarily

Fig. 9.7. Pleasure–pain gap, Geneva Motor Show. (Source: Gast and Van Moorst, 2009, presentation, unpublished, adapted by the authors.)

during the pleasure moments. These are displayed in dark purple. It is therefore of crucial importance to identify and orchestrate these moments carefully, the magical moments.

The black touchpoints are not important, neither to the organization nor to the visitor. The small open circles are the satisfiers and/or dissatisfiers.

As we will see in the following example of a visit to the Geneva Motor Show, the visitor experience process (or the customer journey) consists of three phases:

- Pre-exposure phase:
  gathering information about the event;
  registering for the event; and
  travelling to the event.
- Direct exposure phase:
  arrival at the event;
  being at the event;
  visiting stands at the event; and
  leaving the event.
- Post-exposure phase:
  returning home; and
  arrival at home.

This customer journey shows that it is essential for exhibitors to allow interested visitors to actually experience their products, which means offering visitors the possibility to test-drive new cars. Test-driving a new car that is not yet in production certainly qualifies as a magical moment. Suppose that the visitor test-driving the new car gained a negative experience earlier at the event when he had to wait for what seemed like forever queuing for a certain exhibitor. And suppose he gets stuck in a 10-km traffic jam on the way home. The overall experience may still be thought of in a positive way, thanks to a photograph of the test ride and a brochure containing detailed information that is sent to his home address afterwards. So, as it turns out, heterogeneity makes for a more intense experience.

Value-oriented objectives

The intensity of the visitor experience is achieved because the brand, product or service creates a meaningful experience by means of an event. In this respect, objectives are decisive to the nature and form of the event, and as such, to the experience too. If some 'dorky' engineering business wants to become exciting and innovative, the event to be organized will have to convey a different kind of image and lead to a different kind of experience from the ones commonly associated with the business.

It is difficult to focus purely on the experience. Intensive and effective experiences are developed through personalization. As we have seen already, the specific details of the experience depend on the type of company, the situation (which is perpetually changing) and the objectives. That is why objectives are increasingly formulated in a value-oriented manner.

Well-chosen touchpoints

Each individual is unique and has a different frame of reference, as we have shown already in Chapter 8. Since designing individual experiences would be too expensive, the process of creating the ideal experience often involves making certain choices. This involves looking for cheaper alternatives that are comparable experience-wise. Which touchpoints will have to be applied in which phase? What emotions do we want to evoke? How big is the target range? How many participants will there be? What is the duration of the event? Can the target group be accessed easily, and what costs does this involve? It goes without saying, for instance, that a clearly defined target group within a certain company can be accessed and engaged more easily than a vaguely identified target group.

The Customer Journey

The individual journey that a visitor makes (the customer journey) is an important point of departure to determine touchpoints for an event, as we have seen in the previous subsection on the Geneva Motor Show.

The journey is packed with sensory perceptions and attendant emotions that determine how visitors are going to perceive the physical environment in all its aspects (touchpoints) and how they are going to respond to that; for example, the directional signage and reception area at an event like a trade fair. After all, there is a whole list of things you do not want to happen to your visitors when entering the complex: being sent in the wrong direction due to poor signage, then – after a long search – having to wait in line checking in their coats at the cloakroom and being served by uninterested hostesses. Situations like these will cause emotions like discontent, irritation, anger and disappointment, which will undoubtedly affect the experience of the rest of the event. If, on the other hand, visitors were directed to the car park by means of clear directional signs on the motorway and, after that, were given a warm welcome on entering, this would be a much better start.

Paying attention to the sequence of touchpoints is very important. Do the touchpoints make up a consistent whole and are they interconnected? Are they based on the concept that underlies the total chain of experiences?

Optimization of touchpoints

It has to be clear, for every touchpoint, which emotion exists in the visitor and which emotion is elicited. Only then will it be possible to determine whether the touchpoint applied is the right one or whether another touchpoint should be applied.

How can you make the customer's journey as comfortable and as easy as possible? We have already mentioned in Chapter 5 the use of applications for mobile phones so as to keep visitors updated on all performances, things worth knowing, news, and a floor plan of the venue.

Table 9.1 presents a touchpoint form that organizations can use to analyse and improve the experience process, possibly by means of a mystery guest. The mystery guest goes through the entire process that the customer goes through and writes down his findings on a form designed especially for this purpose. Based on the outcome, an improvement plan can be set up.

Organizational Consequences of Orchestrating Experiences

In creating visitor experiences, the organizer must be able to empathize with the visitor – seeing what the customer sees, feeling what the customer feels – and, if necessary, optimize the process. It requires real skill and ingenuity to design the visitor experience in a real and virtual experience environment: the experience setting. This section will explore the consequences of touchpoints for internal and external processes, for the design process and for people.

In Chapter 8, we emphasized that the solid foundation of an experience is made up of a vision, mission, values and the experience concept. This is demonstrated by, among other things, the guest experience model in Fig. 9.8. Between the foundation and the visitor experience, there are three pillars: people, setting and process. Each of these three pillars contains touchpoints that affect both the virtual and the real visitor experience.

Table 9.1. Touchpoint form. (Source: Remmers, 2010, unpublished, adapted by the authors.)

Touchpoint	Issues	Current situation	Ideal situation	Item requiring improvement	Marketing opportunity	External impact	Internal impact	Priority	Go/No-go
1. Parking space	Safety Sufficient parking spaces Queue signage Ease of parking	There is sufficient parking space at the venue, but the parking attendants do not let the traffic flow properly. Access to the car park is limited due to poor traffic flow	Give parking attendants better instructions, so that they will be able to improve the traffic flow. Appoint a coordinator. Access gates with greater capacity	High	Low	High	Medium	High	Go
2. Physical environment	Hall entrance	The hall access doors only open partially (often only one door or even half of it). The position taken by the door attendant prohibits smooth visitor entrance. Control/screening is unclear. This leads to discussions or even to some degree of aggressiveness	Open doors earlier. Instruct staff earlier. Appoint duty officer	High	Low	High	High	High	Go
	Level of chair comfort	The atmosphere and technical aspects of the hall are in order. The chairs, however, are not comfortable for long sitting	Buy or rent other chairs	High	Low	High	Medium	High	Go
	Staff recognizability	Some staff members do not have a neat, well-groomed appearance	Uniform clothing for staff	High	Medium	High	Medium	High	Go

Fig. 9.8. Guest experience model. (Source: Lier and van Wijngaarden, 2015.)

People

The parking attendant, the security guard, the hostess or the stage performers are all part of the people pillar. They have influence on the experience and are factors that organizations should take into account, constantly reassessing the desired behaviour of all people involved in the context of the customer's wishes and needs. The organization's responsibility is to train its staff to comply with these performance and conduct standards.

Setting

The setting is formed by the physical and virtual environment; for example, the natural environment of the amphitheatre of Verona in Italy during a classic opera like *Aida*, or the facilities of Bella Centre in Copenhagen. Decor, layout, communication and ambiance also fall into the setting category. A website launched in the preliminary stage is an example of a touchpoint that makes an indirect contribution to the total setting of the event.

Process

The *process* contains all visitor–organization interaction required to facilitate the event, through personal interaction or otherwise. In other words, the process may involve the setting as well as the people.

The model by Lier & van Wijngaarden concerns interaction at front office level. We believe that the process pillar also affects the back office procedures (see Fig. 9.9) of an event or organization. In this respect, one may think not only of booking systems and transport arrangements but also the volunteer workforce. The choice for certain touchpoints has consequences for the organization of the front and back office, the required information technology (IT) and the behaviour that the personnel will have to display.

Figure 9.9 is a brief schematic outline of the Geneva Motor Show example. The figure illustrates the visitor journey along the physical touchpoints, from direct front office contacts to back office, supporting processes and IT. We have left a few blank spaces in the figure.

Touchpoints

Customer journey	Gathering information	Registering	Travelling to the event	Event	Event	Event	Event	Returning home	At home	
Touchpoints	◉	◉	◉	◉	◉	◉	◉	◉	◉	
Physical evidence	Website	Website	…….	Building	…….	…….	…….	…….	…….	Interaction line
Front office	Website; floor plan; list of exhibitors	Registration form	…….	…….	…….	…….	…….	…….	…….	
										Visibility line
Back office	Server	Server	…….	…….	…….	…….	…….	…….	…….	
										Internal interaction line
Support and IT	Database	Ticket system	…….	…….	…….	…….	…….	…….	…….	

Fig. 9.9. From visitor journey to supporting processes. (Source: Gast and Van Moorst, 2009, presentation, unpublished, adapted by the authors.)

#EventCanvas

Another practical method to look at the fundamentals of event design is the #EventCanvas (Frissen *et al.*, 2016). The #EventCanvas is a strategic management template for developing new or documenting existing events and conference models. It gives answers in terms of the expected return on investment and provides a common visual language to discuss events in a more strategic manner than in the past. It allows you and your team and/or client to jointly develop event designs. Applying the #EventCanvas methodology will create transparency across the different layers of your organization. Those who map out tactics, manage people and execute plans now have a common language at their disposal to talk about events, about what's important from their perspective and how they would like to secure their responsibilities.

The model articulates how behaviour changes as a result of having participated in the event as well as stating the required levels of satisfaction against expectations. Additionally, the canvas outlines the costs and expected revenues in relation to the customer journey (service design) and the instructional design of the event.

Based on various empathy maps (an analysis tool per stakeholder), the wishes, requirements and expectations regarding the event are analysed and presented in a visual framework, in consultation with all stakeholders. After that, the event organizer will be able to develop and execute several event prototypes. Figure 9.10 displays the #EventCanvas. The model can be downloaded free of charge under Creative Commons 4.0 license via https://edco.global/download/.

Source: www.eventcanvas.org

Fig. 9.10. #EventCanvas.

Summary

The individual event visitor, with his individual needs, is becoming increasingly important and should be the primary point of departure in planning and organizing events. The visitor embarks on a journey (the customer journey), calling in at touchpoints that are instrumental to an optimal visitor experience.

Touchpoints are points of contact: moments when a visitor or customer has contact with an organization or company. Touchpoints are becoming increasingly important in the events industry, and they are applied to control the points of contact, taking the customer's values and needs as the guiding principle (value addition and value fit).

Touchpoint models can be set up from the organization's perspective, as well as from the customer's perspective; however, the customer's perception of the touchpoints is always the guiding principle. Touchpoints should be diversified, inspire memorable experiences, evoke emotions, stimulate several senses, be value oriented, be mutually consistent and be well chosen.

Organizations can direct the visitor experience by means of the setting, the people and the process of interactions. Several touchpoint models have been developed for trade fairs and corporate events. See the Appendices on the following pages.

Appendices to Chapter 9
Touchpoint Models for Trade Fairs and Corporate Events

Empirical data produced by research into trade fairs and corporate events served as the starting point in the development of two touchpoint models. Both models are based on the vision of professionals working for leading companies. Planning and organizing fairs and events is something that these people are involved in on a daily basis. They were asked to provide as complete as possible a description of touchpoints within their area of expertise. In addition, they identified priorities within each of the three phases of an event: the pre-exposure, direct exposure and post-exposure phase. The visitor's perspective of the visitor experience is a subject of current research and has not been incorporated in the two touchpoint models presented here.

Appendix 1
Touchpoint Model for Trade Fairs

As we have already seen, there are generally three parties involved in trade fairs: the organizer, the exhibitor and the visitor. The touchpoint model (see Fig. 9.11) was developed on the basis of research among organizers of trade fairs. Their views of what touchpoints are, which touchpoints should be prioritized and in which particular phase, and which ones allow you to excel have all been taken into account. The following matters are crucial to a correct interpretation of the model:

- The details of a trade fair must always be considered carefully (e.g. programme, exhibitors).
- Co-creation is increasingly used to optimize experiences. In this process, the exhibitor's and the visitor's views are taken into account.
- The model contains only the most important touchpoints.
- It is still important to continue managing the various dissatisfiers.
- This model focuses on professional trade fair organizers. It is also possible to construct a model from the exhibitor's point of view.
- The organizer operates on the basis of the visitor's objectives: networking, familiarization, gathering information.

The core of the model is the trade fair organizer and his set of values. The trade fair will be successful if it satisfies or – preferably – exceeds the visitors' expectations. This is achieved through an accurate insight into the customer journey and by choosing the right touchpoints by means of questions such as: What do visitors find important? What do they hope to achieve by visiting the trade fair? What are the needs that lead them to visit the fair?

As is the case with any event, a trade fair can be classified into pre-, direct and post-exposure phases: the phases before, during and after the fair (the second layer from the core). The third layer represents, for each phase, the building blocks that the trade fair organizers think are the most important; the concrete touchpoints can be found in the outer layer. On the following pages, the pre-exposure phase of trade fairs will be set out in more detail.

The Pre-exposure Phase of Trade Fairs
Communication
Website
The website is often the first touchpoint. It takes mere seconds for visitors to form a first impression. Obviously, the website has to be up-to-date and contain relevant information: date, location, list of exhibitors, floor plan, seminar programme and a registration tool. When a potential visitor can find the information he is looking for easily, he will be more readily inclined to return to the site. Website designers have to take into account the various visitor objectives.

Fig. 9.11. Touchpoint model for trade fairs.

Newsletter/direct mail

Newsletter and direct mail campaigns involve information being sent by the trade fair organizer (via regular mail or e-mail) to potential visitors who have visited a trade fair before, or to people who have indicated a desire to be kept updated. In our current Internet age, direct mail is cheaper than other means of advertising; for instance, paper-based mail. Direct mail should have a catchy subject title, as this will increase the probability of your mail being opened. It also has to contain valuable and useful information, but not an overload of information. During the period leading up to the trade fair, the information becomes more specific, and so more interesting. The first message, for instance, discloses that there will be a seminar programme, the second message provides a list of seminar speakers and the third one sets forth the various subjects. This will arouse curiosity in potential visitors. It is also possible for visitors to be informed about the trade fair programme, trends and developments, novelties and registration options.

Personal invitation

The next important touchpoint in the pre-exposure phase in the area of communication is the personal invitation. Since one-to-one communication is becoming increasingly important, potential trade fair visitors generally appreciate a personal invitation. It increases their feeling of involvement. Some trade fair organizers design and distribute these invitations themselves, in keeping with the overall 'look and feel' of the trade fair; other organizers leave the matter up to the exhibitors. The fact is that personal communication in the pre-exposure phase is very important to stimulate favourable expectations in trade fair visitors.

Trade fair details

Exhibitors

In the pre-exposure phase, prospective visitors examine both the subject area of the trade fair and the exhibitors that will be present. It is very important for the trade fair organizer to communicate the list of exhibitors in good time, because prospective visitors will use this list in their decision on whether or not to visit the trade fair. A good trade fair has a list of high-quality exhibitors. Co-creation with sector organizations, for instance, may be an important contributive factor in this respect. The exhibitors present will obviously determine the greater part of the expectations regarding the fair.

Floor plan

In the pre-exposure phase, many potential visitors often take a look at the floor plan to get an idea of what they will find where at the trade fair. The floor plan displays the names of the exhibitors and the locations of their exhibition stands, so as to enable the visitor to plan his route beforehand, preparing a personal stand-visiting schedule. This personal schedule will contribute to the expectations of the individual trade fair visitor.

Programme

Trade fair visitors want to meet exhibitors who are interesting to them, and this means that the trade fair programme is also very important. This programme consists of activities organized by the trade fair organizer. As the programme is distributed in the pre-exposure phase, visitors know what to expect at the trade fair.

Seminar programme

Not every trade fair has a seminar programme. If there are not going to be any seminars during a certain trade fair, it is important to communicate this early in the pre-exposure phase, so that visitors do not come to the fair with the expectation of attending a seminar. If seminars are held, it is obviously the speakers and subjects that will be important to the visitor's expectations. Seminars should comply with certain standards in terms of quality and subject matter, and they should be in keeping with the overall theme of the trade fair.

Exhibitors

Preparation by exhibitors

Exhibitors are an important part of the trade fair, and it is important that they prepare for the trade fair in the pre-exposure phase. As a trade fair organizer, you have no full control over this process, but you can exert some influence by offering standard exhibition stands, furniture and trade fair training. In addition, it is important for exhibitors to establish targets for themselves with regard to the trade fair; otherwise, they will be unable to measure any effects afterwards.

Personal invitation sent by exhibitors

Potential visitors will get a much greater sense of one-to-one communication if they receive a personal invitation from exhibitors, rather than from the trade fair organizer. Moreover, the exhibitor can attach information about any novelties he will be presenting at the trade fair.

Identity

Name/trade fair title
The name of the trade fair conjures up expectations, too. The name is mostly linked to the theme of the fair. The longer a trade fair has been in existence, the more its name will turn into a brand.

Logo
A logo is the symbol that gives the trade fair title its identity. It is the graphic representation of the fair title. As time goes by, a logo will also become part of the trade fair brand; it exudes the values and identity of the trade fair.

House style
The house style is used on the website, in brochures, direct mail and invitations. Use of colour, typeface and graphic design should be the same in all these touchpoints. As a result, the recognizability of the trade fair will be increased.

Appendix 2
Touchpoint Model for Corporate Events

The touchpoint model for corporate events (see Fig. 9.12) has been developed by means of expert interviews and case study analyses. Corporate events also generally involve three parties: the client/company, the visitor and the event management agency. A corporate event supports the strategic goals that have been determined by the company. For the purpose of a correct interpretation of the model, there are a few matters that require clarification first.

- The client determines the objectives, the message, the preconditions, the value and the budget.
- The choice and details of the touchpoints should be tailored to the company, the culture and the mindset of the company as well as the visitor: or in other words, the values. It will be the project manager, however, who gets to determine the creative details.

Fig. 9.12. Touchpoint model for corporate events.

© Dorothé Gerritsen and Ronald van Olderen 2020. *Events as a Strategic Marketing Tool*, 2nd Edition (D. Gerritsen and R. van Olderen)

- If the client wishes, the event management agency can take charge of the creation and/or execution of the event.
- The model shows the most important touchpoints. This does not mean that the touchpoints not mentioned are not important.
- The visitor experience is not an explicit part of this model.

The inner layer represents the organization/company and its values. The pre-exposure phase is used to provide information, encourage visits, arouse curiosity and build tension. The direct exposure phase is the event itself, and the post-exposure phase serves to sustain the experience. The third layer displays the pillars for the various touchpoints, and the outer layer contains the actual touchpoints. Below, we will give you a more detailed explanation of the direct exposure phase of a corporate event.

Direct Exposure Phase of a Corporate Event
Atmosphere
The atmosphere is critical to the visitor experience. The 'atmosphere' pillar consists of touchpoints in the form of experience optimization tools: location, decor, furnishings, technological aspects, format and setting, and entertainment.

Location
The location is often determined by the preconditions set by the client. Accessibility, immediate environment and professionalism are important aspects in choosing a location.

Decor
The interior design and the use of decoration are key determinants in the pillar called 'decor'. It should be in keeping with the concept and theme of the event. An eye for detail is important, as is creating a visually attractive and coherent atmosphere.

Technology
Technology can be classified into lighting, sound, visual aids and show elements.

Lighting
Light is an important factor in atmosphere perception. With the right light effects, an ugly location can be transformed into a beautiful location. Light colours and intensity levels are tailored to the programme contents and the concept or theme. Light also determines the focus (either on the stage or the audience).

Sound
Everything must be clearly audible. In addition, sounds can be used to create excitement or enthusiasm, for instance.

Visual aids
A picture is worth a thousand words. A certain combination of music and images may convey a feeling that needs no further explanation. Visuals may support a presentation. Live registration is also very functional. Speakers, performers and visitors themselves are displayed on big screens.

Show elements
The use of laser, fireworks or disco effects has an impact on the atmosphere. Moreover, show elements can be used to appeal to people's senses; for example, a fragrance machine or a snow cannon.

Format/setting
The choice of a format/setting is an important atmosphere component. This involves, for instance, opting for a plenary setting or an informal setting with the speakers seated at tables. Or, you can have the speakers and the presenter sit on a stage. The focus may be on the stage, but also on the audience.

Entertainment
Entertainment may be provided at the entrance and may be related to the event or its various components.

Logistics
Logistics is an element that is noticed only when things go wrong. In other words, it is important to handle the logistics properly. Logistics in corporate events involve the touchpoints of routing, transport and parking facilities.

Routing
It is important that there is a clear visitor route. That is why efficient signage, which is checked on a regular basis, is essential. If visitors come by car, it is important that there is clear signage to direct them to the event venue. Additionally, it is important to give visitors directions from the location where they arrive to the location where the event takes place, possibly by hostesses. Bus and other public transport departure times must also be displayed clearly.

Transport
The mode of transport that visitors use to get to the event may be a car, coach, public transport or bicycle. The transport component can become an experience when it is given a little extra attention; for instance, playing a film or serving refreshments on the coach. If visitors come by car, a text messaging service may be an option; for instance, to announce a later start time for the plenary programme if many visitors are unable to arrive in time due to traffic congestion.

Parking
There must be sufficient parking space, obviously. Depending on the location, there will be parking attendants to show visitors a place to park.

Facilities/organization
To put it briefly: visitors simply expect the facilities and organizational infrastructure to be arranged adequately. If any aspect falls short of their expectations, this will be detrimental to the total experience. This component comprises the touchpoints of toilets, cloakroom, personnel and temperature.

Toilets
The toilets must be clean. Moreover, the toilets must be directly accessible from the entrance area.

Cloakroom
Cloakroom facilities must be organized efficiently. Visitors must not only be able to deposit their coats but also their laptops, for instance. The cloakroom must be directly accessible from the entrance area.

Personnel
High-quality personnel are important. All personnel who come into contact with visitors must be friendly and courteous; this particularly involves catering personnel and hosts. All relevant

information, in the form of a briefing session, must be provided to the personnel. If necessary, personnel clothing can be tailored to the theme of the event.

Temperature
In the case of outdoor activities, the temperature is a decisive factor. And in the case of indoor activities, there must be an adequate climate control system: in other words, not too warm and not too cold.

Event details
The way in which the details of the event are reflected in the various touchpoints is also crucial to the optimization of the experience. It involves the way in which the objectives and the message to be conveyed are integrated in the touchpoints of entrance, programming, programme contents and catering.

Entrance
It is important for visitors to feel welcome straight away. The entrance is an important factor in this respect. Interpersonal contact is one of the most effective ways to make visitors feel welcome. In addition, it has to be possible for visitors to register themselves, and drinks and snacks should be served. All activities in the entrance area must be service oriented.

Programming
There are plenary parts at every event, often either a plenary opening or a closing session. It is important to indicate when the plenary part begins. Festive events often have plenary closing sessions. In addition, the timing of the various activities is crucial, creating just the right balance between activity and rest.

Programme contents
The programme contents obviously differ with each event. As the contents should convey the message, this component is extremely important. The message can be communicated by artists, speakers, activities, and so on. Celebrities attract visitors.

Catering
Catering is important to the event as a whole. Drinks and snacks must be served to visitors on arrival at the entrance, as well as during the plenary activities. There are also events in which catering makes up the most important part of the event.

Part III

Check

Part III

In this part of the book, we discuss the 'check' phase of the strategic use of events, so the right-hand part of the EVENTS model.

In Chapter 10, we deal with effect measurement and evaluation. In the Appendices, examples of methods can be found that can be used to do this, together with examples from practice.

10. Effect Measurement and Evaluation

Appendices to Chapter 10: Effect Measurement and Evaluation

Appendix 1. The ROI Model of Jack Phillips

Appendix 2. Economic Impact Study of the World Cyclo-Cross Championships 2014, Hoogerheide, the Netherlands

10 Effect Measurement and Evaluation

Dorothé Gerritsen and Ronald van Olderen

The central issues of this final chapter are effect measurement and evaluation. How do you study the impact of events? In the EVENTS model and in Chapter 1, the *Plan–Do–Check–Act* (PDCA) cycle was discussed briefly. Here, we will do that in more detail, because measuring effects and evaluation are only useful when the PDCA cycle is taken as a starting point. We will also describe effects and types of effects in relation to events. In this context, the key question is 'Who wants to know what, and why?' The formulation of proper objectives is crucial to measuring effects, as we will demonstrate. At the end of the chapter, we will describe how effect measurement and evaluation can be carried out.

Learning Targets

After studying this chapter, you will have learnt:
- what is meant by effect measurement and evaluation;
- what types of effects of events can be distinguished;
- what you must take into account when measuring effects and evaluating;
- how to build up a hierarchy of objectives;
- the methods and techniques regarding effect measurement and evaluation;
- how to design the measurement of effects on the basis of objectives; and
- how measuring effects and evaluation can be carried out.

The Importance of Effect Measurement and Evaluation

Cities that put themselves forward as candidates for the title of Cultural Capital of Europe get back double what they invested and believe in impacts other than economic ones. That is clear from the newspaper article with which we opened this chapter (see Box 10.1). It mentions the effects of (cultural) events in those cities: more overnight stays, higher revenues for the catering industry and an increase in business tourism. It could also have mentioned another effect: a greater feeling of pride among the inhabitants of those cities. But how do you measure that?

Effect measurements and evaluation take money, time and effort. However, effect measurements are becoming increasingly important, for the very reason that events are deployed more and more on the basis of strategic objectives. Clients want to know if, and to what extent, those objectives are attained. It is then crucial to be able to show what the contribution of the event has been.

Box 10.1. Leeuwarden, Cultural Capital of Europe 2018

Together with the Maltese capital of Valetta, the city of Leeuwarden carried the title of 'Cultural Capital of Europe' in 2018. The city was chosen by the jury, consisting of representatives from the European and Dutch cultural fields, over Eindhoven and Maastricht. Leeuwarden was the jury's preferred choice thanks to the innovative approach presented in the bid book. The jury opted for the story of a shrinking region that believes that the status of Cultural Capital of Europe can bring dynamism. The title is intended to 'show the richness and diversity of European cultures' and offers cities an opportunity to put themselves on the map. The city of Eindhoven engaged Greg Richards, Professor of Leisure Studies at Tilburg University, to conduct a study into the effects of the title. The professor concluded that the European cities are making double returns on their investments. When you read the bid books, you will see that the candidate cities not only believe in economic benefits, but also in less measurable benefits such as a growing sense of community, more cultural diversity, and a better relationship between city and countryside. Every year, two countries are allowed to designate a city as cultural capital.

Source: Huiskamp, 6 September 2013, www.nrc.nl

Of course, to attain the objectives, more (communication) efforts are required than simply organizing events. Budgets are under pressure when the economy is doing less well. However, clients are usually still prepared to put money and time into events, if their efforts generate enough profits (return on investment – ROI). The organizer of an event is accountable for the results of an events policy. *Accountability* means that the contribution of an event to the strategic objectives is made clear to financiers and other interested parties on the basis of systematically collected data.

The Plan–Do–Check–Act Cycle

Assuring the quality of an event and being able to show what an event contributes to the objectives requires a continual process of improvement and innovation modelled on the PDCA cycle (see Fig. 10.1), from which a company can learn by looking at the actions taken before, during and after an event. On the basis of the PDCA cycle, you can make interim adjustments, show the results afterwards and, with the help of a good evaluation, formulate new objectives for a new event.

The planning phase is meant to determine the course you take, set goals and formulate plans. The objectives may arise from a city marketing policy, for example, or a relationships marketing strategy (see Part I). You also identify the target group and interested parties (stakeholders), and how you want to reach your target group.

In the 'do' phase, you develop the concept and the design of the event, based on the objectives, target group and stakeholders (see Part II). This should include the execution of the event in the pre-, direct and post-exposure phases. In the 'check' phase, you monitor the implementation of the plans. Depending on what the client wants to know, you measure the effects, interim or post-event, on the target group and/or stakeholders. This enables you to measure whether an event has attained the set objectives.

In the 'act' phase, you analyse the collected data to be able to provide feedback for strategy making and to formulate new objectives.

Effects

Effects are reactions to actions that are performed. If you deploy an event (an action = stimulus = experience), you can expect reactions. There are intended and unintended effects. The intended effects of an event ensue from the predetermined objectives. Unintended effects refer to consequences you could not have foreseen in advance. This may concern unintended negative effects such as bad weather or traffic jams, but also unintended positive effects like extensive media attention that you had not counted on.

We have already pointed out that it is impossible to determine beforehand whether an event will deliver the desired results. Sometimes, an event has no effect at all on an individual person, even if it has been organized perfectly. If, for example, a visitor has just heard that he has lost his job, this will have a great impact on how he experiences an event. Or the reverse: residents of the inner city appear not to be bothered at all by the enormous noise nuisance of a musical event close to where they live, whereas this could indeed have been expected to be a negative effect.

Fig. 10.1. PDCA cycle. (Source: Truscott, 2003.)

Types of effects

Various theories and models of the effects of events have been developed, and described in the recent literature. They emphasize the economic effects or economic importance of events. Hall (1992) has devised an effects matrix for public events in which other types of effects are included as well, together with the ways in which these effects show themselves. This provides an indication of how the effects can manifest themselves in practice. Local and national governments, for instance, want to make their city or country better known, or portray a city as a sports city. These effects are related to tourism and the economy, and the ultimate goal is: developing new tourist facilities, organizing annually recurring events and stimulating repeat visits.

The matrix shown in Table 10.1 mentions both positive and negative effects: positive effects often have a negative counterpart. This matrix shows possible effects that can occur. Of course, this does not mean that the entire range of effects will occur. Which effects do occur depends on the size, theme and type of event. The matrix does not tell you anything about the impact of the effects. This differs from event to event. For all of those involved, it is, of course, essential that positive effects are worked out and communicated as well as possible and that negative effects are offset as much as possible.

Several of the effects mentioned can also occur when business events are organized. An example is the inconvenience to residents as a result of heavy traffic near the location of the event. A recent example is the Nuclear Security Summit in The Hague. Apart from the city's organizational potential, in which security was obviously a hugely important issue, the identity and image of the city of The Hague were decisive factors in the organizers' choice of The Hague as a location for their summit. The Hague, with its International Court of Law and Peace Palace, reflects the values of a crucial summit on any international political topic. International media attention for this summit contributed greatly to the image of The Hague as a city deeply involved in world politics. The summit was attended by 58 world leaders from 53 different countries and four leading international organizations.

Table 10.1. Effects matrix for public events. (source: Hall, 1992.)

Effect	Manifestation Positive	Negative
Economic	Increase in spending by visitors Increase in employment	Price increases Better alternative investments
Touristic/commercial	Awareness of potential as tourist destination Awareness of development potential	Bad reputation due to bad facilities, prices that are too high Competition with existing businesses
Physical (infrastructure)	Construction of new facilities Improvement of existing infrastructure	Damage to environment Destruction of heritage Too crowded with visitors
Sociocultural	Increase in participation in type of activity connected to event Strengthening regional tradition	Commercialization of traditions Adaptation of traditions to commercial requirements
Psychological	Improvement of civic spirit and sense of community Awareness of non-local views	Defensive reactions in host region Culture clashes Risk of enmity between visitors and residents
Political	International interest Improvement of planning skills	Increase in public spending Legitimation of existing ideology

The effects of public and business events

Measuring the effects of public events is slightly different from measuring them at business events. Business events are generally organized in closed spaces, and their principal goal is the achievement of an objective regarding a particular target group. In addition, effect measurement is usually focused on the intended target group. As a result, effects can be better identified and controlled. As we have shown in Chapter 1, public events are often a vital platform for business events. There is an increasingly important role for objectives in relation to public events; for example, in the context of a city marketing policy. But the various stakeholders of public events can also benefit from measuring the consequences of an event at the regional, urban or national level. What makes the measurement of effects a tough proposition is that stimuli external to an event must be excluded: how do you know that effects are from the event and not from other stimuli? We will discuss this in further detail in the section below that deals with methods and techniques.

Table 10.2 lists the different points of emphasis in a comparison of business events with public ones. It includes the consequences for measuring effects, but it is not an exhaustive list.

Effect Measurement

Effect measurement comprises the collection of data for the analysis of an event to be able to: make adjustments before, during and after an event; account for everything; improve processes; and formulate new objectives. The question that arises in connection with effect measurement is, of course, whether you want to measure everything and whether you can. The answer is: no. A stakeholder who wants a record of the effects of an event must give a very clear indication of the goals for which the effects should be measured. In the context of the World Championship Football in Qatar, issues can be media attention and economic spin-offs for the local catering businesses, but also security or being proud of the country. When Samsung wants to organize festivities for all its employees because of its anniversary, the objectives will be quite different and, as a consequence, other effects have to be measured, such as thanking the employees and bolstering the image of Samsung as an employer in order to reinforce the feelings of loyalty and pride in its employees. What is required to measure the effects of an event is a clear focus and knowing what should be excluded.

Table 10.2. Effect measurement of business and public events.

Corporate event	Public event
Invitees	Not exclusively for invitees
	Possible side events with no public admission
	Public admitted
	Admission tickets/no admission tickets
Usually business–economic goal, entertainment may be part of the programme	Entertainment of all sorts is usually the goal and the principal part
Direct communication possible to target groups	Less direct communication/mass communication
Consequence of effect measurement	**Consequence of effect measurement**
Effect measurement can be managed better	Harder to manage well
More control over event	Less control because of many activities in public space
Generally smaller scope	Often many people; crowd management is more complicated
Those who attend are known	Those who attend are diverse and unknown

Effects can occur in the short term, during and immediately after an event, for instance. Strategic objectives often require more time and will usually be attained in the longer run. For that reason, it is important not to restrict measurements to the periods during and immediately after an event. We will discuss this in more detail in the section below that deals with the hierarchy of objectives.

Who wants to know what, and why?

Each interested party wants to know what the effects of an event are from that party's own angle. The important question that should be asked before effect measurement and evaluation is: *who* wants to know *what*, and *why*? It is crucial to know from which angle measurements should be made. Do the city authorities want to know what the effects of an event are, or is it the sponsor who wants to know? The cities of Torrevieja (Spain) or Pamplona (Spain), for example, want to know what the impact of the Vuelta a España starting there has been. The Amstel (beer brand) sponsor wants to know what the benefits of organizing the Amstel Gold Race, a 1-day classic cycling race, have been. For some, 'what' stands for hard cash; for others it is about feeling and name recognition. The organizer of the Amstel Gold Race, for instance, is curious to know about the impact of the event on the host community. Can you rely again on the necessary cooperation of those involved in that region? The interested party that carries out the effect measurement decides which effects have to be measured and who has to be measured.

Why Effect Measurement and Evaluation?

Effect measurement and evaluation can be used to find out whether the investments involved in organizing an event have yielded sufficient returns (ROI).

Another reason may concern accountability for the policy pursued. Interim measurements can be helpful to make adjustments if necessary, and/or to change plans.

Accountability

Regarding business and public events, effect measurement is used to account for the policy pursued and investments. Public events, for example, often take place in public spaces and make use of public resources. In view of retaining commitment and getting support, it is of great importance to city leaders to be able to show the positive effects of public events to the various stakeholders. Both quantitative and qualitative measuring methods are used.

Appendix 2 as well as the website for this book provide examples of effect measurement and evaluation with regard to major public sports events and demonstrate the vital role of accountability.

Return on investment

Budgets are under pressure and organizations want to know whether the policy that has been pursued produces any ROIs. How much is budgeted for, what is the return and does this meet the predetermined objectives? Having a good feeling about an event is no longer enough. It is very clear: an event must make money, or be cost neutral at the very least. Appendix 1 deals specifically with the ROI model that has been developed from the meetings industry.

Making adjustments

Measuring the interim results of an event and those after an event is very useful. It is a tangible form of self-reflection, turning opinions into facts. A negative result should be a reason for finding out how things can be done better next time. The result can be used not only to dot the i's and cross the t's regarding a supplier, for example, but also to inform customers about improvements that are being made. The results are used to assure quality and to improve it continuously. Measurements are not only useful for making adjustments but also they can serve as input for the next time. Carrying out measurements is, then, a starting point and not something of a conclusion. After all, results are useless if nothing is done with them: take, for example, the PDCA cycle in this connection.

Looking back
Effect measurement and evaluation ensure structure in the design of an event. It is a way of thinking and structuring. Thinking about measurement forces an organization to consider consciously the 'what' and the 'why'. This not only applies to the objective, important as that may be, but also in deciding which indicators will be the basis of measuring the objective. By reviewing an objective during the course of planning an event, it can be improved. The point here is a detailed description of an event.

Objectives of Effect Measurement: The 'What' Question
We have already pointed out that it is important to know from what perspective an effect measurement is carried out: who wants to know something? The next question is: what should be measured?

Providing an answer to the 'what' question appears to be easier than it is in practice. It seems like an open door, something very obvious. However, it turns out that it is often not easy for clients to indicate exactly what an event is supposed to achieve and what exactly the effects are that should be measured. Take, for instance, the Geneva Motor Show, which is a leading trade fair for the car sector in the Netherlands. Nearly all brand dealers present themselves with novelties and actions to their colleagues, the trade press and the consumer. But how can you tell whether this trade fair is successful when there is the same number of visitors as 2 years earlier? Or is a client only satisfied when the number of visitors is relatively higher? Or do you want to attract target groups that have been ignored up to now? Or are you not satisfied until all brands have submitted x quotations? In other words: what are the goals, strategic or otherwise, that the Geneva Motor Show wants to achieve? What do the various parties involved want to accomplish? So, the 'what' question can be used to determine what the effects are that should be measured and whether or not an event is successful.

The hierarchy of objectives
Objectives can be set at various levels, and therefore we can speak of a hierarchy of objectives. The strategic effect objectives are at the top of the hierarchy, the operational effect objectives are in the middle and the attainment objectives are at the bottom (Dreimüller, 2002).

Strategic effect objectives
Strategic effect objectives are formulated on the basis of corporate objectives and the marketing and communication objectives derived from them. They are based on the long-term vision and mission of an organization and indicate the contribution of event marketing to attaining those objectives. What was the effect on the target group or stakeholders? It is, in fact, about measuring the effects of an event on the brand, the relations, the staff of the organization, the visitors to a city, and so on. The ultimate effect is the effect on money: has an event contributed to an ROI?

You have seen that events can be utilized for many different reasons; for example, to reinforce customer relations, increase loyalty or swell the feeling of pride in the residents of a city where a public event takes place. An event may also be intended to promote brand loyalty, increase sales and consolidate business relationships. All these examples relate to objectives that ensue from the strategic goals of the enterprise in question. The effects will generally become manifest only in the course of time. The impact of an event on the commitment and loyalty of a relation will not be noticeable at once. In this context, the importance of the pre- and post-exposure phases should not be forgotten. Improved customer relations and loyalty are objectives that cannot be realized in the short run: it takes time and requires more than merely an event marketing strategy. Besides, other factors may be involved, factors that cannot, or can hardly, be influenced, like developments in the market.

To be able to measure effects, it is necessary to record information continuously and keep it up to date in an information system, define concrete behaviour and, if necessary, compare measurements to see if there are any changes.

At the beginning of Chapter 4, we presented the fictitious company of Insurance Direct as an example of a company applying a clear relationship marketing strategy. We return briefly to this example here to indicate what is strategic in the objective. Insurance Direct is a retail bank and insurer that wants to position itself differently in relation to intermediaries as a result of changing developments in the market: as a partner in business. This is linked to an important development, that of consumers increasingly bypassing intermediaries when buying insurance and banking products. It has become harder and harder for intermediaries to sell their products. Moreover, it turned out that the intermediaries knew nothing, or very little, about the marketing support that Insurance Direct offered them. By using event marketing, Insurance Direct not only ensured that its positioning as a partner in business got through to the intermediaries, but also that they were now actually making use of the new ideas in the field of marketing, apps and the use of social media and the marketing support provided to them by Insurance Direct staff. This has eventually boosted the sales of the banking and insurance products of Insurance Direct.

Operational effect objectives

Operational effect objectives refer to the process of an event. Among other things, they concern the degree of satisfaction and appreciation on the part of visitors and other stakeholders. The satisfaction approach is based on the assumption that satisfaction is a cognitive, calculating process: afterwards, the visitor reasons, mainly rationally, what he thought of an event and whether it came up to his expectations.

Effects occur before, during and after an event. Measuring those effects in the short and medium term involves processing information, attitude and behaviour. As a rule, the focus is on the organizational aspect, the logistics, the facilities, customer satisfaction and appreciation. In other words, the operational part of an event is measured, often by means of questionnaires, feedback from the client, interviews and observation.

Measuring how an experience actually feels is a more problematic matter. It is rather hard to measure emotions. One method that is used in practice is interviewing the consumer during the experience. Another option is an interview before the experience, observation during the experience and an interview after the experience. The section below on methods and techniques provides information on other methods to measure emotions.

A perfectly organized event is the basis for achieving objectives in the longer run. If the visitors highly appreciate an event and are satisfied with it, it will be much more likely that the strategic effect objectives will be attained. For example, if customers or staff feel appreciated and identify with a brand or company, the likely effects can be seen in lower absenteeism, greater commitment to the company, a higher turnover, and so on.

The graph in Fig. 10.2 shows the relationship between customer satisfaction and customer loyalty. The graph sets off the degree of satisfaction and retention (keeping customers and customer loyalty) against each other. The degree of loyalty increases substantially as the degree of satisfaction increases (from 4 to 5).

Fig. 10.2. Impact of customer satisfaction on customer loyalty. (Source: van Tilborgh, 2008.)

The likelihood of satisfaction leading to loyal customers is high, but in practice things may work out differently, as the example of the Soundwave festival in Australia will demonstrate. Soundwave is an annual music festival held in major cities around Australia. The festival originated in Perth, Western Australia, and began travelling to the other Australian capital cities in 2007. It features a number of international and Australian music acts, from various genres including rock, metal and punk (http://soundwavefestival.com). A visitor to Soundwave may be very satisfied about the programme in a particular year because it includes a performance of his favourite band, but this does not mean that he feels connected to the brand and the values of the Soundwave festival. Or the reverse: a regular visitor to Soundwave is not satisfied about the line-up of the programme in that same year, but he still attends because he is a regular, loyal visitor and has felt a connection with the Soundwave brand for years.

Attainment objectives

Attainment objectives are objectives aimed at the quality and quantity of the target group to be reached at an event. Which part of the target group comes into contact with an event and in which way? Attainment objectives involve potential reach and effective reach: there is a target group and of the people in that target group, a certain percentage attends an event. The potential reach comprises the entire target group for which an event is organized. The effective reach refers to that part of the target group that actually attends the event. So, this is about quantitative data on reach. The question of whether the visitors to an event are actually the people targeted by the supplier is a qualitative matter.

What are good objectives?

An objective should:

- be embedded in the strategy of the organization/supplier of the event;
- have measurable units (= performance indicators);
- be logical, transparent and lucid; and
- be formulated in terms of SMART (specific, measurable, acceptable, realistic, time bound).

A good objective is formulated from the perspective of a company or organization and comes from the heart of that organization. Based on its mission and vision, an organization decides in what areas it wants to be successful; or, what are the critical success factors? The list is headed by the financial–economic success factors. Then there are critical success factors derived from the fields of, among other things, marketing, personnel, quality and processes. Indicators are linked

Box 10.2. IMEX

IMEX is a trade fair for professionals in the event industry, where suppliers and firms offering innovative concepts present themselves. At this fair, Messe Frankfurt pulls out all the stops each year at a big stand where visitors receive a warm welcome. The objective Messe Frankfurt wants to achieve by taking part in the trade fair is making contact with 60 serious prospects out of 11,000 visitors. This is a clear indication of the quantity of the target group to be reached. Not every one of those 11,000 people fits the target group of Messe Frankfurt: visitors include staff of agencies that organize events, marketing communication professionals, managing directors or owners, but not all of them have the power of decision, nor are they all in search of a big location for an event like that of Messe Frankfurt. In contrast, qualitative reach means focusing on those of the 11,000 visitors who have concrete plans for an event between now and 1 year's time and who make their decision on the location of the event in the centre of Germany.

The preparations for participation in the trade fair on the part of Messe Frankfurt are aimed both at the quantity and the quality of the visitor target group, and include registration of the visitors' details. The team manning the stand of Messe Frankfurt succeeds in making about 40 good contacts. The effective reach is 40 serious potential clients. All sorts of details about those persons have been collected, including name and address, function, budget, interests, and so on.

---

to critical success factors, which are then made measurable by setting a performance level or standard. Thus, an objective emerges in which the performance indicators are interwoven. Performance indicators are variables on the basis of which an organization can be analysed and results can be measured. They are, in fact, objectives formulated in terms of SMART.

Effect Measurement and Evaluation

SMART stands for:

S = Specific: what exactly should be accomplished where.
M = Measurable: link to statistical performance indicators.
A = Acceptable: with some ambition.
R = Realistic: formulated in such a way that the objectives are attainable.
T = Time bound: linked to a certain moment in time or a deadline.

Formulating a good objective is essential as a starting point for the concept and design of an event, but also as the basis for proper effect measurement. The interpretation of an objective should be unambiguous. An unambiguous interpretation is harder to arrive at when measuring psychological effects such as loyalty or commitment. Concepts are often interpreted in different ways; therefore, they should be defined clearly in advance, so that they mean the same thing to all parties concerned.

There are two important reasons for formulating proper objectives for an event, as we said above.

1. It puts you in a better position to work out a concept and design for an event that fits the target group and the stakeholders.
2. It is easier for you to demonstrate to what extent an event has contributed to attaining the objectives because you can measure the effects better.

Figure 10.3 shows the relationship between formulating objectives and setting up effect measurement and evaluation.

Here is an example to clarify the SMART principle in relation to a critical success factor. Insurance Direct wants to inform its intermediaries of a crucial change in its product portfolio. The vital relations of Insurance Direct are (in)dependent partners of the company. They are part of the distribution chain that sells Insurance Direct's products to the consumer.

For Insurance Direct, the critical success factor is 'professional and well-informed sales people/intermediaries'. The performance indicator in this example is 'knowledge', and knowledge is an indicator that can be measured. The SMART objective in this example is: after the new product portfolio event for the intermediaries/sales people of Insurance Direct, 95% of them are fully informed of the extension of the product portfolio, have all the necessary information and are able to advise (potential) policyholders.

Fig. 10.3. Relationship between objectives and effect measurement.

By formulating proper objectives that contain measurable units and are embedded in the strategy of an organization, those objectives are formulated along SMART lines and their effects can be measured. Critical success factors and objectives can be formulated at several levels. Similarly, you can go through the PDCA cycle (see Fig. 10.4) at several levels. At the highest level, we find the strategic effect objectives as discussed in the preceding section. The operational effect objectives can be found one step down, and the attainment objectives are at the bottom. Figure 10.5 shows the hierarchy of objectives in diagram form.

Qualitative objectives are often formulated within event marketing. An effect measurement must then convert the feelings and emotions evoked during an event into data that show that those feelings and emotions have brought about a different attitude, and sometimes even different behaviour, in people. An effect measurement can obviously also assess quantitative objectives, such as the number of visitors, number of spin-off deals, customer appreciation, or *Net Promoter Score* (NPS) (a simple method to establish if the customer would recommend

Fig. 10.4. PDCA cycle including SMART objective. (Source: Truscott, 2003, adapted by the authors.)

Fig. 10.5. Hierarchy of objectives.

you to friends, colleagues or relatives; www.allesovermarktonderzoek.nl). Naturally, an effect measurement also shows whether the financial objectives have been achieved, or achieved to a substantial extent.

Methods and Techniques: The 'How' Question

The quality of an effect measurement depends on the way in which the measurement, or the collection of data, is organized. So, the focus is on the 'how' question. There should be a predetermined plan for evaluating an event.

Drawing up a plan for effect measurement and evaluation

For the purpose of effect measurement, the objective must be worked out in indicators and measuring tools. Each situation is different, and each event has different starting points and objectives. Moreover, each visitor perceives and experiences an event in his own way. So, each event requires a unique approach focused on a specific situation. Four steps can be helpful:

Step 1. Knowing what you want to measure.
Step 2. Selecting indicators.
Step 3. Making measuring tools operational.
Step 4. Collecting data.

Knowing what you want to measure

Effect measurement starts with the client. What does the client want to be measured? Is it the satisfaction of participants right after the event? Is it satisfaction on the part of the staff? Is it a change in behaviour? Is it numbers of visitors? Is it emotions during the event? Is it an increase in turnover or staff loyalty? Plenty of questions, which all have an impact on the initial phase of a measurement and determine the nature of the measurement. Does the measurement refer to the attainment level only or to the operational effect objective, or does it include both? As a rule, the measurement of strategic effect objectives takes a longer period of time. So, the client specifies the questions to be answered, and this determines the selection of indicators and measuring methods.

Selecting indicators

The selection of indicators depends on what you want to know, as we saw before. For measuring an experience in the short run (operational effect objectives and attainment objectives), possible indicators are:

- the layout of the space available;
- the atmosphere;
- the number of visitors;
- the quality of catering; and
- security.

This concerns basic experience. Measuring an experience in the longer run (strategic effect objectives) requires indicators that are related to the behaviour and conduct of the target group or stakeholder with regard to a company or organization. This is, then, about a memorable or transformative experience. Possible indicators in this case are:

- commitment;
- loyalty;
- trust; and
- social behaviour.

Making measuring tools operational
Indicators have little practical meaning without the operationalization of a measuring tool. The specific application of a measuring tool determines its development. Is it an international, national or regional event that has to be assessed? What is the available budget? What is the number of respondents? Is the measurement feasible? On the basis of the answers to questions like these, a choice of method is made: surveys, interviews, observation, 360 degree feedback, emotional measurement, an experience report or a number of other methods. A combination of measuring tools is possible as well, of course.

Collecting data
When the measuring tools have been selected and operationalized, it is time for Step 4: collecting the data on the basis of which the analyses are made. For example, when the commitment of employees is the objective of an event, a survey of these employees can be conducted besides assessment interviews and observations during the performance of their tasks, to find out to what degree the employees show different behaviour.

Baseline, first and second measurement
It is crucial to establish the baseline, the starting point of the measurement. This cannot always be done properly. In that case, a first effect measurement can serve as the baseline for the second measurement. Thus, it can be shown whether and to what extent an event has had an impact on the expected effects, such as stronger loyalty, a stronger brand preference or stronger ties to a city. Three months before 3FM Serious Request in Breda, for example, a baseline measurement was made among the city's residents with regard to certain statements. The statements covered a range of issues relating to the experience of the city, such as sense of pride, the degree to which residents visit the event and how they feel about it. However, it is not always possible to perform a baseline measurement. In that case, a first effect measurement may serve as the baseline measurement for the second measurement.

The first measurement is done during or shortly after an event. As for 3FM Serious Request, this was done a week after the event, using the same aforementioned statements. What is examined here is what the event has inspired in visitors or in residents. At this point, feedback should be provided to the objective, or objectives.

The second measurement is done at a later time on the basis of questions like: To what degree does the experience leave a lasting impression? Has the event actually changed the visitor? So, the point here is measuring whether and to what extent the experience during and after the event has brought about a change in attitude, or even in behaviour, in the visitor. To make it possible for measurements to be compared, identical performance indicators should be used. As for 3FM Serious Request, the second measurement was not performed, because it was not part of the assignment.

Quantitative and Qualitative Research
Assessing events involves doing properly prepared research. A combination of qualitative and quantitative methods is often the best approach to substantiating the effect of an event. For example, a researcher who wants to have a complete picture of how a programme was appreciated by the public would like to have a representative picture of the opinion of the entire audience. In practice, most measurements are quantitative, due to accountability requirements and the need to show ROI.

To conduct in-depth research into the values and experience of an event, it is necessary to have extensive interviews with the respondents (visitors or groups of stakeholders) to find out

> **Box 10.3. Diesel**
>
> In discussions with several important internal key people, the brand Diesel has formulated a new mission for the coming years. A part of that mission is a greater display of social responsibility. Top management would like to see that all employees are aware of this part of the new mission, in particular, assume a positive attitude towards that mission and conform to it in their conduct. They also want employees to come up with initiatives and ideas themselves regarding a greater contribution to society on the part of Diesel. This is, in fact, about an objective at the transformative level. A transformation does not occur just like that. It takes time and an intensive campaign, with a staff event as its highlight.
>
> The initial situation is analysed: the employees know nothing, or hardly anything, about the new mission, are still not aware of the desire to create more social commitment among the employees and still do not act in accordance with the new mission. The campaign starts with a number of (communication) activities, and there is a follow-up after the staff event.
>
> The first measurement takes place shortly after the event and measures whether and to what extent the employees know about the new mission and what the event has contributed (the memorable experience). About 6 months later, the second measurement is done to find out to what extent the employees actually think differently and conduct themselves differently, in line with the new mission. Has there been a transformation?

why an event has had certain effects on an individual and why other effects had no impact at all. This is what qualitative research is about.

Quantitative measurement

If you want to know how large groups of visitors have experienced an event and what has been its impact, your first step obviously involves quantitative research. In most cases, you will then take a random sample requiring the respondents to fill out a questionnaire. If you want to measure strategic effect objectives, you will have to take several measurements: this is referred to as monitoring. Besides, the effects will then only be visible in the longer term, which makes it necessary to undertake a measurement some time after the event as well, as we discussed earlier.

Surveys

Research based on surveys means that data are collected with respect to a large number of research units through systematic interviews or observation. Surveys are applied to several types of effect measurement, and, as a rule, a random sample is taken from the research population and chance determines who will be part of the sample. If this is not possible, a select sample will be taken.

A questionnaire must be drawn up in such a way that it can comprise several types of questions and scaling methods: open-ended and closed-ended questions; the Guttman or Osgood scale; and Likert scale method.

Closed-ended questions come with possible answers, whereas a respondent has to produce an answer himself in the case of open-ended questions. The Guttman scale provides respondents with a statement in combination with 'yes' and 'no' options. The Likert scale is an ordinal ranking scale.

The respondent can indicate to what extent he agrees with the statement, often on a 5- or 7-point scale ranging from 'strongly disagree' to 'strongly agree'. The Osgood scale (semantic differential) is an ordinal scale enabling respondents to indicate on a 5- or 7-point scale to what extent they think that certain qualifications correspond to the subject in question. This is a method that is used frequently to test attitudes to products.

A questionnaire is more than the sum of a large number of questions. It is vital that the questions that belong together are indeed grouped together. Questions should also be asked in a proper sequence and cause no irritation on the part of the respondent. In this respect, the tunnelling technique may be useful: start with the more general questions and continue with more specific (hard/personal) ones.

This description of research into effects is a general one and only describes frequently applied methods. When conducting proper research, it is, of course, advisable to consult the available literature.

Qualitative measurement

There are several methods that can be used to measure whether the objectives of events have been attained. Interviews, observations and laddering are methods frequently used in qualitative research. Qualitative research is intended to find out what the underlying thoughts, values or motives are of the respondents, usually when objectives have been formulated that are related to feelings such as pride, commitment and preference. Getting a complete picture that is representative of the entire group is not the primary aim in the first place. Apart from that, qualitative research is also quite useful in the concept development phase of an event, as we said in Chapter 8. The information from quantitative research can be tested in the context of qualitative research.

In-depth interview

Qualitative research can be done by using in-depth interviews. They are meant to track down unconscious thoughts. A list of topics is used in conducting in-depth interviews. This list has a fixed structure: introduction, research subject, questions and conclusion. Questions may be different from respondent to respondent, and they may be not only open-ended questions (in relation to so-called probing questions) but also statements on which the respondent gives his opinion.

Laddering

Laddering, or meaning structure analysis, is a research technique that can, for instance, be used in the course of an in-depth interview. This technique is based on the *means–end chain theory* (Reynolds and Gutman, 1988), which starts from the premise that consumers buy products and services to achieve important goals in their lives; this refers to values that people find important. This was illustrated in Chapter 6 by the example of the Black Cross event.

The laddering technique comprises three phases: finding out what are the essential attributes, the interviewing process and analysis.

During the first phase, the attributes of a product or service essential to the consumer are tracked down to become the items of research. This can be done by asking spontaneously for essential attributes, and also by using a sorting task. The most essential attributes, with a maximum of four, are the input for the second phase: the interview phase.

The interview phase is intended to reveal the meaning structure: the meaning that a consumer attaches to the essential attributes. With each question, the interviewer probes deeper and deeper into the answer of the respondent. The starting point is quite explicit (concrete attributes). Subsequently, the interview shifts to the more abstract terminal values that are important to a consumer by way of abstract attributes, functional consequences, psychosocial consequences and instrumental values. What is derived from this are meaning structures called 'ladders'. When there are 20 respondents and 4 ladders per respondent, 80 meaning structures will have been drawn up at the end of the interview period to be used for later analysis.

In the analysis phase, the researcher transfers each individual ladder to a value map, in which the most frequently mentioned attributes, consequences and values, and the relationships between them, are displayed graphically.

This process of analysis is fairly complicated and takes much time. To be able to make a value map, code lists have to be made first on the basis of the answers of the respondents. Then, each individual ladder is codified. The result is input for a matrix that displays how often the attributes, consequences and values are mutually connected. With the help of this matrix, a value map can be drawn up so that it is clear at a glance what the meaning is that consumers attach to a product or service.

The value map can serve as input for strategies regarding communication, segmentation or positioning. In advertisements, for example, the most important psychological consequences or terminal values can be accentuated. However, the value map can also be used for feedback on the objectives of an event.

Please note that conducting an in-depth interview with 'why' questions does not mean that you apply laddering. There is no laddering until you really uncover meaning structures and transfer them to a value map. Laddering is so popular because this technique enables you to transform qualitative interviews into a neat and clear value map that you can put to use immediately.

Observation

By observation, we mean the systematic study of the particular behaviours of a person. This includes only those aspects of behaviour that are relevant to the research. If you intend to make use of observation during an event, you will have to plan beforehand who you are going to observe and when. You also have to decide on the basis of which aspects you want to make your observations.

Other methods

We have already described the most frequently used and helpful methods with regard to the effect measurement and evaluation of events. There are still quite a number of other methods, of which we mention a few here:
- experiment, with or without control groups;
- camera registration of emotional expression;
- having visitors keep a diary or journal; and
- feedback without hypotheses or tested questionnaires.

Neuromarketing

The rise of the field of neuromarketing, in which knowledge about the functioning of our brains is used to better align products and services with the needs of consumers and to make marketing campaigns more effective, is also expected to have an increasing influence in events (van Zeeland, 2016). In the advertising and marketing (and communication) sector, various advanced methods to measure emotions are used. The PrEmo test is one of them. This is a tool that allows a respondent to give expression to his emotions with the help of animations on seeing and hearing certain forms of communication such as logos, advertisements, packaging and products. Thus, it is possible to register the emotions evoked in the respondent by the logo belonging to an event. Yet another method is the IRP technique: measuring appreciation by registering physical changes; for instance, in eye reflexes and blood circulation in the skin.

In neuro-research, a baseline measurement is always performed. After all, the workings of the nervous system are different in each individual. Neuro-research studies the attention for and perception of the message (the communication message), assuming that the communication expression has actually reached the target group. The advantage of neuro-research is that it provides insight into conscious and unconscious reactions. This makes it a suitable tool for charting the emotional experience of a brand or a certain product (van Zeeland, 2016). This research method is not yet applied in events, but this is likely to change in the near future.

> **Box 10.4.** Research: the practice of measuring at corporate events.
>
> Research among various event agencies (members of IDEA (Independent Dutch Event Organization), the sector organization for independent event organizers) has shown that there are considerable differences in the way effect measurement and evaluation of events are carried out. Some organizers evaluate extensively, whereas others ask their clients for feedback in a quick phone call and get on with their daily routines sooner rather than later. It is true that, in general, short-term evaluations are made, but the longer-term effects are often not measured. Below we will describe the most significant research results.
>
> **Personal talk**
>
> Most event agencies reported a preference for having a personal talk with their clients to determine compliance with the objectives. In this process, the organizational (process-related) parts of the event are discussed. Both parties, client and event agency, give their opinions on the event, and the joint conclusions are recorded for future reference. Some agencies do these talks by phone, often due to a lack of time of either of the two parties.
>
> **Methods of effect measurement and evaluation**
>
> Methods of evaluation used by the agencies include:
> - questionnaires;
> - online surveys for visitors (as soon as possible after the event);
> - asking questions by phone;
> - evaluation forms;
> - intuitive evaluation, i.e. a talk based on experience and observation during an event; and
> - personal interview with the client.
>
> **Subjects of effect measurement and evaluation**
>
> In general, the agencies do quite a lot in the way of effect measurement and evaluation. The emphasis is mainly on the proceedings that make up the event, the organizer's role, the visitors' experiences and, of course, the client's opinion. The agencies agree that an evaluation should be done, or that at the very least, there should be a moment of contact to sustain the relationship with the client.
>
> Possible subjects of effect measurement and evaluation:
> - logistics;
> - share of artists;
> - programme;
> - catering;
> - parking policy;

> **Box 10.4.** Continued.
> - commitment to the company;
> - baseline measurement;
> - reactions of visitors;
> - customer satisfaction;
> - client's objectives;
> - process; and
> - experiences of customers and visitors.
>
> The emphasis here is on measuring the operational effect objectives.
>
> **Objectives**
>
> What various event agencies discovered through their effect measurement and evaluation efforts was that the client did not always have a clear-cut objective in advance. Almost every agency said that the conclusions of their evaluation would be included in the organization of the next edition of the event for the same client.
>
> **Added value of effect measurement and evaluation**
>
> Many agencies agreed that effect measurement and evaluation could be a value add to them. Effect measurement can be offered as an additional service or – and this is a minority view – it can be a standard component of the event agency's responsibilities, a service that is included in the initial quotation.
>
> **Applicability of effect measurement and evaluation**
>
> There is a consensus on applicability among the agencies: effect measurement and evaluation are useful instruments in major events or events that are part of a communication mix. However, if an event is a modest business party or an anniversary celebration, for instance, there is little enthusiasm for effect measurement and evaluation on the part of the agencies and clients. In the end, the client always has the final say in this matter, because, after all, it is the client who pays the bill.
>
> Source: Nyenrode project group, 2009, edited by the authors.

Summary

Effect measurement is becoming increasingly important for the very reason that events are exploited more and more on the basis of strategic objectives. In this context, the PDCA cycle is a vital tool. Hall (1992) devised an effect matrix for public events that, as well as the economic effects, measured touristic/commercial, physical, sociocultural, psychological and political effects.

Possible reasons for an effect measurement are: determining whether the investment has been profitable (ROI) and accountability for the policy pursued. Moreover, interim effect measurements are useful when adjustments have to be made.

Several objectives can be distinguished regarding effect measurement (hierarchy of objectives): strategic effect objectives, operational effect objectives and attainment objectives (the 'what' question). A proper objective is logical, clear, transparent and formulated in terms of SMART. Methods and techniques used in effect measurement are related to the 'how' question: it must be decided which indicators and measuring tools are relevant to the objective. The baseline of the measurement should be established in advance.

Effect measurement can be both quantitative and qualitative. A combination of qualitative and quantitative methods, with the emphasis on qualitative methods, often works best. Examples of qualitative methods to measure effects are the in-depth interview, laddering (with the value map as its graphic result) and observation.

Appendices to Chapter 10
Effect Measurement and Evaluation

There is not yet an extensive body of literature on the effect measurement and evaluation of events. Most practitioners/people involved in day-to-day practice increasingly appreciate the importance of measurements, and this is something that cannot be separated from the formulation of proper objectives. There is no ready-made model of effect measurement and evaluation, as we have already pointed out in this chapter. Each event is unique, and therefore it is necessary to construct a made-to-measure evaluation model on each occasion. Existing methods can then be a source of inspiration. That is why we describe examples of models for effect measurement and evaluation in these appendices.

Appendix 1. The ROI model of Jack Phillips

Appendix 2. Economic impact study of the World Cyclo-Cross Championships 2014, Hoogerheide, the Netherlands

Appendix 1
The ROI Model of Jack Phillips

Background of the ROI Model

An event should make money or demonstrably reduce the expenditure of a company. That is the idea behind the ROI model devised by Phillips *et al.* (2007). ROI stands for return on investment. Elling Hamso, founder of the European Event ROI Institute, advocates the introduction of this model in the meetings and events industries. It must bring about a change in behaviour among organizers and clients in the sense that they continually ask themselves: why do we organize a meeting or an event? Within the sector of business events, courses are provided at the moment to put this model into practice.

The development of the ROI model for the events sector has everything to do with the professionalization of this sector and developments in the 1990s that saw a rise in the need for recognition of the profession of organizing. A project within an organization called Meeting Professionals International (MPI) was part of those developments and it provided professionals in the meetings sector with training to teach them how to demonstrate the value of events to customers and employees. The logic behind it was that if top management understood the values of an event or conference in the light of organizational and business objectives, they would be more willing to fund meetings. In addition, the event organizer would become more of a 'strategic team member'. This approach has proved itself so far. Times have changed, and today it is essential in business and industry to account for goals, expenditure and values, using proven methodologies. This holds good for events as well.

An Analysis Tool

The ROI model devised by Phillips *et al.* (2007) has become more sophisticated over the past 20 years, also with respect to the events sector. As we showed in Chapter 10, it is becoming more and more important to demonstrate what an event has achieved and also to pay attention during the decision process to the expected returns prior to an event. In the light of these developments, it is only logical that systematic methodologies are also introduced in the events sector to prove that an event is a professional tool of increasing strategic importance. This means that professional analysis tools are required.

Target Group

The clients are the most important target group for the output of the calculations, the report in fact. The data collected to make those calculations concern the visitors to an event.

What is the ROI Model About?

The ROI model comprises several steps: planning, data collection, data analysis and reporting. These four steps are displayed in Fig. 10.6.

THE ROI MODEL

Fig. 10.6. The steps of the ROI model. (Source: Phillips *et al.*, 2007, adapted by the authors.)

Fig. 10.7. ROI pyramid. (Source: www.roiinstitute.net.)

Planning

The goal of an evaluation should be clear from the beginning, because this largely determines the scope, the tools to be used and the data to be collected. This step is about the formulation of the needs of the target group and the objectives of the organization. This may involve several levels, as we said earlier in our discussion of the hierarchy of objectives in Chapter 10. The model presents a ranking order of objectives ranging from preference needs via learning needs, performance needs, business needs to pay-off needs. These objectives are used to define the levels of measurement, and the last one mentioned, pay-off needs, makes it possible to measure ROI. The other objectives refer to *impact*, *application*, *learning* and *reaction*, respectively.

Hamso's method (see Fig. 10.7) involves a pyramid, or a *chain of impact*. The bottom section of the pyramid is linked to *satisfaction and planned action*, also referred to as preference needs, so this is about measuring participants' satisfaction: with catering and hospitality, for example. It concerns preconditions (satisfiers) that have to be met first to get any response at all from the visitors and participants of an event. In relation to this, it is the wishes of those who attend an event that are decisive with respect to structure, location, time required, and so on.

The second level from the bottom of the pyramid is about *learning*: has the event achieved its aims as far as the visitors are concerned? For example, after an event, the visitor should have a better idea of new policy intentions, or make new contacts, or make use of a new system. In other words: learning goals have been formulated for the target group of an event. And in this vision, each event has an over-arching learning goal. In the case of so-called network events, relationship learning can be measured; this should be clearly defined to make a later assessment possible.

Application, the third level, is about the result of what has been learnt. How do employees who have attended an event, for instance, deal with what they have learnt? After a visit to a stand at a trade fair, will those visitors really start using that energy-saving product? The rule of measuring predetermined goals applies here as well.

The fourth level is related to the *impact* of an event. What is the meaning of an event to an individual? What does that which has been learnt and its practical application produce in hard cash? Hamso emphasizes that, at this level, it is important to determine the period over which the effects of an event must occur.

The final level at the top of the pyramid (*ROI*) concerns the financial result. Once the financial result is known, the ROI percentage can be calculated. Thus, ROI can be calculated by the following simple sum: divide profit by costs and multiply by 100. To be able to draw the conclusion that a particular ROI percentage is indeed the one originally aimed at, the objectives must have been formulated in clear and concrete terms.

The first two levels of the ROI pyramid are always there and, as a consequence, can be measured. The levels above level 2 can really only be measured in the case of large-scale events or a series of events as part of a campaign.

The ROI model as a planning tool

At first sight, the ROI model appears to be a tool for measuring the results of an event afterwards. But it is also intended as a planning tool. The idea behind this is that properly thinking through in advance which objectives should be measured later at various levels is very useful to the design of an event. This means that the model can make an event better and more effective from the start. An online tool is now available that enables the organizers of events to measure the impact of events without much of a problem: www.eventroi.org.

Data collection

Both hard data (such as sales, costs and time) and soft data (such as customer satisfaction and brand awareness) are collected with the help of questionnaires and interviews, among other things. So, this is data collection as referred to in Fig. 10.6. The trick is in selecting the most effective method for the event in question, one that is feasible within the constraints of time and budget. There are various items that must be measured:

- input and indicators;
- responses and perceived value;
- learning; and
- application and implementation.

These items will be explained further below.

Effect Measurement and Evaluation

Measuring input and indicators

When measuring input and indicators, you can take into consideration the total number of participants in an event, the number of days and hours, cost per participant, and so on. As an event organizer, you should, of course, know how much money it takes to organize an event, taking into account that there are various types of events. This can be included in the analysis. Another obvious indicator would be the visitors of an event. Data on the target group, for example, require an answer to the question of what percentage of the total target group has participated in the event. Naturally, the target group can be divided into further segments and then analysed. Visitors can also be monitored to see how much time they spend on an activity, which can be done per segment as well. Another kind of analysis, one that is made less often, is an analysis of the reasons for organizing an event. The list of indicators may also include the extent to which technology and the Internet are used, efficiency and the degree of outsourcing.

Measuring responses and perceived value

Measuring responses and perceived value is the start of the first operational phase of the ROI model. This involves the actual collection of data during and at the end of an event. So, here the focus is on responses and perceived appreciation. This is about feedback, of course. Feedback from the public is crucial to gaining an insight into the way in which an event has been experienced. Customer satisfaction is the central point here. Though many event organizers measure the success of an event only on the basis of data on the reactions of visitors, the ROI method shows that this is merely *one* item of the entire data collection. Success is determined not only by the participants, as an interested party, but also by speakers and facilitators. There are also sponsors, of course, who are not directly involved in an event but who do have an interest. And the client, as the one who pays for an event, should not be forgotten either. The client has asked for an event, has initiated it, supports it, approves budgets, taps sources and is very much dependent on the success or failure of an event.

Collecting data is, in practice, often about aesthetic issues (*non-content*), but the focus should be on *content*. Examples of non-content data are location, transport and catering. Examples of content data are new information, the quantity and quality of new contacts and the quality of speakers.

Measuring learning

Especially when an event revolves around learning, knowing the number of participants who say they have learnt something is of great importance. In this model, learning is an essential success factor.

If no learning goals are linked to a meeting or event, it is merely about entertainment. Many measurements of events are still done from the entertainment perspective, and questions are asked about whether there was a nice atmosphere and a good experience. But, of course, this does not tell you anything about learning. Especially in light of the past two decades, during which organizations have slowly been transformed into learning organizations in order to be able to survive in competing *global markets*, and also in light of economic changes, learning should be at the top of the agenda, also with respect to meetings and events. Continually finding new ways to serve customers is what this is all about. Organizations have to become more innovative and anticipate technological developments with a view to more efficiency, restructuring and reorganization processes. Therefore, meetings and events are becoming increasingly important as *learning tools*, as platforms for teams and larger groups where individual people can cooperate and create new knowledge. In this context, networking will continue to grow in importance, both within and outside organizations.

The rate of learning can be measured, for instance, by means of a quiz or test, although participants sometimes find this rather intimidating. Questionnaires, with a combination of questions on *non-content* and *content*, are often useful in this case, too.

Measuring application and implementation

Some events are intended to spur people into action, but quite often this is not achieved. For example, participants do not use afterwards what they have learnt at a congress. Without a successful implementation (i.e. after the event), no changes will occur at the next level of the ROI pyramid, the level of impact. Especially when participants are expected to take action after an event and tackle things differently (behavioural objectives), it is necessary to measure application and implementation. This is valuable, because it provides data on the success of an event, but also on the factors that have contributed to this success: information that can be used for future events – factors such as a stimulating environment, an inspiring speaker, workshops that seamlessly match the level of the participants, to mention a few. Measurements at this level are carried out with a view to the long term and concern the question of to what extent the participants apply at a later time, in the context of work or leisure (the post-experience phase), the knowledge and skills they have gained during an event. The measurement can be done by the use of questionnaires, observations, interviews and focus groups.

Data analysis

Isolating effects

This step, *data analysis* in Fig. 10.6, specifically *Isolate effects of meeting*, deals with specific techniques for measuring the impact of an event. Take, for instance, an analysis of a group of persons that has attended an event and a group that has not (control group). If, after an event, a significant improvement can be found in *business performance* on the part of the participants, the issue becomes one of demonstrating the relationship with the event in question.

Whenever the performance of an organization does not come up to expectations, or there seems to be a chance of improvement, the feeling that there should be a meeting or event will often spring up. If business needs are the driving force, these business needs and the objectives linked to them are the most important subjects of evaluation, during or after an event. Think back to hard and soft data, as described earlier. An example: a team of employees in a department does not cooperate adequately and, as a result, productivity is too low. Obviously, the business objective is clear: productivity must be raised. An event is used as a tool to realize this goal. Consequently, this productivity goal is then the crucial indicator to be measured after the event. The event is utilized as a strategic tool and it is essential to measure whether this goal has indeed been attained.

When an event is organized at a company for the reason given above, an analysis of the event should make it clear whether productivity has increased, quality improved, cost savings or work satisfaction achieved in relation to a predetermined objective. Available data collected within an organization, business unit or department can also be used for analysis. Customer relationship management (CRM) systems and databases for the systematic collection of data are tools that come to mind in this respect. They can be used for evaluation, or questionnaires can be used again, but whatever method is used, the question should always involve the link between the objective and the contribution that the event has made to achieving this objective, according to the participants.

Control groups, trend line analysis and estimates

To demonstrate that changes have actually been effected by an event, use can be made of control groups, trend line analysis and estimates.

Control Groups

As a researcher, you compare the group of people who have participated in the event (the experimental or pilot group) with the control group (the group for comparison) that has not participated. Conditions should be the same as much as possible, to exclude other influences. Such research is hard to conduct in practice.

Trend Line Analysis

The performance of an employee may be the basis of trend line analysis. We return to the example of labour productivity. Productivity is recorded by a company over the course of a year and plotted on a timeline. After the event, actual performance is compared to what it was before the event on the timeline. If there is a clear upward or downward deviation in the line, you can reasonably assume that the event is a primary cause of this deviation. It is not an exact method, but trend analysis presents a plausible picture of the (probable) impact of a meeting.

Estimates

Estimates can contribute to measuring the impact of an event, but this is not really a precise method of analysis and should at least meet a number of criteria. A primary condition is the use of the most credible source; in the case of events, this may be not only a participant but also the organizer or the media. These parties can often provide good estimates of the impact of an event. They know the market.

An example: when you ask exhibitors at a trade fair about the quality of visitors to their stands, it will give you a fairly reasonable picture of the visitors to the trade fair in question. On the basis of, for example, follow-up appointments, interest shown and business cards handed out, an exhibitor is quite capable of indicating whether the objectives of the trade fair have been achieved, as far as he is concerned.

Translating data into financial results

To calculate ROI, the data collected have to be translated into economic values and compared to the cost incurred for an event. In Fig. 10.6, this is referred to as *Convert data to monetary value*. According to the model, this can be done in several ways, such as using experts, databases and estimates. To return to the example of a company with a stand at a trade fair, the obvious question is whether the company can tell how many follow-up appointments actually result in a quotation, and eventually in a sales order. Naturally, the company itself sets the economic value of the order, or orders.

Identifying less tangible effects

In addition to economic value, there are less tangible effects after an event. The ROI model attempts to convert the value of both tangible and less tangible data into financial results. Sometimes, this is not possible, which does not mean that an event has been less valuable. The economic value will often become visible only over the course of a longer period of time. This is also referred to as an indirect effect.

Direct and indirect costs

This concerns all the costs incurred, direct and indirect, for organizing a meeting or event. This is referred to in Fig. 10.6 as *Tabulate meeting costs*.

Calculating ROI

ROI is calculated by dividing the revenues of an event by the costs incurred: the *cost–benefit ratio* (CBR). This is *Calculate the return on investment* in Fig. 10.6.

$$BCR = \frac{\text{Meeting benefits}}{\text{Meeting costs}}$$

$$ROI(\%) = \frac{\text{Net meeting benefits}}{\text{Meeting costs}} \times 100$$

This is the basic formula that is also used for other investments.

Reporting

The reporting step is a crucial one, because conclusions are drawn on the basis of all the data from the preceding steps (*Reporting* in Fig. 10.6). An account is rendered to various parties who have an interest in the effects and impact of an event, and the organizer, too, can profit from it the next time. Reporting may also lead to the implementation of quality improvement to obtain a higher return on the objectives formulated. The Love & Marriage trade fair, for example, carries out continual quantitative and qualitative research into the needs or wishes of visitors and reports the results to its exhibitors. They are then in a better position to align their own objectives to (potential) visitors and get more out of their participation in the trade fair.

A Critical Note

Calculating ROI is certainly not suitable for all events. This is also acknowledged by the developers of the ROI model and by the European Event ROI Institute. Moreover, not every event lends itself to a measurement at five levels. It is, for instance, useful to calculate the ROI with regard to approximately 5% of all congresses organized. All other events must be measured at level 1 of the pyramid (*Satisfaction and planned action*): 30–40% can be measured up to and including level 3. Effect measurement costs money, which is why only the most important events are singled out.

Within the framework of the ROI model, all sorts of data are collected and quantified. However, on closer inspection, it turns out that estimates are still used in several steps of the model. This makes the outcome less reliable and precise than you would expect at first sight. Moreover, various data collection methods are mentioned for which it is not very clear how they should be integrated.

Appendix 2

Economic Impact Study of the World Cyclo-Cross Championships 2014, Hoogerheide, the Netherlands

Key Factors

Characterization of the event:

- Two-day sports events in the category of bicycle racing (cyclo-cross is not an Olympic sport).
- An event held in public space, involving road closures and detours.
- A world championships event with international participants, visitors and media attention, in a different city every year.
- Live broadcasting of the cross on Sunday, on radio and television at home and abroad.
- An event with 50,000 visitors, spread across Saturday and Sunday, with emphasis on Sunday.

The client of the study is the Dutch foundation of cyclo-cross championships in Hoogerheide (chairman: Jan Prop).

In General

The World Cyclo-Cross Championships 2014 Hoogerheide were held on Saturday 1 and Sunday 2 February 2014 in Hoogerheide in the Dutch province of Noord-Brabant. It is an international cycling event that is organized in a different city every year, and has taken place in the Netherlands several times already (Hoogerheide hosted the event in 2009 too). The juniors and the ladies had their races on Saturday 1 February. Sunday 2 February was the day of the young talented cyclists and the men's elite race (professional riders). The races were held on the streets and there was an off-road part in the fields of the rural area surrounding Hoogerheide. A part of Hoogerheide was closed off in the week prior to the cycling weekend and there were detours to ensure adequate traffic access. Based on the evaluation of 2009, the street circuit was redesigned to reduce inconvenience to local residents. Visitors rated the event with a score of 8.3, which is a very good score compared to other sporting events. The Net Promoter Score (NPS) of the event was + 36. On a scale from − 100 to + 100, this is a very good score. The event had many 'ambassadors'; in terms of media reach there were 47 million viewers and listeners and a total broadcasting time of 40 h.

Who Wants to Know What, and Why?

The World Cyclo-Cross Championships were very important to the municipality of Hoogerheide and the province of Noord-Brabant within the framework of the sports agenda. Top sports events play an important role in this agenda. From this point of view, there was a need to evaluate the event extensively on the basis of questions such as: How are Hoogerheide and the western part of Noord-Brabant put on the map both nationally and internationally, and how does this affect the region's image? What is the economic impact of this event? How did local residents experience this event? These and other questions were presented to various parties in two surveys. The results of these surveys were described in an extensive evaluation report that can be used by the client to account for the subsidy received and the use of the public space.

In this example, we will focus on the economic impact of the event on the western part of Noord-Brabant. Relevant questions in this respect are:

- How much did the organizers and visitors spend in the region? What part of this spending is additional and what is its economic impact?
- How did the residents of Hoogerheide experience the event?

Contracted Party

Breda University of Applied Sciences (BUas) has years of experience in the field of research into sporting events and other types of events and is often asked to undertake impact studies for organizers, sponsors or government authorities. Thanks to the systematic working procedure, it is possible to compare the various studies against each other.

COROP Area and Input–Output Model

In order to determine the economic impact of the event, the spending behaviour of the visitors to the event, the cyclists and their supporting staff, the journalists and the organizers was analysed. The study used the input–output model for the COROP area that includes Hoogerheide, in this case the western part of Noord-Brabant (one of the 40 regional areas in the Netherlands within the COROP classification that is used for analytical purposes). Statistics Netherlands (CBS) has input–output model data available, broken down by COROP area. The model consists of a system of multipliers that indicate the extent to which national income changes as autonomous spending changes – and indicates the economic structure of the region. On the basis of the defined input (spending), the model calculates the output. This output is the potential economic output in the area as a result of the event. In other words, if the event had not taken place, there would have been no additional output.

The economic impact relates to the additional spending amount – additional, in the context of this study, means that only those interviewees who would not have been in Hoogerheide if the cyclo-cross championships had not taken place there were included in the calculations. This means that spending by visitors from outside the COROP area who would have been in Hoogerheide if the event had not taken place (substitution effect) and the subsidy from the local authority are not regarded as additional expenditure. This spending would have been incurred in the region anyway (see Fig. 10.8).

Research Method Economic Impact

First of all, the average spending and the number of participating teams, companies and journalists were determined on the basis of interviews with the organization concerned. A quantitative

Fig. 10.8. Additional spending. (Source: Van Schendel, 2014.)

study was then carried out by means of exit surveys among the event's visitors. These surveys were conducted among approximately every fifth visitor who left the event, spread over Saturday and Sunday, taking into account sold-out races and taking more surveys on Sunday than on Saturday. Sunday is the busiest day, so more surveys were conducted on that day. Surveys have a limited capacity of surveyors and a certain sample size is sufficient to provide a reliable picture. Based on the number of visitors (50,000) and the size of the sample (469 visitors), the statements can be said to be generally applicable with a confidence level of 95% and a confidence interval of 5%. This means that you can be 95% confident that the results could be 5% higher or lower.

The questions for this survey were based on the client's objective and on the input required for the model: visitor profile (including living inside or outside the COROP area) and spending profile (overnight stays and number of days, travelling within the region, food and drink, merchandise), taking into account the substitution effect.

Conclusions on Economic Impact

Of those surveyed, 73% would not have come to the region if the cyclo-cross championships had not taken place there. The expenditure of this group is therefore additional (Table 10.3).

The additional spending of €3,363,243 was then entered into the input–output model. When money is circulating in a certain sector, production in other sectors is boosted as a consequence. For example, if the hotel and catering industry generates a lot of turnover, suppliers of meat, fish, vegetables and fruit will also see their sales figures increase. These mutual economic relationships were incorporated into the input–output model.

The spending of the various target groups of the study were then divided over the various sectors of industry, after which the model did its work. Potential production as a result of the sports event amounted to €3,867,697, as shown in Table 10.4.

The conclusions with regard to the economic impact are:

- The event provided an important economic stimulus of around €3.9 million, which corresponds to 31 full-time equivalents worth of employment.
- The economic input came from visitors, press, participants and organizers.

A Critical Note

It is very hard to be exhaustive in a study of the impact of an event. There are always external factors that can hardly be controlled. Companies or sponsors, for example, can develop activities

Table 10.3. Additional spending.

		Average (€)	Spending (€)
1	Overnight stays	52.39	917,856
2	Food and drink	28.03	907,223
3	Merchandising	7.12	132,545
4	Travel	8.83	375,436
	Subtotal		**2,333,060**
	Of which additional		1,982,153
5	Organization and media		1,381,090
	Additional spendings		**3,363,243**

Table 10.4. Input–output model.

	Input per business sector (€)	Output per business sector (€)
1. Agriculture, forestry, fishery	0.00	21,952.00
2. Mineral extraction	0.00	6,729.00
3. Industry, energy and water companies	0.00	45,490.00
4. Construction	0.00	8,554.00
5. Commerce	259,880.00	302,262.00
6. Catering	1,691,068.00	1,930,476.00
7. Transport, storage and communication	322,295.00	337,641.00
8. Financial institutions	0.00	15,645.00
9. Lettings, business services	1,090,000.00	1,137,233.00
10. Government, defence, social services and sub-education		25,384.00
11. Health and welfare	0.00	26,496.00
12. Environmental services, culture, services	0.00	9,835.00
13. Imports	0.00	0.00
Total	3,363,243.00	3,867,697.00

in the context of the World Cyclo-Cross Championships, which the organizer or researcher has no knowledge of. As a consequence, this spending is not included in the input–output model.

Exit polls were conducted with every fifth person leaving the event. But not every visitor was willing or able to cooperate, so sometimes it was the sixth or seventh person leaving who was surveyed, which is a risk with regard to the reliability of the study.

Finally, it is always hard to pin down exactly what the additional spending is. With respect to this study, a deliberate choice was made for the COROP area and the substitution effect. Moreover, no account was taken of the crowding-out effect (which is typically difficult to determine): as a result of the event, residents leave the region or regular visitors avoid the region. It should be noted, however, that during this period of the year (February) there are normally few regular visitors from outside the region (Van Schendel, 2014; www.evenementenevaluatie.nl).

Illustrations

Information as well as illustrative and photographic material was kindly provided by:

- Robert Aarts, photographic design;
- Olga Kappel-Boekhorst, Deloitte;
- Jacco van Mierlo, Breda University of Applied Sciences;
- Frank Ouwens, Breda University of Applied Sciences and f2o creative studio;
- Margo Rooijackers, Breda University of Applied Sciences;
- Albert van Schendel, Breda University of Applied Sciences;
- Thesis authors and student project groups of Academy for Leisure;
- International Event Management study track;
- Placemaking and Events research group, Breda University of Applied Sciences;
- Thomas van Velthoven, Breda University of Applied Sciences and Resultive; and
- Moniek Hover, Breda University of Applied Sciences.

Cover photo, photo page 1, all photos at the beginning of the chapters:
Robert Aarts/www.robertaarts.com

Preface: Olympic Games – Lazyllama/Shutterstock.com

Chapter 1: Volvo Ocean Race – Leightonoc/Shutterstock.com
Tennis tournament – mr3002/Shutterstock.com
Vuelta – Jan de Wild/Shutterstock.com

Chapter 2: Pathe specials – © Pathe © The Metropolitan Opera House
Cruyff – Catwalker/Shutterstock.com

Chapter 3: Heineken Experience Shop – karenfoleyphotography/Shutterstock.com
New York City Marathon – Steve Broer/Shutterstock.com
Nuclear Security Summit – Robert Paul van Beets/Shutterstock.com

Chapter 4: Gouden Giraffe – www.gouden-giraffe.nl

Chapter 5: Containers – Ruud Taal
Logos: tanaha2001/Shutterstock.com
André Rieu – JuliusKielaitis/Shutterstock.com
Eetafoor – Sanne van Arnhem

Chapter 6: Zwarte Cross – Loes Kampshof en Ilja Vaags of the Feestfabriek
Red Bull Air Race – Pfeiffer/Shutterstock.com
Audi – Jne Valokuvaus/Shutterstock.com

Chapter 7:	Marqt Rotterdam – Gerard Koudenburg/Shutterstock.com
	London – Songquan Deng/Shutterstock.com
	Bloemendcorso – Daniel Leppens/Shutterstock.com
Chapter 8:	Coldplay – yakub88/Shutterstock.com
Chapter 10:	Messe Tradefair Frankfurt – orinoco-art/iStock

All other photos © Shutterstock.com

Bibliography

Alberts, P. and Buitendijk, N. (1995) *Relatiemarketing; hoe het echt werkt*. Amsterdam: Jubels Cobypoint.

Ashworth, G.J., Pellenbarg, P. and Voogd, H. (2004) *Place Marketing. Marketing in the Planning and Management of Places*. London: Routledge.

Baarda, D.B. and de Goede, M.P.M. (2006) *Basisboek Methoden en Technieken; handleiding voor het opzetten en uitvoeren van kwantitatief onderzoek*. Groningen, the Netherlands: Wolters-Noordhoff.

Ballantyne, D., Christopher, M. and Payne, A. (2002) *Relationship Marketing : Creating Stakeholder Value*. Oxford, UK: Butterworth-Heinemann.

Barendse-Schijvens, S. (2009) *Van medewerkers naar medemerkers. Internal branding in de praktijk*. Deventer, the Netherlands: Kluwer.

Berci, F., Mommaas, H. and Synghel, K. van (2002) *City Branding. Image Building and Building Images*. Rotterdam, the Netherlands: NAi Publishers.

Beunders, N. and Boers, H. (1997) *De andere kant van de vrije tijd (derde, herziene druk)*. Leiden, the Netherlands: ToerBoek.

Biel, A.L. (1999) Exploring brand magic. In J.P. Jones (ed.), *How to Use Advertising to Build Strong Brands* (pp. 157–176). Thousand Oaks, CA: Sage.

Boom, E. and Weber, A. (2001) *Consumentengedrag. Beslissen, gedrag en marketingstrategie*. Groningen, the Netherlands: Wolters-Noordhoff.

Boom, M. (2006). Op weg met geur. *Geurbeleving in de vrije tijd*. Breda, the Netherlands: NHTV.

Bos, N. (2009) Van Evenement naar belevenement; een onderzoek naar de touchpoints in de bedrijfsevenementenbranche. NHTV internationaal hoger onderwijs Breda, Breda, the Netherlands [unpublished].

Boswijk, A., Thijssen, T. and Peelen, E. (2008) *Een nieuwe kijk op de experience economy. Betekenisvolle belevenissen (tweede editie)*. Amsterdam: Pearson Prentice Hall.

Boswijk, A., Peelen, E. and Olthof, S. (2012) *Economy of Experiences*. Bilthoven, the Netherlands: European Centre for the Experience Economy.

Buuren, R. van (2006) *Beleef je eigen verhaal. Onderzoek naar impliciete en expliciete storytelling in oorlogsmusea*. Breda, the Netherlands: NHTV.

Buursink, J. (1991) *Steden in de markt. Het elan van citymarketing*. Muiderberg, the Netherlands: Coutinho.

Chernatony, L. de and McDonald, M.H.B. (1992) *Creating Powerful Brands. The Strategic Route to Success in Consumer, Industrial and Service Markets*. Oxford, UK: Butterworth-Heinemann.

CLC-Vecta (2016) *Rapportage Toekomstscenario's door Stefan Hartman*. Leeuwarden, the Netherlands: Stenden Hogeschool. [Unpublished]

Curry, J. (1991) Customer marketing. *Een praktisch antwoord op de vraag: 'In welke business zitten we eigenlijk?'* Amsterdam: Management Press.

Dekker, E.L. (2006) *Belevingsonderzoek naar geur als belevenisinstrument. Ik ruik je wel maar ik zie je niet*. Breda, the Netherlands: NHTV.

Diener, E. and Biswas-Diener, R. (2008) *Happiness. Unlocking the Mysteries of Psychological Wealth*. Malden, MA: Blackwell.

Dijkhuis, J.J.G. (1999) *Een albeheersend streven. Zeven filosofen over het menselijk geluksverlangen*. Amsterdam: Sahara.

Disney Institute (2003) *Be Our Guest : Perfecting the Art of Customer Service*. New York: Disney Editions.

Dreimüller, A.P. (2002) *Het ondernemersplan en de balanced scorecard. Over richting en verrichting*. Den Haag, the Netherlands: Academic Service.

Duif, L. (2016) *De magie van Bosch. Oude schilders, nieuwe citymarketing*. MM Nieuws (themanummer Cities in transition and leisure), pp. 14–15.

Farquhar, P.H. (1989) Managing brand equity. *Journal of Advertising Research* 30(4), 7–12.

Fatingan, A., Pancham, A., Niamat, Z. and Govers, R. (2009) Evenementen, media en de invloed op place image. *Vrijetijdsstudies* 27(3), 35–45.

Floor, J.M.G. and Raaij, W.F. van (2006) *Marketingcommunicatiestrategie*. Amsterdam: Stenfert Kroese.

Florida, R. (2002) *The Rise of the Creative Class*. New York: Basic Books.

Franzen, G. (1996) *Het merk op weg naar de 21e eeuw*. Amsterdam: SWOCC.

Franzen, G. and Berg, M. van den (2002) *Strategisch management van merken*. Deventer, the Netherlands: Kluwer.

Franzen, G. and Bouwman, M. (1999) *De mentale wereld van merken*. Alphen aan den Rijn, the Netherlands: Samsom.

Frijda, N.H. (1986) *The Emotion. Studies in Emotion and Social Interaction*. New York: Cambridge University Press.

Frissen, R., Janssen, R. and Luijer, D. (2016) *Event Design Handbook. Systematically Design Innovative Events Using the #Eventcanvas*. Amsterdam: BIS Publisher.

Gabriel, Y. (2000) *Storytelling in Organizations. Facts, Fictions and Fantasies*. Oxford, UK: Oxford University Press.

Getz, D. (2009) Policy for sustainable and responsible festivals and Events. Institutionalization of a new paradigm. *Journal of Policy Research in Tourism, Leisure and Events* 1(1), 61–78.

Groenendijk, J.N.A., Hazekamp, G.A.T. and Mastenbroek, J. (2000) Public relations. *Beleid, organisatie en uitvoering*. Alphen aan den Rijn, the Netherlands: Samsom.

Hall, C.M. (1992) Hallmark tourist events. *Impacts, Management and Planning*. London: Belhaven.

Hart, H.W.C. van (1998) Van massamarketing naar one-to-one marketing en relatiemarketing. *Bedrijfskunde* 70(3), 24–29.

Hasanoglu, A. and Dopheide, P. (2016) *Technologische trends en ontwikkelingen in de live communication branche. Tips, tricks en tools*. Breda, the Netherlands: NHTV.

Havitz, M.E. and Mannell, R.C. (2005) Enduring involvement, situational involvement and flow in leisure and non-leisure activities. *Journal of Leisure Research* 37(2), 152–177.

Hench, J. (2003) Designing Disney. *Imagineering and the Art of the Show*. New York: Disney Editions.

Herlé, M. (1999) *Te kijk staan*. Alphen aan den Rijn, the Netherlands: Samsom.

Herlé, M. and Rustema, C. (2005) *Corporate Communication Worldwide*. Groningen/Houten, the Netherlands: Wolters-Noordhoff.

Hesselmans, K.H.N. (2005) *Thematisering als belevenisinstrument. Onderzoek naar succes- en faalfactoren van thematisering in de attractieparkensector*. Breda, the Netherlands: NHTV.

Hover, M. and Horsten, P. (2004) *Handleiding cursus imagineering*. Breda, the Netherlands: NHTV. [Unpublished]

Hover, M. and Mierlo, J. van (2006) *Imagine Your Event. Imagineering for the Event Industry*. Breda, the Netherlands: Event Management Expertise Centre NHTV.

Hurst, A. (2014) The purpose economy. *How Your Desire for Impact, Personal Growth and Community is Changing the World*. Boise, ID: Elevate.

Ind, N. (2007) Living the brand. *How to Transform Every Member of Your Organization Into a Brand Champion*. London: Kogan Page.

Kapferer, J.N. (1992) Strategic brand management. *New Approaches to End Evaluating Brand Equity*. London: Kogan Page.

Keller, K.L. (1993) Conceptualizing, measuring, and managing customer-based brand equity. *Journal of Marketing* 57(1), 1–22.

Kempen, S.G.G. van (2005) *Evenementen. De oplossing van relatiemarketing*. Breda, the Netherlands: NHTV.

Kneepkens, S.J.R. (2005) *Eventmarketing. Geen real goods maar feel goods*. Breda, the Netherlands: NHTV.

Kotler, P., Haider, D.H. and Rein, I. (1993) *Marketing Places. Attracting Investment, Industry and Tourism to Cities, States and Nations*. New York: The Free Press.

Kralingen, R. van (1999) *Superbrands. Merken en markten van morgen*. Deventer, the Netherlands: Samsom.

Kuiper, G. and Kamp, D. (red.) (2015) *Basisboek eventmanagement. Van concept naar realisatie (tweede, herziene druk)*. Bussum, the Netherlands: Coutinho.

Kuiper, G. and Smit, B. (2011) *De imagineer. Ontwerp beleving met betekenis*. Bussum, the Netherlands: Coutinho.

Lafferty, X. and Chalip, L. (2006) Effects of hosting a sport event on destination brand. A test of co-branding and match-up models. *Sport Management Review* 9(1), 49–78.

Landuyt, I. and Ummels, T. (2008) *CityMakers. Marketing the City*. Nederhemert, the Netherlands: De Nieuwe Aanpak.

Lane, K. (1993) Conceptualizing, measuring and managing customer based brand equity. *Journal of Marketing* 57(1), 1–22.
Laurel, B. (1993) *Computers as Theatre*. Boston, MA: Addison-Wesley.
Layard, R. (2011) *Happiness. Lessons from a New Science*. London: Penguin.
Levitt, T. (1980) Marketing success through differentiation – of anything. *Harvard Business Review* 58(1), 83–91.
Liebregts, S. (2007) *Medewerkers worden medeMerkers*. Breda, the Netherlands: NHTV.
Lier, H. and Wijngaarden, P. van (2015) *Nieuwe business modellen voor de toeristisch-recreatieve sector*. Nieuwegein, the Netherlands: NRIT Media.
Mark, M. and Pearson, C.S. (2001) *The Hero and the Outlaw. Building Extraordinary Brands through the Power of Archetypes*. New York: McGraw-Hill.
Michels, W.J. (2013) *Communicatiehandboek. Identiteit, imago, merk, media*. Groningen/Houten, the Netherlands: Noordhoff.
NHTV Minorgroep CLC-Vecta (2015) *Tussentijdse rapportage 2015*. [Unpublished]
NIDAP (2016) *Bedrijfsevenementenonderzoek*. Amsterdam: NIDAP.
Nijs, D. and Peters, F. (2011) *Imagineering. Het creëren van beleveniswerelden*. Amsterdam: Boom.
Noordman, T.B.J. (2004) *Cultuur in de citymarketing*. Den Haag, the Netherlands: Elsevier Overheid.
Notten, P.W.F. van, Rotmans, J., Asselt, M.B.A. van and Rothman, D.S. (2003) An updated scenario typology. *Futures* 35(5), 423–443.
Oldenboom, E. (1999) *Brood & Spelen; de economische en maatschappelijke waardering van grote sportevenementen*. Amsterdam: MeerWaarde.
Ooijen, M. van (2009) *De juiste weg van doelstelling naar concept. Put yourself into everything you create*. Breda, the Netherlands: NHTV.
Pappot, S. (2008) *Merkwaardig*. NHTV internationaal hoger onderwijs Breda, Breda, the Netherlands.
Phillips, J.J., Myhill, M. and McDonough, J.B. (2007) *Proving the Value of Meetings and Events. How and Why to Measure ROI*. Birmingham/Dallas: ROI Institute/MPI.
Pine II, J. and Gilmore, J.H. (1999) *The Experience Economy : Work is Theatre and Every Business a Stage*. Boston, MA: Harvard Business School Press.
Pine II, B.J. and Gilmore, J.H. (2000) *De beleveniseconomie. Werk is theater en elke onderneming creëert zijn eigen podium*. Schoonhoven, the Netherlands: Academic Service.
Pine II, J. and Gilmore, J.H. (2011) *The Experience Economy : Work is Theatre and Every Business a Stage*. Boston, MA: Harvard Business School Press.
Prahalad, C.K. and Ramaswamy, V. (2004) *The Future of Competition. Co-Creating Unique Value with Customers*. Boston, MA: Harvard Business School Publishing.
Projectgroep IDEA (2007) *Event Rendement Meter. Een onderzoek naar het meetbaar maken van (psychologische) effecten van bedrijfsevenementen*. Breda, the Netherlands: NHTV. [Unpublished]
Projectgroep NHTV (2014) *Onderzoeksrapport Sponsorwaardemodel*. Breda, the Netherlands: NHTV. [Unpublished]
Projectgroep Nyenrode (2009) *Onderzoek naar de rol van eventmarketing*. Breda/Breukelen, the Netherlands: NHTV/Nyenrode Business Universiteit, IDEA-leerstoel Eventmarketing en -communicatie. [unpublished]
Rennen, W. (2007) *CityEvents. Place Selling in a Media Age* (proefschrift Universiteit van Amsterdam). Amsterdam: Vossiuspers UvA.
Reynolds, T.J. and Gutman, J. (1984) Laddering. Extending the repertory grid methodology to construct attribute-consequence-value hierarchies. In Pitts, R.E. and Woodside, A.G. (eds), *Personal Values and Consumer Psychology* (pp. 155–167). Lexington, MA: Lexington Books.
Reynolds, T.J. and Gutman, J. (1988) Laddering theory, method, analysis, and interpretation. *Journal of Advertising Research* 28(1), 11–31.
Richards, G. and Palmer, R. (2010) *Eventful Cities. Cultural Management and Urban Revitalization*. Oxford, UK: Butterworth-Heinemann.
Riel, C.B.M. van (1996) *Identiteit en imago. Grondslagen van corporate communication (tweede, herziene editie)*. Schoonhoven, the Netherlands: Academic Service.
Riezebos, H.J. (1995) *Unravelling Brand Value. A Conceptual Model on Consumer- and Producer-based Brand Value*. Rotterdam, the Netherlands: Erasmus Universiteit.
Rijkenberg, J. (2005) *Concepting. Het managen van Concept-merken in het communicatiegeoriënteerde tijdperk (zevende druk)*. Den Haag, the Netherlands: BZZTôH.
Rijnja, G. and Jagt, R. van der (2004) *Storytelling. De kracht van verhalen in communicatie*. Alphen aan den Rijn, the Netherlands: Kluwer.
Rokeach, M. (1973) *The Nature of Human Values*. New York: The Free Press.
Rooijackers, M. (2007) Beleving? Geluk! *Leisure Trends* 1(4), 24–26.

Rotterdam Festivals (2012) *Festival ambities 2013–2016. Dieper in de stad, verder in de wereld*. Rotterdam, the Netherlands: Rotterdam Festivals.

Schendel, A. van (2014) *Economische impact-studie WK Veldrijden 2014 Hoogerheide*. Breda, the Netherlands: Event Management Expertise Centre NHTV.

Schijns, J.M.C. (2000) *Relatiemarketing. Stapsgewijs naar customer loyalty*. Alphen aan den Rijn, the Netherlands: Adfo Specialists Group.

Schreuder, G. and Gosman, B. (1997) *Relatieversterkende evenementen*. Alphen aan den Rijn, the Netherlands: Samsom bedrijfsinformatie.

Schulz von Thun, F. (1982) *Hoe bedoelt u? Een psychologische analyse van menselijke communicatie*. Groningen, the Netherlands: Wolters-Noordhoff.

Seligman, M. (2002) *Authentic Happiness. Using the New Positive Psychology to Realize your Potential for Lasting Fulfillment*. New York: The Free Press.

Sterk, R. and Kuppenveld, E. van (2007) *Organisaties en hun bedrijfscommunicatie, relatiegericht aangepakt*. Groningen, the Netherlands: Wolters-Noordhoff.

Storm, C.M. (1992) Complicaties in communicatie. Breng uw brouwerij tot leven. *Harvard Holland Review* 31, 17–28.

Tilborgh, N. van (2008) *Event Rendement Meter. Van gevoel naar feiten*. Breda, the Netherlands: NHTV. [Unpublished]

Truscott, W. (2003) *Six Sigma. Continual Improvement for Business. A Practical Guide*. Oxford, UK: Butterworth-Heinemann.

Verhaar, J. (2014) *Projectmanagement. Een professionele aanpak van evenementen* (negende, herziene druk). Amsterdam: Boom.

Verhage, B.J. (2009) *Grondslagen van de marketing* (zevende, herziene druk). Groningen, the Netherlands: Noordhoff.

Verhagen, D. (2006) *Cocreatie wordt groot!* Breda, the Netherlands: NHTV.

Verhoeven, P. (2006) *Meten of gemeten worden; hoe kunnen (zachte) doelstellingen van een bedrijfsevenement het beste gemeten worden?* NHTV internationaal hoger onderwijs Breda, Breda, the Netherlands [unpublished].

Vyncke, P. (2002) Lifestyle segmentation. From attitudes, interests and opinions, to values, aesthetic styles, life visions and media preferences. *European Journal of Communication* 17(4), 445–464.

Wiegerink, K. and Peelen, E. (2013) *Eventmarketing (tweede editie)*. Amsterdam: Pearson Education.

Zande, T. van der (2007) *De toegevoegde waarde van live communicatie*. Breda, the Netherlands: NHTV.

Zeeland, E. van (2016) *Basisboek neuromarketing. Neuro-onderzoek voor marketing- en communicatieprofessionals*. Bussum, the Netherlands: Coutinho.

Zwaag, I. van der (2009) *Van bereiken naar beRAKEN. Een onderzoek naar touchpoints in de vakbeursbranche*. Breda, the Netherlands: NHTV.

Zwol, C. van (2010, 1 April) Film + prosecco + meezingen. NRC.next, p. 14.

Professional Journals

Adformatie
Experience magazine
Expovisielive
Feestelijk zakendoen
High Profile Events
Marketingtribune
Quality in Meetings
Tijdschrift voor Marketing

Websites

All websites accessed in June 2017, unless stated differently.
- www.10000hours.nl
- www.teamnl.org, accessed August 2016
- www.2interact.nl
- www.3fm.nl
- www.accelerom.com
- www.ah.nl
- www.ahoy.nl
- www.allesovermarktonderzoek.nl
- www.artishockevent.nl, accessed October 2016
- www.belastingdienst.nl
- www.bogra.nl, accessed September 2005
- www.boomfestival.org
- www.burningman.com
- www.calanza.com
- www.cappeu.org
- www.castlebar4dayswalks.com
- www.centerparcs.nl
- www.cgr.nl
- www.clcvecta.nl, accessed October 2016
- www.cliniclowns.nl
- www.corsozundert.nl, accessed November 2016
- www.cosmit.it
- www.cruyff-foundation.org
- www.db-online.nl
- www.dirkkuytfoundation.nl
- www.eetafoor.nl, accessed September 2016
- www.effectmeting.nl
- www.efpia.eu
- www.escaperoomkvl.nl, accessed June 2016
- www.estrelladamm.com
- www.eubeafestival.com, accessed May 2016
- www.evenementenevaluatie.nl

https://eventsummit.nl/
www.eventmodelgeneration.com, accessed June 2016
www.eventmarketer.com
www.eventroi.org
www.expoproof.com, accessed June 2016
www.expovisie.nl
www.fz.nl
www.gouden-giraffe.nl, accessed October 2007
www.grand-am.com
www.greenevents.nl, accessed November 2016
www.heineken.nl
www.heinekenthecity.nl
www.hema.nl
www.high-profile.nl
www.hypsos.com
www.ifeaeurope.com
www.imex-frankfurt.com
www.ippanetwork.org
www.itb-berlin.com
www.jaarbeurs.nl/meetup
www.jdvhotels.com
www.libellezomerweek.nl, accessed June 2016
www.maisonvandenboer.com
www.mananamanana.eu, accessed October 2016
www.marketingfacts.nl
www.marketingonline.nl
www.marketingtribune.nl
www.meetingmoods.nl
www.miele.nl
www.miele.de
www.mindz.com, accessed January 2017
www.nidap.nl
www.nrc.nl
www.nu.nl, accessed October 2016
www.nojazzfest.com
www.oxfamnovib.nl
www.patheinternational.com
www.plasticwhalefoundation.com, accessed October 2016
www.redbullairrace.com, accessed October 2016
www.rockinriolisboa.sapo.pt
www.roiinstitute.net, accessed June 2016
www.rolandgarros.com
www.rotterdamfestivals.nl

www.salon-auto.ch
www.sensation.com
www.snsbank.nl
www.spoorzone013.nl, accessed November 2016
www.stichtingskyway.nl
www.stichtingvlinders.nl
www.stukafest.nl, accessed July 2016
www.surveymonkey.com, accessed June 2016
www.sziget.hu
www.ted.com, accessed October 2016
www.tennisdailynews.net
www.trendslator.nl
www.visma.nl, accessed July 2016
www.volvooceanrace.com
www.wikipedia.org
www.wimbledon.com
www.worlddatabaseofhappiness.eur.nl
www.world-peace-foundation.org, accessed October 2016
www.yo-opera.nl
www.yourevent.nl, accessed September 2005
www.your-sencity.com
www.zwartecross.nl, accessed October 2016

Index

Agrarian economy 17

Bernstein's spiderweb method 113
   Deloitte 114–115
   emotion 114
   ideas and stories 114
Bogra 37
BrabantStad 110
brand-identity prism
   culture 103
   personality 102
   physical and personal characteristics 102
   physical aspect 102
   reflection 103
   relationship 103
   self-image 103
brands 88–115
   'a good feeling' 92
   Black Cross Festival 91
   brand-added value 94–95
   brand equity 95
   'branding game' 93
   characteristics 92
   definition 92
   entertainment products 99
   event on its own staff 110–115
   events, image transfer 90
   factors 96
   features 100–101
   identity prism 101–103
   image transfer 104–110
   inside-out positioning 105
   intensity 97
   Internet, television and print media 89
   ladder 98
   legal and economic property 92
   Mañana Mañana 107
   marketing 93
   marketing tool 104, 105
   means-end analysis 97
   motocross 90
   person's memory 97
   positioning, strategies 103
   positive associations 96
   principles 93
   product and service 93
   product/corporate 99
   product/service attribution 107
   psychosocial and functional consequences 107
   public's trust 89
   Quattro 108–109
   Red Bull 103–104
   sensual 99
   strategies 105, 106
   terminal and fundamental and instrumental values 107
   unicity 97
   value patterns 99–100
business-to-business events (BtoB) 7, 8, 12
business-to-consumer events (BtoC) 8, 12
business-to-employee events (BtoE) 8, 9, 12

CBR *see* cost–benefit ratio (CBR)
Centre for Applied Positive Psychology (CAPP) 22
city branding 121–123
   advantages 122–123
   diversity, distinctiveness and profundity 121
   self-expression, marketing tool 121
   urban development and creativity 121–122
   urban renewal 121
city marketing 116–138
   attractive city 120
   companies 128
   consuming and producing 120
   definition 123
   description 117
   developments 119
   emergence of
     changes, society 119
     history 117
     industrial revolution 117
     opportunities and plans 118
   market-oriented thinking 119
   price, politics, personnel and presentation 119–120

city marketing (*continued*)
  product, place and promotion 119
  promotion 118
  residents 128
  Rotterdam festivals 124
  sustainability 136–138
  visitors 128
CLC-VECTA 27–28
consumers' pursuit of happiness 16–29
  experience economy 17–20
  happiness economy 21–25
  innovation 25
  scenario analysis 26–28
  social cohesion and personal well-being 29
corporate events 7–9, 12
  aesthetic and idealistic objectives 9
  atmosphere 189–190
    decor 189
    elements 189
    entertainment 190
    format/setting 190
    lighting 189
    location 189
    sound 189
    visual aids 189
  BtoB 7, 8, 12
  BtoC 8, 12
  BtoE 8, 9, 12
  catering 191
  description 188–189
  entertainment and commercial objectives 9
  entrance 191
  facilities/organization 190
    cloakroom 190
    personnel 190
    temperature 191
    toilets 190
  logistics 190
    description 190
    parking 190
    routing 190
    transport 190
  pre-exposure phase 189
  programme contents 191
  programming 191
cost–benefit ratio (CBR) 221
customer journey 178
customer relationship management (CRM)
  communication 64
  corporate strategy 60
  economic value 63
  knowledge 61–63
    companies 62
    'customer value' 62

  emotional data 61
  individual and demographic data 61
  precondition 63
  products/services 62
  pyramid 62
  small, top and medium 62
  psychological nature 63
  social strategies 63
  value proposition 64
customer relationship marketing 51–66
  advantages 57
  appreciation 64
  characteristics 56
  communication developments 54
  CRM 59–64
  dual challenge 65
  emotional grounds 58
  exchange transaction 66
  growing competition 53
  high-quality services 58
  individual transactions 58
  Insurance Direct 52
  interactive process 57
  limitation 66
  mass communication 54
  pre-trade 65
  price 51
  profit 58
  reciprocity 57
  reputation 55–56
  society individualization 54
  target group 57–59
    competitors 59
    employees 59
    financial institutions 59
    government 59
    internal/external 58
    press 59
    prospects and customers 58
    suppliers 59
  technological advancements 53
  transaction 53

DESTEP model 26

effect measurement and evaluation 195–214
  accountability 200
  adjustments 200–201
  Amstel Gold Race 200
  attainment objectives 203
  baseline, first and second measurement 208
  cultural capital of Europe 196
  customer satisfaction and loyalty 202–203
  data collection 208

Index

Geneva Motor Show 201
IMEX 204
indicators selection 207
intended and unintended 197
matrix 198
measuring tools operational 208
objectives and effect measurement 201
operational effect objectives 202–203, 207
PDCA 197
public and business events 199
qualitative measurement 210–212
   behaviour observation 211
   corporate events, research 212–213
   description 210
   in-depth interview 210
   laddering technique 210–211
   objectives 206
quantitative measurement 209
   closed-ended questions 209
   description 209
   Osgood scale 209
   surveys questionnaire 209–210
ROIs 200
SMART 205
stakeholder 199
strategic effect objectives 201–202
thinking and structuring 201
3FM Serious Request 208
World Cyclo-Cross Championships 2014 223–226
Environment, Value, Effect, New, Touchpoint and Strategy (EVENTS) mode 13–15
eventful cities 126–127, 131–135
   advantages 126–127
   business relationships and partnerships 133–134
      cultural parties 133
      media 133–134
      stakeholders 133
   culture 131–132
   factors, event programmes 131
   magic of Bosch 127
   media impact 134
   negative effects 127
   place 132–133
   planning 135
   power 133
   resources 134–135
   Spoorzone project 135
event marketing 5–15, 30–49
   advantages 44–46
      consumer attention 45–46
      emotions 46
      integrated communication 45
      networking opportunities 46
      personalized approach 45
      target groups 45
      trade journalists 46
   business practices 33
   characteristics 6
   city 37
   coffins 37–38
   communication professionals 4
   communication tools 31
   consumer 32–33
   corporate and public events 7–12
   customization 48
   definition 32
   disadvantages
      complexity 47
      costs 48
      one-offness 46
   discipline matrix 38
   Do–Check–Act cycle 13
   economic objectives 36
   elements 6
   EVENTS model 13–15
   experience 34
      economic progress, products and services 34
      non-tangible and memorable 34
      sing-along cinema 35
   external and Internal branding strategy 36
   factors 48
   follow-up 48
   international trade show 38
   management process 13
   marketing communication developments 34–35
   marketing communication strategy 36
   marketing mix 38–39
   marketing through events 36
   message 47
   Nintendo Wii 83
   objective 47
   one-offness 46
   organizations 32
   personnel 38
   product orientation 33
   products and services 4
   psychological processes 7
   quality of life 4
   relationship 36
   sensory impressions 6
   sporty and adventurous image 5
   target groups 4
   target market 47
   theme and programme 32
   tools, means and media 47–48

event marketing (*continued*)
  touchpoints 7
  traditional and communication 32
  types 6, 39–44
    conceiving and organizing 39–41
      teaming up 41–43
  use of
    message 47
    objective 47
    target market 47
    tools, means and media 47–48
events
  strategic marketing tool 4
  strategic use 4
events policy
  contemporary role 125–126
  description 124
  Fringe festivals 125
  municipal authorities 124
  Rotterdam city 124
  urban traditions 125
experience concept 153–156
  abdominal phase 155–156
  creative process 154
  creativity aspects 154
  description 153
  dreams 155
  knowledge acquisition 155
  Lego's corporate vision 156
experience economy
  agrarian and industrial 17
  co-creation 19–20
    consumers and producers 19
    'secret events' 20
  consumer orientation 17
  devaluation of 20
  explosive growth 18
  organizers 18
  service 17
  sharing economy 19–20
  suppliers 18
  theatre and cinema branch 18
experience tools 157–163
  co-creation 160–162
  personnel 163
  play elements 160
  senses stimulation 158–160
  storytelling 158
  thematizing 157

guest experience model 178, 180

Hamso's method 217
'happiness economy' concept 21–25
  corporate social responsibility 25
  emotions, commitment, meaning and purpose 22
  feeling of 23
  guiding principle 22
  individual psychological condition 21
  IPPA 22
  leisure products 23–24
  management and organization sector 22
  positive psychology 22
  purchase criterion 17, 21
  Rafael Nadal Foundation 24

IFEA *see* International Festivals and Events Organization (IFEA)
image transfer 105–110
  brand-specific events 105–107
    financier 105
    pre- and post-exposure phases 107
    Red Bull Air Race 106
    wings 106
  co-branding 110
  ingredient branding event 109–110
  sponsor 107–109
    Audi 108–109
    Dutch 108–109
    meaning structure analysis 106, 108, 109
    naming company 107
    upper value areas 109
Insurance Direct 52
internal branding events 110–115
  aim 111
  Bernstein's spiderweb method 113
  brand image 110
  business model 110
  communication 111, 112
  corporate identity 111, 113
International Festivals and Events Organization (IFEA) 51, 65
International Positive Psychology Association (IPPA) 22
Internet 82

Jheronimus Bosch 500 127

laddering technique 98, 210–211
Libelle 168

marketing communication 68–87
  advertising firms 81
  Albert Heijn's musical 78
  APM terminals MVII 70
  attitude 77
  audio-visual means 83
  AutoRAI 85
  behaviour 78

Index

catering 87
charity event 79
communication model 68–69
  definition 68
  digital and print 84–87
  direct/virtual 69
  EETAFOOR 86
  IMEX 80
  Internet 82
  knowledge influence 78
  live 69
  location 87
  mass and interpersonal 76–77
  media attention 81
  media, news 80
  message 71, 74
    appealing aspect 74
    business aspect 74
    expressive aspect 74
    relational aspect 74
  mobile applications 82
  modalities
    advertising 75
    education 75
    internal and external 75
    public relations 75
    sharing knowledge 75
    tool 75–76
  multi-channel strategy 80
  news value 80–81
  old and new media 82
  one-to-one 69
  organization agencies 84
  printed matter 84–87
  professionals 69
  social media 82
  television 70–71
  video gaming 83
  'Yacht 2402' 72–74
marketing communication developments 34–35
  one-to-one communication 34
  producers 34
  production methods 34
marketing, definition 32
marketing mix 38–39
mass and interpersonal communication 76–77

Olympic Experience event 42

peak-end rule 175–176
  Club Vega 175–176
  post-exposure phase 175
  pre-exposure phase 175
Plan–Do–Check–Act (PDCA)
  cycle 197

SMART 205
public events 9–12
  attractions 10
  commemorations and ceremonies 10
  commercial interests 12
  concerts/musical performances 9
  culinary events 10
  exhibitions/trade shows 9
  festivals 9
  markets 10
  parades 10
  rallies and sports 10
  'trade day' 10

Red Bull 5, 104
Remmers' touchpoint model 170–171
returns on investment (ROIs) 216–222
  analysis tool 216
  application 217
  application and implementation
    measurement 220
  CBR 221–222
  content 219
  control groups, trend line analysis and
    estimation 220–221
  data collection 218
  development 216
  direct and indirect costs 221
  Hamso's method 217
  input and indicators 219
  isolating effects 220
  learning measurement 219–220
  less tangible effects identification 221
  online tool 218
  planning 217–218
  reporting step 222
  target group 217
  translating data, financial results 221
ROIs *see* returns on investment (ROIs)
Rokeach's value model 150
Rotterdam Festivals 124

Samsung theme park 60
scenario analysis 26–28
  CLC-VECTA 27–28
  DESTEP model 26
senses stimulation 158–160
  colours 158–160
    meeting moods development 159
  scents 160
sing-along cinema 35
Smart car 31
specific, measurable, acceptable, realistic, time
  bound (SMART) 203, 205
storytelling 158

strategy translation, concept 141–163
  definition 152
  event setting 156–157
  experience tools 157–163
  NPO 3FM/Serious Request 152
  Possibilize Foundation 143–144
  psychosocial framework 146–151
    description 145
    expectations and past experiences 146–148
    expressive values 150
    functional values 150
    impressive values 151
    involvement 148–149
    knowledge 146
    lowlands 151
    moods 148
    motives 148
    personality and competencies 149
    Rokeach's value model 150
    social context 149
    social value 151
    symbolic values 150
    terminal values 151
  staged and true experience 144
  supply and demand analysis 142–144
  target group values 142
  true experience levels 144–146
sustainability
  domains 136
  economic effects 136
  Green Deal 137
  visitors 136

thematizing 157
touchpoints 165–194
  audience development research 166
  'check' 194
  contexts 165
  customer experiences 167
  customer journey 178
  definitions 165
  #EventCanvas 181–182
  events to experiences 173–178
    Expoproof corporate vision 174
    magical moments 174–175
    peak-end rule 175–176
    pleasure–pain gap 176–177
    positive visitor experience 173
    satisfiers and dissatisfiers 173–174
    value-oriented objectives 177

  experiences, organizational consequences
    #EventCanvas 181
    guest experience model 180
    people 180
    process 180
    setting 180
    visitor experiences 178
    visitor journey 181
  form 178–182
  ING 169
  Libelle Zomerweek 167–168
  optimal visitor experience 172–173
  organization's and visitor's perspective 165
  organization's values 170
  physical contact 169
  planning and communication 165
  Remmers' touchpoint model 170–171
  Reykjavik pure energy 166
  value addition 167
  value fit 169
  visitor perception 171, 172
trade fairs 184–187
  communication
    newsletter/direct mail 185
    personal invitation 185–186
    website 184
  description 184
  exhibitors
    personal invitation 185–186
    preparation 186
  floor plan 186
  house style 187
  identification 187
  logo 187
  name/trade fair title 187
  programme 186
  seminar programme 186

Veed YouTube event 76
Visma 19

World Cyclo-Cross Championships 2014 223–226
  additional spending 225
  description 223
  desk research and interviews 224–225
  exit polls 226
  Hoogerheide 223
  input–output model 224, 226

Zundert Flower Parade 129–131